LE BONE FLORENCE OF ROME

OLD AND MIDDLE ENGLISH TEXTS
General Editor: G. L. BROOK

Le Bone Florence of Rome

Edited by

CAROL FALVO HEFFERNAN

MANCHESTER UNIVERSITY PRESS

BARNES & NOBLE BOOKS · NEW YORK

178678

© MANCHESTER UNIVERSITY PRESS 1976

Published by Manchester University Press
Oxford Road, Manchester M13 9PL

UK ISBN 0 7190 0647 3

USA
HARPER & ROW PUBLISHERS INC
BARNES & NOBLE IMPORT DIVISION
US ISBN 0 06 492790 3

Library of Congress catalog card No. 76 7656

Printed in Great Britain by T. & A. Constable Ltd., Edinburgh

PREFACE

Seven manuscript versions of the story of Florence—one in English, five in French, and one in Spanish—as well as the many related tales of innocent, persecuted high-born women, both in eastern and western literature attest to the fascination the story held for the medieval imagination. Also, the tale's relationship to Chaucer's *Man of Law's Tale* makes it a useful touchstone against which to measure Chaucer's greatness.

Despite the scholarly attention given to the tale of Florence in the nineteenth and twentieth centuries,[1] there is no adequate, accessible edition of *Le Bone Florence of Rome*. Both nineteenth-century editions have long been out of print. The romance first appeared in a collection by Joseph Ritson[2] which provided readable texts of manuscripts most of which had not appeared in print before. Ritson did not produce consistently reliable scholarly texts, but he did provide a real service to readers of his generation interested in medieval romance.

While comparatively free of errors, a later nineteenth-century text, that of Wilhelm Vietor,[3] is not easily readable, nor is W. A. Knobbe's introduction[4] to it in all points reliable. In addition, the absence of a glossary and explanatory notes is a significant shortcoming.

In its original form this edition was approved as a dissertation for the Ph.D. degree at New York University in 1973 and I am pleased to acknowledge my great debt to Professor

[1] Lillian H. Hornstein, 'Le Bone Florence of Rome', *A Manual of the Writings in Middle English 1050–1400*, ed. J. Burke Severs (New Haven, 1968), Fasc. 1, I, 290–1.

[2] Joseph Ritson, ed. 'Le Bone Florence of Rome', *Ancient English Metrical Romances*, 3 vols. (London, 1802), III, 1–92.

[3] Wilhelm Vietor, ed., *Le Bone Florence of Rome*, Diss. Marburg, 1893 (Marburg, 1899). I disagree with his readings in only eighteen instances and I introduce several emendations which challenge Vietor's interpretation of words or phrases.

[4] W. Albert Knobbe, 'Über die Mittelenglische Dichtung *Le Bone Florence of Rome*', Diss. Marburg 1899 (Marburg, 1899) (Introduction precedes Vietor's text).

Lillian Hornstein, who first kindled my interest in medieval romance literature, and whose guidance was constant and generous over the full period I was engaged in writing the dissertation. I would also like to thank my readers at that time, Professors Jess B. Bessinger, Jr. and Robert R. Raymo, for their valuable suggestions for the improvement of my work. Thanks are also due for the courtesies extended to me by Miss Jayne Ringrose and Miss Margaret Pamplin, Assistant Library Officers of University Library, Cambridge. The staff of the Adelphi University Computer Center was of invaluable assistance in helping me to compile a complete list of the words in the romance and the lines in which they occurred. I was, thereby, enabled to check every appearance of every word, so that accuracy in the glossary, I hope, has been more nearly achieved. My colleagues in the Department of Humanities of the U.S. Merchant Marine Academy, Kings Point are also to be thanked for their encouragement of this project.

I am grateful, finally, to my parents, who have always applauded my scholarly interests, and to my husband and son, who cheerfully endured the preparation of this book.

CONTENTS

ABBREVIATIONS

Archiv	*Archiv für das Studium der neuren Sprachen und Litteraturen*
EETS, OS, ES	Early English Text Society, Original Series, Early Series
ES	*Englische Studien*
JEGP	*Journal of English and Germanic Philology*
MÆ	*Medium Ævum*
MED	*Middle English Dictionary* (Michigan)
MLN	*Modern Language Notes*
MP	*Modern Philology*
MLR	*Modern Language Review*
OED	*Oxford English Dictionary*
PAPS	*Proceedings of the American Philosophical Society*
PQ	*Philological Quarterly*
SATF	*Société des Anciens Textes Français*
Spec.	*Speculum*

INTRODUCTION

THE MANUSCRIPT

MS Cambridge Ff. 2.38 is a folio, on paper, of 247 leaves, $11\frac{3}{4}$ in. $\times 8\frac{1}{8}$ in. For the most part, the manuscript contains religious literature[1] and didactic romances, suggesting that it may have been a tale book copied in a monastery.

The manuscript was number 690 in the collection of John Moore (1646–1714), Bishop of Ely, whose library was purchased by King George I and presented to the Cambridge University Library in 1715. Nothing further is known about its provenance.

The foliation of the entire manuscript as assembled until June 1972 was originally numbered 1–247 throughout. However, Henry Bradshaw, who was Librarian from 1867 to 1886, realised that the first thirty-three leaves had been bound out of order and, moreover, that the original fol. 1, 2, 22–7, 141, 144 and fol. 157r–160r were lost. He accordingly renumbered the folia, leaving two sets of handwritten numbers in the upper right-hand corner of each leaf.

In June 1972 the old nineteenth-century brown calf binding was replaced by boards covered with marble paper and a red leather spine. Also, the disorder in the early leaves of the manuscript was rectified.

The *Catalogue of Manuscripts* describes the handwriting as 'uniform';[2] however, my study of a microfilm copy of the manuscript and, later, personal examination of the actual folio in Cambridge reveal that this is not the case. Although the hands are quite similar, there are certainly variations from page to page in the evenness of the hand and in the colour of

---

[1] Among the religious pieces there are twenty short poems—one of these a saint's life—and eight prose narratives, three of these also saints' lives. Of the sixteen long narrative poems in the manuscript nine are romances: *The Erle of Tolous, Syr Egyllamoure of Artas, Syr Tryamoure, A Tale of the Emperor Octavian, Sir Beves of Hampton, Dioclesian the Emperor . . ., Guy, Earl of Warwick, Le Bone Florence of Rome, Robert of Sicily, Sir Degaré.*

[2] H. R. Luard *et al., A Catalogue of the Manuscripts Preserved in the Library of the University of Cambridge* (Cambridge, 1857), II, 404.

the ink, a major change to blacker ink occurring on fol.
64r–67r and on 42r where the ink becomes darker, but reverts
to the usual brown on the verso of the leaf. The marked
change occurring at fol. 93r–156v does tempt one to conclude
that there has been a change of scribes, as the handwriting
becomes very heavy and widely spaced. The light hand which
begins *Guy, Earl of Warwick* at fol. 161r is probably the same
hand that wrote *Le Bone Florence of Rome* which follows.
Besides the similarity in the graphs, both romances average
thirty-six lines per column and contain marginal scribbles, writ-
ten in the same hand as the text, which are boxed in the same
way ('4 gat tyn haste', fol. 180v.; 'full grete othys', fol. 241v.).

The handwriting of *Le Bone Florence of Rome* is essentially
a blend of two kinds of cursive script. The first has usually
been referred to in England as 'court hand' or 'charter hand'.
Parkes[3] names it 'Anglicana' book hand since the varieties of
this hand are peculiar to English manuscripts of the fourteenth
and fifteenth centuries. The second type of cursive script is
secretary hand, a continental script which possessed letter
forms and stylistic features which had no counterparts in
traditional English hands. It was introduced into England
during the third quarter of the fourteenth century.

Mixed hands are particularly difficult to date unless one is
able to relate enough separate details to those in datable
examples of the script. The results of my comparison of the
individual ingredients of the hand in *Florence* to other dated
scripts indicate that it is probably a late fifteenth-century
copy.[4] However, the fullest reservations must be added as to
the possible persistence of old forms. There was, in fact, some
resemblance to early sixteenth-century hands.[5]

[3] Malcolm B. Parkes, *English Cursive Book Hands, 1250–1500*
(Oxford, 1969), 21–4.

[4] Cf. especially the plate in Wright's *English Vernacular Hands: From the
Twelfth to the Fifteenth Centuries* (Oxford, 1960) and the sketches based
on dated manuscripts in Charles Johnson and Hilary Jenkinson, *English
Court Hand A.D. 1066–1500* (1915; rpt. New York, 1967), I, 3–55.

[5] Cf. the sixteenth-century hands in G. E. Dawson and L. Kennedy-
Skipton, *Elizabethan Handwriting, 1500–1600* (New York, 1968), pp.
29 (Plate 1B), 33, 35.

Among the late fifteenth-century features of the handwriting the most notable is, perhaps, the mixed hand itself. Another striking end-of-the-century feature is the habit the hooks of ascenders have of trailing into the body of letters. Also descenders tend to be longer than ascenders and frequently run into the letters in the line below.

Some of the shapes of individual letters are particularly characteristic of the late fifteenth century; for example, double *f* sometimes has the curious compass-like appearance in the downstroke which is noticeable toward the end of the century.

Finally, there are two special signs in *Florence* which can be fairly well dated; the Tironian sign for *and* (1478) and the final curl which stands for *-ys* (1488).[6]

There are no markings to indicate punctuation. We have only the capitals at the beginning of each line to mark the individual verses of the poem.

VERSIONS AND ORIGINS

Versions. 'The unfortunate, persecuted maiden! The subject is as old as the world . . .';[7] and there are hundreds of permutations of the tale in popular folk legend as well as in romance. The version to which Florence gives her name is distinguished from the other tales about persecuted women, such as Emaré, Constance and Griselda, by two characteristics: (i) exile is always caused by the accusations of a rejected brother-in-law, and (ii) after numerous persecutions and sufferings, the heroine's healing powers bring together her persecutors, who confess their crimes.

Wallensköld[8] bases a reconstruction of the outlines of a lost Sanskrit version of the Florence story on three extant Oriental texts: the *Touti-Nameh*, the *Thousand and One Nights*, and

---

[6] Johnson and Jenkinson, 62–3. These pages contain sketches of dated symbols.

[7] Mario Praz, *The Romantic Agony* (London, 1933), 97.

[8] A. Wallensköld, 'Le Conte de la Femme Chaste Convoitée par son Beau-frère', *Acta Societatis Scientiarum Fennicae*, 37 (Helsingfors, 1907), 9.

the *Thousand and One Days*. It is Wallensköld's belief that the original may have been transmitted to Europe before the end of the eleventh century. The earliest extant version, the Persian *Touti-Nameh* (1330) of Nakhchabi, derives from a portion of an earlier *Touti-Nameh* which was a twelfth-century translation of a Sanskrit original, now represented by the *Soukasaptati*. There is a Turkish version of the primitive *Touti-Nameh* dating from the beginning of the fifteenth century in which our tale is called the 'Tale of Merhuma'.[9] In the Arabic *Thousand and One Nights*, the earliest manuscript of which dates from 1400, there are three versions of the story represented by the 'Adventures of the Cauzee, His Wife . . .',[10] 'The Jewish Cadi and His Pious Wife',[11] and 'The Pious Woman Accused of Lewdness'.[12] The story of chaste Repsima[13] occurs in the third branch of the Oriental versions, the *Thousand and One Days*, which is probably a translation from Persian; the earliest redaction is a fifteenth-century manuscript in Turkish.

Two features distinguish the Oriental stories from the two hundred and sixty European versions. First, the husband in the western tales is always a man of high rank: an emperor or king,[14] and second, the heroine has her brother-in-law imprisoned after his attempted assault on her virtue.[15] The oldest European version is the story of Crescentia, whose name is frequently used to describe the general type of 'la femme chaste convoitée par son beau-frère'. Crescentia first appears

---

[9] *Tuti-Nameh*, ed. George Rosen, 'Geschichte der Merhuma' (Leipzig, 1858), I, 89–108.

[10] *Arabian Nights Entertainments*, ed. Jonathan Scott, 'The Adventures of the Cauzee, His Wife . . .' (London, 1811), VI, 396–408.

[11] *The Book of the Thousand Nights and One*, ed. John Payne, 'The Jewish Cadi and His Pious Wife' (London, 1883), V, 9–13.

[12] *Tales from the Arabic*, ed. John Payne, 'The Pious Woman Accused of Lewdness' (London, 1884), III, 263–74.

[13] *Mille et un Jours*, trans. Petis de la Croix, 'Histoire de Repsima' (Paris, 1840), V, 241–95.

[14] See *infra*, p. 13: I argue that the profession of the husband in the Oriental versions—that of judge—seems to be a significant factor in determining origins.

[15] Wallensköld, 23–4.

in the Old High German *Kaiserchronik*[16] (*c.* 1150). The tale
also occurs as a derivative *chanson* in several fourteenth-
century manuscripts.[17] According to Wallensköld, the story of
Crescentia is probably a variant of a Miracle of the Virgin
which appeared in a collection of quasi-historical tales about
the Roman emperors. Other scholars, for example Stefanovic,
consider the Miracle part of an independent group.

It was inevitable that a tale about the vindication of a
falsely accused woman should become a Miracle of the Virgin;
by the twelfth century Mary had become the Mother of Mercy
whose privilege it was to intercede for justice from God.[18] The
presentation of the Florence story as a miracle occurs at least
as early as the second half of the twelfth century in a *mariale*
of the Bibliothèque Nationale (MS 14463).[19] It is an anonymous
prose account in Latin which appears as the forty-fifth tale.
Wallensköld identifies four classes of this miracle—in Latin,
French, Dutch, and Icelandic;[20] he seems to have overlooked
the English rendering of the miracle.[21] Hilka also points to
three additional Latin versions of the twelfth-century Miracle
in fourteenth- and fifteenth-century texts.[22] The Miracle was
evidently a popular tale. Since the heroine of the story is an
empress of Rome and we know that she has Oriental ante-
cedents, it seems likely that this Miracle may be an example of
what Evelyn Wilson describes as the 'quickening interest of the
twelfth century in the matter of ancient Rome' prompting 'the
transformation of some highly pagan tales into Mary legends'.[23]

Vincent of Beauvis incorporates the Miracle into his

[16] *Die Kaiserchronik*, ed. Edward Schröder, 'Crescentia' (Hannover,
1892), 289–314.
[17] A. Wallensköld, *Florence de Rome: Chanson, D'Aventure du Premier
Quart du 13ᵉ Siècle*, Société des Anciens Textes Françaises (1909; rpt.
New York, 1968), I, 125.
[18] *The Stella Maris of John of Garland*, ed. Evelyn Faye Wilson
(Cambridge, Mass., 1946), 4.
[19] Wallensköld, 'Le Conte de la Femme Chaste', 33.
[20] *Ibid.*, 36.
[21] This version is anthologised by Beverly Boyd in *The Middle
English Miracles of the Virgin* (San Marino, 1964), 64–7.
[22] Alfons Hilka, 'Zum Crescentiastoff', *Archiv*, 133 (1915), 136.
[23] Wilson, 8.

Speculum Historiale (1244–7), and many subsequent anthologisers of exempla for sermons used it. Although it usually appears as an exemplary story under the heading *castitas*, it should be noted that the story has also been used to illustrate *pietas*—a point I shall return to.

Gautier de Coinci produced a famous French poetic version[24] of the Latin Miracle before 1222. A French miracle play[25] of the end of the fourteenth, or beginning of the fifteenth, century, is more or less based on an account in *Les Vies des Pères* which is an abbreviated version of the twelfth-century Miracle in which the empress is exposed on a rock in the middle of a river.[26]

Closer to the original Latin Miracle is a seventeenth-century Italian drama[27] based on Giovanni Briccio's poem, 'La Historia di Flavia Imperatrice'[28] (sixteenth century). Also in Italian is a prose narrative in which the heroine is named Guglielma[29] (fourteenth century), and a sacred play based on this narrative by Antonio Pulci[30] (end of the fifteenth century).

On the Iberian peninsula, a Galician translation of De Coinci's work probably served as a basis for one of Alfonso el Sabio's *Cantigas de Santa Maria*.[31] Balthasar Dias (sixteenth century) may also have based a Portuguese romance on the same translation.[32] According to Wallensköld, Juan Timoneda,

---

[24] 'De l'Emperirix qui Garda Sa Chastée par Moult Temptacions', *Nouveau Reueil de Fabliaux et Contes Inédits*, ed. Dominique Martín Méon (Paris, 1823), II, 1–128.

[25] Louis Monmerqué and F. Michel, eds., *Théâtre Français au Moyen Age*, 'Mystère de l'Empereris de Rome' (Paris, 1814), 365–416.

[26] This abbreviated version is told in prose as 'De La Bonne Imperatrice' in *Fabliaux ou Contes du XIIe et du XIIIe Siècle*, ed. P. J. B. Legrand, 3rd ed. (Paris, 1829), V, 125–9.

[27] Wallensköld, 'Le Conte de la Femme Chaste', 48.

[28] Giovanni Briccio, *La Historia di Flavia Imperatrice* (Venice, 1812).

[29] Wallensköld, *Florence de Rome*, I, 121.

[30] 'Santa Guglielma', *Sacre Rappresentazione*, ed. Alessandro d'Ancona (Firenze, 1872), III, 208–34.

[31] *Cantigas de Santa Maria*, ed. Walter Mettman (Coimbra, 1961), II, 7–12.

[32] 'Historia da Imperatriz Porcina' in *Floresta de Varios Romances*, ed. Theo. Braga (Portugal, 1869), 104–49.

a fifteenth-century writer of novellas from Valencia, based a tale in his *Patrañuelo*[33] directly on the Latin Miracle.[34]

A German poem[35] by the fifteenth-century poet Hans Rosenblut is also largely based on the Latin Miracle. It is notable, however, for naming the emperor Octavianus, the name of the emperor in the Continental *Gesta Romanorum*, which contains still another rendering of the Florence story.

The *Gesta Romanorum* was intended as a compendium of edifying stories for the use of preachers. Its nucleus may have been an actual series of stories derived from Roman history, though in its extant forms it is a mélange of folklore and pseudo-history. In the fourteenth century, an abridged version of the Florence story appeared in the *Gesta* and was included in the Continental and Anglo-Latin manuscripts. The *Gesta* version was given also in a metrical paraphrase by Thomas Hoccleve in 1421.[36]

Florence of Rome gives her name to seven manuscripts. In enumerating these, I will adopt the letters first assigned to them by Rudolph Wenzel.[37] There are two manuscripts which present the *chanson* of *Florence de Rome*[38] in its entirety: MS Nouv. acquis franc. 4192 of the Bibliothèque Nationale (P.), belonging to the end of the thirteenth or beginning of the fourteenth century, and a late thirteenth-century manuscript owned by the d'Arcy Hutton estate. There is also a badly mutilated fragment of the *chanson*, Lansdowne 362, ff. 75–6, 77 of the British Museum (L.).

Besides these three manuscripts, there are four other redactions of the story about Florence of Rome: an early

---

[33] 'Patraña Veintiuna' in *El Patrañuelo* (Madrid, 1958), 201–10.

[34] Wallensköld, 'Le Conte de la Femme Chaste', 55.

[35] 'Ein Liepleich History von Groszer Schone, Gedult und Kuscheit einer Edeln Keyseryn' in *Fastnachtspiele aus dem Funfzehnten Jahrhundert*, ed. Adelbert Keller (Stuttgart, 1853), III, 139–49.

[36] 'Fabula de Quadam Imperatrice Romana' in *Hoccleve's Works*, ed. F. J. Furnivall, EETS, ES, 61 (London, 1892), 140–73.

[37] *Die Fassungen der Sage von Florence de Rome*, Diss. Marburg, 1890, 5–6.

[38] The definitive edition has been published by Wallensköld, *Florence de Rome*, II. He collates the manuscripts.

fourteenth-century *Dit de Flourence de Rome* in quatrains of
the Bibliothèque Nationale, Paris (Notre-Dame 198) (D.);[39]
MS 24384 of the *fond français* of the Bibliothèque Nationale
which contains a long fifteenth-century version of *Florence de
Rome* in alexandrines (Q.);[40] a Spanish prose version (S.),
based on a late fourteenth-century manuscript in the Biblio-
teca Escorial;[41] and the fifteenth-century unique Middle
English version (R.).

A consideration of the relationship of the English version to
the oldest extant French text follows later in this Introduction.

While all the other versions of the Florence story are patently
about fictitious women, Hildegard, the heroine of a well-
known sub-group,[42] was said to be Charlemagne's wife.
According to one theory, represented by Wallensköld,[43] the
story of Hildegard goes back to a Bavarian schoolmaster,
Johannes Birck, who introduced it into his chronicle of the
Abbey of Kempten in 1484 or 1485. He attributed the role of
the heroine to the patroness of the abbey, Queen Hildegard.
This theory has been strongly contested by Stefanovic,[44] who
maintains that the Hildegard story is based on a popular
tradition independent of, and earlier than, Birck's version.

Origins. Five scholars have advanced as many theories in an
effort to establish the origin of the Florence story. The easiest
to defend—though not solely with the arguments the author
offers—seems to be that of Wallensköld.

Since all five suggestions hinge ultimately on the essential

---

[39] *Dit de Flourence de Rome* in *Nouveau Recueil de Contes, Dits,
Fabliaux et Autres Pièces Inédits des XIIIᵉ, XIVᵉ, et XVᵉ Siècles*, ed.
Achille Jubinal (Paris, 1839–42), VI, 88–117.

[40] Wallensköld, *Florence de Rome*, I, 4.

[41] *Historia Critica de la Litteratura Española*, ed. Amador de los Ríos,
'Cuento Muy Famoso del Enperador Ottas de Roma' (Madrid, 1864),
V, 391–468.

[42] The brothers Grimm include the tale in *Deutsche Sagen* (Leipzig,
1818), II, 83–5.

[43] Wallensköld, 'Le Conte de la Femme Chaste', 65 ff.

[44] S. Stefanovic, 'Die Crescentia–Florence Sage: eine Kritische
Studie ueber ihren Ursprung und ihre Entwicklung', *Romanische
Forschung*, 29 (1908), 461–557.

elements of the different versions, it may be useful here to enumerate the nine principal incidents: (i) the wooing of the heroine by her brother-in-law; (ii) the heroine's rejection of him and his accusation of adultery; (iii) her condemnation; (iv) her exile; (v) refuge in a household where she is accused of murdering the child of her protector by a rejected, revengeful, and murderous suitor; (vi) the second exile; (vii) a debtor, freed from the gallows by the heroine, sells her to a ship's captain; (viii) her escape after a storm wrecks the boat; (ix) her reputation as a healer draws all her afflicted persecutors together.

Grundtvig[45] rejected absolutely the hypothesis of an Oriental origin for the story. He regarded *le conte de la femme chaste convoitée par son beau-frère* as closely related to stories which actually fall within the more general cycle of tales about innocent persecuted women. As a result of his too unrestricted classification of the story, he concluded that the Danish ballad *Ravengaard og Memering* represented the oldest version of the Florence story. The Scandinavian ballad is actually related to the English *Sir Aldingar*.[46]

Stefanovic[47] also defended the idea of Germanic origins but, unlike Grundtvig, he addressed himself to the distinguishing elements of the various versions. According to Stefanovic, the core of the story, the episode of the brother-in-law's treachery, is of Germanic origin. He considered the prototype the Old English poem, *The Wife's Complaint*, and argued that the story, having long existed as a popular legend, gave birth to the legend of Hildegard, which was introduced late in the chronicles. By a combination of the story with others in which the heroine is accused of murdering an infant by a rejected suitor (notably the tale of the incestuous father), a new story was produced which has two persecutors. *Crescentia* represents the

[45] Svend Grundtvig, H. G. Nielsen, and A. Olrik, *Gamle Folkeviser*, I (Copenhagen, 1853), 195; III (Copenhagen, 1862), 782; IV (Copenhagen, 1883), 730.

[46] Francis J. Child, ed. *The English and Scottish Popular Ballads*, II (Boston, 1882–98), 33–48.

[47] Stefanovic, 461–557.

oldest version of this stage. The Miracle of the Virgin, which in its most typical form involves only two persecutors, was seen by Stefanovic as a later development of the Crescentia story, resulting from the cult of the Virgin. As for the versions represented by the *Gesta Romanorum* and the Florence sub-group, he regarded them as later amplifications, influenced by the Oriental versions.

If the Old English poem—the crux of Stefanovic's theory—contained the characteristic details of the first episode and the scene of reconciliation which typify the *conte de la femme chaste convoitée par son beau-frère*, it would be easier to accept its seniority. This is not, however, the case. In the Old English poem we infer that a woman, exiled by her husband upon the instigation of malevolent relatives and living alone in a cave, laments her husband and curses a vaguely indicated young man. That is all. The hypothesis that the Hildegard versions are generated from this poem is inadmissible.

The Hildegard story is the most important for Stefanovic's theory. He maintained that Birck, at the end of the fifteenth century, merely introduced into his chronicle at Kempten an old popular story, already in circulation prior to his time. If one considers the fact that there is not the least trace of an atribution to Hildegard as heroine before Birck, this theory becomes less convincing than the point of view represented by Wallensköld, who maintained that Birck simply adapted the twelfth-century Miracle of the Virgin.[48]

As to Stefanovic's suggestion about the evolution of *Crescentia*, it seems plausible, as Wallensköld argued, that by replacing St Peter for the Virgin the Latin Miracle could have generated the type represented in the *Kaiserchronik*. The reverse, however, could hardly have occurred, since the sea voyage in the Miracle during which the sailors try to abuse the heroine is clearly a fragment of the episode involving the fourth persecutor (the ship's captain). To Stefanovic the fact that both the longer European versions and the eastern stories contained the episodes of the debtor freed from the gallows and the ship's captain suggested that these incidents were added

[48] Wallensköld, 'Le Conte de la Femme Chaste', 65 ff.

to the type represented by *Crescentia*, which was then trans-
mitted to the Orient. Stefanovic rejected, *a priori*, the possi-
bility of a classification based on evolution by elimination of
episodes.

The last theory which has been presented in support of
European origins is that of Louis Karl.[49] He attributes the
appearance of Hungry in the European divisions of the story—
the *Gesta*, the Florence sub-group, and the Miracle—to the
influence of St Elizabeth of Hungary (d. 1231). Karl pointed
out that the basic outlines of the saint's life were similar to the
pattern of Florence's persecution, exile, saintliness, and fame
as a healer. None of the versions dating before the second
quarter of the thirteenth century mentions Hungary. Karl's
theory cannot be regarded as more than an exceedingly
interesting explanation of the appearance of a local reference
which in no way precludes the possibility of dissemination from
the east.

In an attempt to refute the theory of Germanic origins,
Adolf Mussafia,[50] in 1865, argued for the priority of the
Oriental versions of the story despite the lateness of the
manuscripts. Mussafia was convinced that the eastern stories
were introduced into the west in the form found in the
Kaiserchronik and the various redactions of the Miracle of the
Virgin. Though he agreed with the theory of eastern origins,
Wallensköld largely discredited Mussafia's view by noting that
the western versions contain an episode absent in all the
Oriental tales: 'le beau-frère, à la suite de ses premiers efforts
pour séduire l'heroine, est enfermé dans un lieu solitaire'.[51] It
is unlikely that two waves of influence could have triggered the
same innovation in the European versions. Wallensköld
maintained that the richest form of the story was found, in
logically combined episodes, among the Persian and Arabic

[49] 'Florence de Rome et la Vie de Deux Saints de Hongrie', *Revue
des Langues Romanes*, 52 (1909), 163–80.

[50] 'Über eine Italienische Metrische Darstellung der Crescentia Saga',
Sitzungsberichte der Phil.-Hist. Classe der Kais. Akad. der Wissenschaften,
51 (Vienna, 1865), 589–692.

[51] Wallensköld, *Florence de Rome*, ii, 107–8.

versions. Although there were some differences between these, Wallensköld tried to prove by analysis and reconstruction that all the Oriental versions were traceable to a common Sanskrit source.[52] One of the eastern versions is in the *Touti-Nameh* of Nakhchabi. It is part of an earlier, lost *Touti-Nameh* (probably of the twelfth century) which is itself a somewhat altered translation of the ancient Sanskrit original, now imperfectly represented by the *Soukasaptati*. This fact alone is a strong argument in favour of an Oriental source and, to my knowledge, the relationship of the *Touti-Nameh* to the *Soukasaptati* has never been challenged.

The western development of the story is easily traced from this point. Since in all the western versions the heroine's husband is a king or emperor and they all include the imprisonment of the brother-in-law in a tower, Wallensköld concluded that the western branches have developed from a common European version which contained these two alterations of the ancient eastern story. He considered the various versions of the *Gesta Romanorum* and the Florence sub-group, all retaining the four persecutors of the ancient eastern versions, the most closely related to the Oriental versions and representatives of a literary tradition. The absence of the two persecutors (the thief rescued from the gallows and the ship's captain) in the Miracle of the Virgin, *Crescentia*, and *Hildegard* sub-groups led Wallensköld to conclude that they were products of the oral transmission of the primitive western source. The Latin Miracle of the Virgin, while omitting the debtor and ship's captain, retains possible evidence of the captain (the sea voyage). Wallensköld, therefore, advanced the notion that the oral versions of the primitive western source ended finally in a written text which was probably some version of the Latin Miracle.

Wallensköld's hypothesis that the longer western versions and the Miracle—among the shorter versions—are most closely related to the Oriental versions is, I think, correct. Besides the reasons he advanced, there is evidence of their close relationship in the very heavy stress they all place on the

[52] Wallensköld, 'Le Conte de la Femme Chaste', 9–23.

idea of justice—an emphasis which is not found in the Hildegard and Crescentia sub-group.

Not only is there the implicit justice of the concluding vindication episode in the eastern versions, together with explicit references to the justice of Allah, but there are also reinforcing details related to the idea of justice: (i) all of them contain a scene in which the brother-in-law falsely charges the heroine with adultery and brings her before a court of law; (ii) the husband in the three versions of the story contained in the *Thousand and One Nights* is actually, by profession, a judge.[53] He does not act judicially as judge or prosecutor in the story, but in 'The Jewish Cadi and His Pious Wife' the husband is characterised as a pious man. In fact, he leaves his wife in order to make a pilgrimage to Jerusalem. The three European versions which are, according to Wallensköld's theory, most closely connected to the Oriental tales seem to have been particularly influenced by these elements in the eastern versions; in the transplanting of the stories the details relating to the idea of justice were adapted for the orthodox theology.

The author of *Le Bone Florence of Rome* lays particular emphasis on the idea of God's justice, which punishes the wicked and preserves the faithful. This is particularly evident in the miracles by means of which God intervenes to save the heroine. In referring to his source, the poet says at one point:

> The boke seyþ God þat vs boght
> Many myrakyls for hur he wroght
> Many a oon and thyckfolde
> [ll. 871-3]

The story reaches a climax when all four men who have injured Florence are stricken with disease and come to the monastery to be healed. Their public confession of their attempts to assault Florence is still another manifestation of the justice of God, and the realistic description of their

---

[53] The husbands in both the 'Tale of Merhuma' (*Tuti-Nameh*) and the 'Histoire de Repsima' (*Thousand and One Days*), while not judges, are described as pious.

painful symptoms (ll. 2020 ff.) stresses the contrast between reward and punishment. The poem concludes with a reminder to the reader that God always metes out justice appropriately to the good and the wicked:

> Forþy schulde men and women als
> Them bethynke or þey be false
>> Hyt makyth so fowle an ende
> Be hyt neuyr so slylye caste
> 3yt hyt schamyþ þe maystyr at þe laste
>> In what londe þat euyr þey lende
> In meene be the iiij fekyll
> That harmed feyre Florence so mykyll
>> The trewest that men kende.

[ll. 2176–84]

There are similar passages in the Spanish and French versions.

The section of the *chanson* which is headed 'Piété de Florence' makes clear that Florence's *piété* consists in giving each man his due. There is a certain justice in the balance of the action in which Florence heals only after having first elicited a confession from each of her persecutors. God the Judge is evident in Florence the healer. The connection between piety and justice, as we shall see in a moment, is consistent with the medieval church's classification of piety as a part of justice.

Like the Florence sub-group, the *Gesta Romanorum* contains a justice motif. In a 'Moral' appended to the conclusion of tale 249 of the Latin *Gesta* ('De Octaviano Qui Super Omnia Uxorem Dilexit') an allegorical equation is set up—the emperor = Jesus Christ = Judge:

> The Emperor is our master Jesus Christ. The Empress is the soul which was entrusted to his brother, Mankind. But alas the Flesh so strongly enticed the soul to sin that it could not rest. What was to be done? Obviously to incarcerate the Flesh by way of penance. But Holy Church recounts to us reports that our emperor is to come out of the Holy Land on the day of Judgement. . . .[54]

[54] Translated from *Gesta Romanorum*, ed. Hermann Oesterley (Berlin, 1872), 652. The standard English translation by Charles Swann includes the story but omits the 'Moral'.

Evidence of the justice motif in the versions of the Miracle is slighter, perhaps because the narrative is so brief. It is particularly noteworthy that in Etienne de Bourbon's collection of exempla the story appears under the heading 'Pietas'. The Greek term for *pietas* is *eusebeia* and was used by the Greek philosophers, especially Plato, and by the Greek Fathers of the Church in the sense of respect for the gods (or God) and one's parents.[55] Among the Roman authors Vergil and Cicero stand out for the frequency of use of the noun *pietas*, or the adjective *pius*. Vergil used the noun twenty-two times in the *Aeneid*[56] where it almost invariably has the sense of the Greek *eusebeia*. Cicero formulated a definition of the word which embraced the main traditions of the term and made them comprehensive and more specific: 'This is pietas: to fulfil one's duty and conscientious service towards our own flesh and blood and those having the interests of our country at heart.'[57] In the Middle Ages Thomas Aquinas, drawing on Cicero, explained *pietas* more fully as a specific form of the virtue of justice:

> Cicero classifies piety as a part of justice. . . . What makes any virtue to be specific is that its relationship to its objective is based on some specific moral value in the objective. Since honouring a debt towards someone else is a function of justice generally, a specific kind of justice arises wherever there is a specific basis for indebtedness to any person. This is the case in regard to anyone who, in the natural course of things, is a source of our life and its development . . . piety is the response towards those sources. . . .[58]

[55] Plato, *The Republic*, trans. Paul Shorey (London, 1935), II, 497 (615c); Clement of Rome, 'The First Epistle of Clement to the Corinthians', *The Ante-Nicene Fathers*, ed. Alexander Roberts and James Donaldson (New York, 1926), I, ch. 11, p. 8; ch. 32, p. 13.

[56] A few examples: 'Aeneid' in *Vergil*, trans. R. Rushton Fairclough (London and Cambridge, Mass., 1954–6), I, l. 151; II, l. 690; VI, ll. 688, 769, 878; X, l. 824.

[57] From Cicero's *De Inventione Rhetorica* as quoted by Saint Thomas Aquinas, *Summa Theologica*, ed. and trans. Blackfriars (Virtues of Justice in the Human Community, trans. T. C. O'Brien (vol. 41)) (London and New York, 1964–), II–ii, Q. 101, Art. I.

[58] Aquinas, II–ii, Q. 101, Art. III.

In short, justice requires that one give every person what is due him. This is probably the sense in which the thirteenth-century Dominican Etienne de Bourbon understood the term as he used it in his collection of exempla. Further it is probably no accident, in the light of these findings about the justice motif, that Chaucer selected the Man of Law as narrator of the tale of Constance, one of Florence's literary cousins.

It goes without saying that the appearance of Mary, intercessor for justice from God, is a constant reminder of the idea of justice which appears in all the Miracles.

It is generally recognised that many tales popular in the west originated or received their present narrative form in the east. Three at least of the *Canterbury Tales* have been shown to have Oriental analogues: the Pardoner's account of the three rioters; the Merchant's pear-tree story; and that of the Manciple, concerning Phoebus and the speaking cow. There are several links in the chain by which Oriental fiction could have been introduced into the west. Certainly by the beginning of the twelfth century the east and west were coming into frequent contact. The pilgrimages and the crusades not only brought east and west together but they stimulated increasing travel in the west itself, whereby travellers in western Europe carried tales from one place to another by word of mouth. The growth of the mendicant orders and the roving character of the monks are additional important links in the chain uniting east and west. Also significant is the development of commerce; merchants undoubtedly could have carried tales back with them from the Orient.

It is likely that stories from the east began to reach western Europe long before the twelfth century. The Moslems, as is well known, were in Spain long before A.D. 800, so that transmission of Oriental stories to the west via Spain would have been a possibility at any time after the ninth century. If advanced developments in astrology, medicine, and chemistry of Arabic origin were introduced into Europe a century at least before the crusades, and if Sylvester II, who died in 1003, brought Arabic numerals to France, then it is not unreasonable to imagine that legendary stories might have begun to extend their influence at the same time. Wallensköld's dating of the transmission of the Oriental version of the Florence story to Europe at the eleventh century is, I think, very likely accurate.

LITERARY ASPECTS

A detailed discussion of the literary aspects of *Le Bone Florence of Rome* may be better understood after this brief summary of the action of the romance:

> Garcy, the old king of Constantinople, moved by tales of Florence's beauty, decides to sue for her hand. After consulting with his barons and Florence, his daughter, King Otes of Rome rejects the offer made by Garcy's emissaries. The returning messengers are full of news about glorious Rome and beautiful Florence. Angry at his rejection, Garcy declares war on Rome and sets sail with an army. Battle begins despite Florence's last-minute offer to marry Garcy in order to save the lives of Roman knights. Mylys and Emere, sons of the King of Hungary, come to King Otes's assistance. Florence and Emere fall in love, and are betrothed. While Emere is engaged in war in Constantinople, his brother Mylys—to whose care Florence is entrusted—tries to win Florence's love after giving a false account of Emere's death. Mylys is put in prison, and then released when news of Emere's return reaches Florence. She and Mylys ride out to meet Emere. While in the woods, the wicked Mylys renews his assaults on Florence's virtue and hangs her by the hair from a tree after being rebuffed once again. Sir Tyrry rescues Florence from the woods and brings her home, where his steward, Machary, attempts to seduce Florence. He too is rejected, and takes revenge by murdering Tyrry's daughter and putting the bloody knife in the hand of sleeping Florence. Tyrry takes pity on Florence and sends her into exile in a forest. After still further adventures and attempts to compromise her virtue, Florence arrives at a convent where she is received by the nuns, one of whom she heals of a serious disease. Her fame spreads. One by one, all of her persecutors come to her for healing. Before helping them, she makes them confess their crimes against her, and is reunited in the end with Emere.

Viewed as a whole, the action of the romance leaves a dual impression. The extensive first section, irrelevant to the moral purpose of the romance, is full of typical romantic elements: the arrival of messengers from distant lands; the detailed descriptions of journeys, clothes, armour, costly gifts, palace halls, and battle scenes; and the love between a conventional chivalric knight and lady. Florence is, throughout the first half of the story, not unlike the traditionally courted ladies of romance literature. The poet is at great pains to describe her beauty, her upbringing, and her aristocratic position as daughter of the king of Rome. Wallensköld views this first part of the romance as a French poet's attempt to create a *chanson de geste* out of Oriental materials: 'C'est que le poète, tout en prenant pour sujet un conte d'origine orientale, qu'il tenait on ne sait d'où, a évidemment voulu composer une véritable chanson de geste.'[59] However near the mark this idea may be, it will hardly do to explain why the English poet retained so many of these romantic elements. It may be simply, as Dieter Mehl suggests, that the variety and swiftness of the first half was intended to 'heighten our interest'[60] in the story. With the sinful demands of Mylys, the type of the faithful, chaste, and holy wife begins to show itself. This aspect dominates the second part of the romance and gives it its exemplary character. It is with the second part that the romance begins to align itself with the legendary Crescentia–Constance material.

The poet gives no indication of some underlying significance connecting the two parts. It would have been possible to relate the suffering of the heroine in the second part to her worldliness in the first. Florence's rejection of Garcy on the very natural grounds of physical abhorrence, for instance, might have been exploited to this end, for initially Florence is selfishly ready to let knights die for her right to a younger, more appealing husband. But the poet was evidently indifferent to creating this kind of unity, and is content to develop the fabliau elements of a May–January situation and nothing more.

The first part does contain some religious elements, notably

[59] *Florence de Rome*, I, 42.
[60] Dieter Mehl, *The Middle English Romances of the Thirteenth and Fourteenth Centuries* (London, 1968), 146.

—as in the French version—long prayers to God and the saints not to disregard the petitioner. These details are, nevertheless, subsidiary to the predominant adventure-story character of the first half, and insufficient as a real link to the exemplary second half.

The poet's perceptiveness about human behaviour, his realistic vigour, and feeling for dramatic poetic effects and narrative pace are most evident in part one, where the hagiological element in his story does not interfere.

Two striking examples of the poet's perceptiveness about human behaviour occur in the presentation of the episode of Garcy's suit. There is first a splendid portrait of Garcy's shrewd ambassador (ll. 205–25). After the initial presentation of gifts, he gets right to the proposal: 'He [Garcy] byddyth, wythowt avysement, / That þy doghtur be to hym sent, / For to lygg hym by.' Almost as if to soften the impact of this demand, the speaker seems to suggest how little, in fact, would be required to satisfy what is really a harmless old man in need of comforting: 'Hys body ys bresyd, hys bones are olde / . . . she may kepe hym fro þe colde.' The rest of the speech continues the pattern of an alternating hard and soft line of attack. *Hurry and follow my instructions!*: 'Haue done now hastelye.' *Your daughter will be well taken care of. And to tell you the truth, I personally would like to see her as my queen; she's very pretty*: 'In comely cloþyng sche shall be cledd, / I haue grete hope he wyll hur wedd, / Sche ys a feyre lady.' *If you don't take my advice, Garcy will ravage your country*:

> And yf þou sende hur not soone,
> Hastelye, wythowten wone,
> > Then ryseth ther a stryfe,
> Ellys wyll he hygh þe nere,
> Wyth hys ryche powere,
> > And feche hur as hys wyfe.
> He wyll dystroye þy bygly landys,
> And slee all þat before hym standys,
> > And lose full many a lyfe.

You see, you have no choice. Decide as I advise: 'Haue done . . . hastelye in hye, / An answare muste we gyf Garcy.' We seem to hear the chameleon voice of the diplomat as he tries to create and react to responses in his listener.

Florence's quick, even witty, answer to Garcy's proposal has the authentic sound of a court lady, made confident of her own worth by a life filled with constant attentions,

> . . . Jhesu forbede!'
> Sche seyde, 'Be God þat boght me dere,
> Me had leuyr þe warste bachylere,
>   In all my fadurs thede,
> Then for to lye be hys bresyd boones.
> When he coghyth and oldely grones,
>   I can not on hys lede.'

[ll. 243–9]

One can imagine that Chaucer's Prioress, had she stayed at court rather than entered the convent, would have reacted with equal abhorrence to such an unequal union. It is only after Florence is confronted by the bloody consequences of her natural inclination to serve her own desires that she offers to sacrifice herself to Garcy. The Florence of the first half of the romance is far from the type of the devout daughter in the *King of Tars* who rejects the Sultan because he is not a Christian.

The poet's considerable skill at realistic description, which in part two is made to serve the exemplary purpose, as in the episode where Florence and Mylys have strongly contrasting reactions to eating the hermit's bread, is used in part one primarily to entertain. For instance, Syr Garcy, a suitor at the age of 100, is presented as the comic antithesis of the chivalric knight:

> Hys flesche trembylde for grete elde,
> Hys blode colde hys body unwelde,
>   Hys lyppes blo forthy;
> He had more mystyr of a gode fyre,
> Of bryght brondys brennyng schyre,
>   To beyke hys boones by,
> A softe bath a warme bedd,
> Then any maydyn for to wedd,
>   And gode encheson why,
> For he was bresyd and all tobrokyn,
> Ferre trauelde in harnes and of warre wrokyn

[ll. 94–104]

The poet is as concrete about enumerating the physical details of the old man's repulsiveness as is Chaucer in his description of January,

> The slakke skin aboute his nekke shaketh,
> [l. 1849]

> In his night-cappe, and with his nekke lene;[61]
> [l. 1853]

or Boccaccio's Agapes on the subject of her husband's senility,

> 'le sue guance, per crespezza ruvide . . .'[62]

> 'il sottile collo ne vend ne osso nasconle.'[63]

The poet was also capable of producing dramatic effects, as in the controlled introduction which builds gradually to Florence's lament for her dead father, 'Allas,' sche seyde, 'þat Y was borne! / My fadur for me hys lyfe haþ lorne' (ll. 826–7).[64] The corpse of the dead king is brought to Rome in silence, 'Wythowten belle or proceson' (l. 797), so as not to attract the attention of the enemy or to shock the unsuspecting Florence. Once safely inside the city, the silence is broken just long enough to raise the standard and vow revenge against Garcy. The focus of the narrative shifts quickly to Florence's chamber, where the ladies-in-waiting announce that a corpse is being drawn silently into the city. Florence looks out; recognises her father's horse being led by a knight; turns pale; and goes with a maid to the receiving hall of the palace. Alone she approaches the bier, and swoons after lifting the cloth from her father's face. The lament follows. With great economy, the poet has moved through four different locations within thirty-one lines, all the time managing large numbers of characters, describing

---

[61] Both lines are from Geoffrey Chaucer's *The Merchant's Tale*, *The Works of Geoffrey Chaucer*, 2nd ed., ed. F. N. Robinson (1957), 115–27. All citations from Chaucer are to this edition.

[62] Giovanni Boccaccio's 'L'Ameto' in 'L'Ameto, Lettere, Il Corbaccio' in *Scrittori D'Italia*, No. 182, *Opere*, v., ed. Nicola Bruscoli (Bari, 1940), 94.

[63] *Ibid.*

[64] Velma B. Richmond discusses the lament in *Laments for the Dead in Medieval Narrative* (Pittsburgh, 1966), 106 ff.

a variety of actions, indicating nuances of emotion, and managing the slow, deliberate pace so that it builds to Florence's collapse and lament. Miss Richmond is put off by what she considers an unfortunate conclusion to this scene which presents the nobles, with nervous wringing of hands, selfishly wondering who will provide them with lands, horses, hawks, and hounds for the hunt now that Emperor Otes is dead. It seems to me, however, that their evident weakness gives the entire scene added point. They sound like helpless children who have lost the generous emperor on whom they depended as on a father. How, indeed, can Rome survive the loss of Otes when the city is left to such weak men?

The death of her father, followed by Mylys's false account of Emere's death, leads Florence to marry herself to God in chastity:

> Furste þen was my fadur slayne,
> And now my lorde ys fro me tane,
>   Y wyll loue no ma,
> But hym þat boght me on þe rode
>   [ll. 1102–5]

The vow sets the exemplary second half of the romance in motion. Florence's flawless beauty, which is in the first part the conventional attribute of the heroine of courtly romance, is raised to a visible symbol of Florence's virtuous nature. Left hanging from a tree by the hair, the sufferer gives off light; expelled from the court of Tyrry, Florence rides through the woods where 'all glemed there sche glode' (l. 1709). The specific virtues which she exemplifies are *castitas*, supported by *pietas* and *fortitudo*. However, the symbolic beauty of the heroine is not the most important means by which the exemplary type is demonstrated in the romance. The virtues indicated by Florence's outward appearance are manifest in her Christian behaviour. Progressively more threatening assaults by Mylys, Machary, the steward, and the sea captain put Florence's vow of chastity to a hard test. Her power to resist in each case comes from her *pietas*, the conviction that God in his justness will protect those who live in Christian virtue, and her *fortitudo*, the sure knowledge that her conduct is consistent with the commands of God. Florence's behaviour at the time of the nadir of her sorrowful history, the sea captain's coming to assert the right he believes he has purchased, is characteristic. Her *pietas* and *fortitudo* enable her to contradict his intentions, stating what she knows to be the position of God: 'Nay that schall not bee / Throw helpe of Hym in Trynyte . . .' (ll. 1846–7). Her prayer to Mary for the protection of her maidenhood indicates, further, that by this point her trust has already been ratified by her experience of heavenly aid, 'Lady Mary free, / Now thou haue mercy on me, / Thou faylyst me neuyr at nede' (ll. 1852–4). And heavenly intervention in the affairs of the deserving *is* immediate. A sudden storm leaves Florence's adversary floundering in the sea while she is washed safely to shore. This happy turn of events, like that in the other episodes, by offering concrete evidence for the heavenly reward of God-pleasing acts and for the effectiveness of prayer, calls the audience to imitate the heroine's virtues.

Without reference to the specific virtues of *castitas*, *pietas*, and *fortitudo*, Florence's conduct is frequently contrasted, in a more general way, with that of her adversaries. There is, for example, the instance of the hermit's reception of Mylys and Florence. Whereas Florence says she considers his water and barley bread a delicious meal, Mylys cannot swallow the stuff ('Hyt stekyth in my hals', l. 1472) and proceeds to beat the hermit.

Her final position as saintly healer in the sanctity of a cloister is in stark contrast to the unhappy lot of her persecutors who go to Florence with the most ghastly diseases. These are all realistically described by the poet who presents them as a strong warning to imitate the other kind of life-style. It should be noted, as Hanspeter Schelp observes, that the exemplary imperative of the 'Romance gode' (l. 2185) keeps the description from being purely realistic, as in the first half of the romance,[65]

---

[65] *Exemplarische Romanzen im Mittelenglischen*, *Palaestra*, 246 (Göttingen, 1967), 127.

Mylys that hur aweye ledd,
He was the fowlest mesell bredd,
  Of pokkys and bleynes bloo.
And Machary þat wolde hur haue slayne,
He stode schakyng the sothe to sayne,
  Crokyd and crachyd thertoo.

[ll. 2020–5]

This description has an obvious didactic function: to express the causal relationship between the horrible diseases and the evil actions of the persecutors.

The French *Florence de Rome*[66] contains a similar episode in which the persecutors recount the misfortunes which befell them after their attempted assaults on Florence's virtue. But the difference between the English and the French versions is instructive. It is not enough for the English poet that the diseased, maimed men recognise their sinful natures by confessing to the saintly lady. No sooner do they admit their sins and become healed than Emere, the man to whom Florence has been faithful, orders that they be burned at the stake (ll. 2116–20). Florence, it seems, manages to bring as much disaster into the lives of men that attempt to tryst with her as any Keatsian *belle dame sans merci*. The poet preserves the impression of Florence's Christian forgiveness, however, by hastening to note her reaction to Emere's orders—'Then was the lady woo' (l. 2121). Nevertheless, Emere has his way. The English poet must keep the exemplary point clear: good is rewarded and evil punished—even if the scene of confession is made to appear senseless.

By a variety of changes and additions, the English adapter

---

[66] The text of this Chanson is in vol. II of Wallensköld. It is generally said that the English poem is a translation of a lost version of the chanson which was closely related to the extant French text. If the lost version was not itself an abridgement, the English poet condensed so ruthlessly that his version would be more appropriately referred to as an 'adaptation'. The English poem contains 2,187 lines as compared with 6,410 in the French. Moreover, very few lines can be regarded as exact translation. For a close study of the relationship between the French, Spanish and English texts, see Wenzel, *Die Fassungen der Sage von Florence de Rome*.

underlines the exemplary character of the romance. He eliminates revelatory dreams and prophesies and other such fantastic elements so that the turn of events will seem to hinge on the effective virtues of the exemplary character worthy of emulation. Thus, no magic brooch protects the English heroine's virginity, only her prayers to the Virgin. The English poet does, however, retain the miraculous ringing of the bells. When Florence, washed ashore after the shipwreck, approaches Beuerfayre, the bells of the cloister begin to ring of their own accord (ll. 1892 ff.). The reason this detail was retained is obvious; bells ringing by themselves are a common sign in hagiographic literature that a saint approaches.[67] The feature is, therefore, consistent with the religious intent of the English adapter.

There are other minor changes by which the English version underlines the religious character of the romance. Pope Simon is said to have composed the tale (l. 2173) and he does, in fact, make several appearances in the poem, most notably with some cardinals in a procession which welcomes Florence back to Rome at the conclusion of the tale (ll. 2143–51). Among some rather local religious details are: the description of the seven deadly sins depicted on the wall of Emperor Otes's palace (ll. 329–33) and the reference to the doctrine of trans-substantiation (ll. 1004–5).

It is evident, as in the French version, that Florence's fate is closely connected to that of Rome. Indeed, her beauty, which inspired Garcy's love in the first part of the romance, very nearly leads to the destruction of Rome. Although the English poet retains the historical opening with the conventional Troy material of romance and announces that he comes to Rome—the second Troy—to speak of Aeneas, the Rome that really interests him is not historical Rome but Rome, the 'chefe cyte of crystendome' (l. 17). It is this Rome which provides an appropriate backdrop for the English poet's conception of the story.

This discussion of the literary aspects of the romance

[67] J. S. P. Tatlock, 'Notes on Chaucer', *MLN*, 29 (1914), 98, and P. Barry, 'Bells Rung Without Hands', *MLN*, 30 (1915), 28–9.

would not be complete without some attention to its metrics.

Le Bone Florence of Rome is a tail-rhyme romance composed in stanzas of twelve lines divided into four groups of three. Each group contains, as a rule, a couplet with four accents to the line and a concluding 'tail' with three accents. Usually the four couplets have different rhymes, while the tail-lines rhyme with one another. The danger in such a rigid stanzaic pattern is obvious. It can become monotonous, and *Florence* does have dull patches. But more frequently than not the poet shows himself capable of exploiting the inherent rhetorical possibilities of the stanzaic arrangement. While the tail-rhyme stanza has a strong tendency to fragment, it can be made, as in stanza 7 of the romance, to build to a conclusion in the twelfth line as smoothly as a well-developed paragraph:

> When Syr Garcy herde seye
> That þe emperowre of Rome had soche a may
>   To hys doghtur dere,
> He waxe hasty as the fyre,
> And gart sembyll þe lordys of hys empyre,
>   That bolde and hardy were.
> He seyde, 'Ofte haue ye blamed me,
> For Y wolde not weddyd bee,
>   Y have herde of a clere,
> Florens þat ys feyre and bryght,
> Jn all þys worlde ys not soche a wyȝt,
>   Y wyll hur haue to my fere.'
>
>   [ll. 70–81]

The poet even manages in a *tour de force* to capitalise on the natural tendency of the stanza to divide into four sections. In stanza 170 the poet uses each of the four three-line units to focus attention on the diseased appearance of one of the four persecutors of Florence:

> Mylys that hur aweye ledd,
> He was the fowlest mesell bredd,
>   Of pokkys and bleynes bloo.
> And Machary þat wolde hur haue slayne,
> He stode schakyng the sothe to sayne,
>   Crokyd and crachyd thertoo.

The marynere þat wolde haue layne hur by,
Hys yen stode owte a strote forthy,
  Hys lymmes were roton hym froo.
They put Clarebalde in a whelebarowe,
That strong thefe be stretys narowe,
  Had no fote on to goo.

[ll. 2020–31]

The tale contains the usual categories of conventional
expressions—especially in the short lines—found in so many
tail-rhyme romances: the summons to attention (*Hende as ye
may here*, l. 1998; *As ye may vnderstande*, l. 1896); references to
authorities (*In Romance as we rede*, l. 645; *And some boke
seyth mare*, l. 84; *As the boke makyth mynde*, l. 2166); assertions
of truth (*The certen sothe to saye*, l. 1359; *To wete wythowten
wene*, l. 1086); pious expressions (*Thorow þe myght of Mary
mylde*, l. 1500; *So Cryste me saue and sayne*, l. 297), etc. It is,
perhaps, not so remarkable that many of these conventional
phrases are alliterative, for, as Trounce suggests, it may be
that 'these . . . are in a special sense the inherited material;
through them the tail-rhyme poems are connected in an
unbroken line with the old epic poetry'.[68]
Sometimes conventional expressions are repeated in the
text with a slight alteration (e.g., *The certen sothe to saye*, l.
1359; *The certen sothe to telle*, l. 306). This kind of substitution
occurs frequently in Old English formulae like *þæt wæs god
cyning, þæt wæs grim cyning*. The location of the romance's
dialect in the north would seem to further support the idea of
influence from an alliterative tradition. Moreover, Knobbe, in
a comment about literary influences, advances the opinion
that the author was familiar with the alliterative *Morte
Arthure*.[69] As evidence he points to the poet's making Sir
Lucius Jbarnyus founder of Beuerfayre (l. 1888) instead of
Julius Caesar, as in the French version; Lucius Iberius is
mentioned in line 86 of the alliterative *Morte*.
What is remarkable, I think, is that alliteration is so per-

[68] A. McI. Trounce, 'The English Tail-Rhyme Romances', *MÆ*, i
(1932), 171.
[69] Knobbe, 'Über die Mittelenglische Dichtung . . .', 9.

vasive in the romance. Eight hundred and forty-nine of the 2,187 lines contain alliteration, that is, more than a third. Of the alliterating lines, 144 contain three words with alliteration on the same sound (ll. 17, 30, 38, 39, etc.), twenty contain four such words (ll. 212, 223, 268, 287, etc.), and fifty-four lines contain alliteration on two different sounds (ll. 12, 87, 112, 133, etc.). There are even forty instances of overflowing alliteration of a single sound into a following line or lines (ll. 98–100, 230–1, 285–7, 352–3, etc.). From these statistics it appears that alliteration is a vital and fundamental part of the author's mode of thought. Basic and extended forms of the alliterative long line occur in the poem: AA/AX (ll. 98. 640, 1345, etc.); AX/AX (ll. 95, 1343, etc.); AA/AA (l. 842, etc.).[70] A very common variation found in the alliterative lines of *Florence* is the placement of the alliteration on unstressed syllables such as prefixes, prepositions, auxiliary verbs, pronouns, and the second element of compounds (ll. 94, 176, 177, etc.).[71] However, in the romance as we have received it, alliteration, while an important aspect of the metrical machinery, seems to be a secondary element superimposed upon the regular stanzaic pattern. It is tempting to wonder—if I am correct in my assumption that we have here a copy of an earlier English version[72]—whether there was more alliteration in the original Middle English text.

Be that as it may, there are concrete things about the use of alliteration which are observable and which can be commented upon with certainty. The alliteration which we have is not primarily structural. It appears often as an unobstrusive undertone in conventional expressions (usually in the short lines) or more interestingly as a stylistic device to give emphasis. The concentration of alliteration does seem to occur in crucial passages.

[70] Marie Borroff, *Sir Gawain and the Green Knight: A Stylistic and Metrical Study* (New Haven, 1962), 170 and her translation of *Gawain* (New York, 1967), 56–7.

[71] See J. P. Oakden's discussion of the 'five types of license' in *Alliterative Poetry in Middle English* (1930–5; rpt. New York, 1968), 178–9.

[72] See p. 41.

Often it turns up in dramatically significant dialogue, as in the speech of the ambassador who comes on Garcy's behalf to sue for Florence's hand (ll. 208–16, discussed above), the lament of the barons for their dead emperor,

> Who schall vs now geue *l*ondys or *l*ythe,
> *H*awkys, or *h*owndys, or *st*edys *st*ythe . . .?
>   [ll. 841–2]

and the revelation of Mylys's wickedness addressed to Emere (ll. 1342–53). It is after this speech that Emere banishes Mylys. The speech is important also for the review it offers of the crimes committed by Mylys against Florence which might be lost sight of by this point in the tale. The technique of recapitulation is, of course, frequently used in oral composition, but it must also be said that this sort of review is likewise employed by writers of literary compositions with an awareness of their audience's need to have its recollections refreshed.

Alliteration serves a decorative function in descriptive set pieces like the portrait of old Garcy (ll. 94–104) and that of Florence and her father, Emperor Otes, in the throne room of their palace (ll. 176–82). Descriptions of battle scenes are unfailingly given emphasis with alliteration, e.g.:

> . . . . *b*odyes *b*rake owt to *b*lede
> *H*edys *h*opped vndur *h*ors fete,
> As hayle*st*ones done in þe *st*rete,
>   *St*ycked was many a *st*ede.
> *F*or *F*lorence loue, þat *f*eyre maye,
> Many a *d*oghty *d*yed that *d*ay,
>   [ll. 639–44]

The use of alliteration in the French chanson of which the English is probably an adaption is very slight and possibly unconscious. Even in the description of battle scenes, which can usually be depended on to contain alliteration, the French version does not employ it.

Can we assume, then, that the English poet came by his technique independently? Is the English version part of an oral tradition and the French part of a literary one? Did an oral poet who understood French hear the literary version read and develop an oral composition in English? These are tantalising questions, but even after the most exhaustive exploration of metrical evidence, clear answers are as elusive as will-o'-the-wisps. While we know that the English oral tradition is an alliterative one, and that conventional expressions and recapitulation of events characterise the oral style, a poem with all the requisite elements may still not necessarily be an oral composition. As Albert C. Baugh has demonstrated in 'Improvisation in the Middle English Romance',[73] it is difficult to make a clear distinction between oral and literary composition, since in the process of copying, translating, or adapting a scribe might feel free to draw on the conventional clichés and other devices associated with oral composition.

If *Le Bone Florence of Rome* is a copy of a more highly alliterated English version belonging to an oral tradition, the copyist was a 'poet' capable of great artistic judgement. When alliteration is no longer a *regular* element in the metrical structure, it can really become a subtle means of giving emphasis. The poet–copyist of *Le Bone Florence of Rome* seems to have discovered one way of writing a tail-rhyme stanza that avoids the metrical pitfalls Chaucer satirises in *Sir Thopas*.

RELATED TALES

It might be well to consider the treatment of the heroine as an exemplary type in three other related romances about Florence's sister-sufferers—the *King of Tars*, *Emaré*, and Chaucer's *Man of Law's Tale*. I have selected the *King of Tars* because it is believed to have been directly influenced by a French version of the Florence story. My reason for choosing the other tales is that they offer the opportunity to compare *Le Bone Florence of Rome* with the two best representatives of a related family of romances, the Constance cycle. Chaucer's Tale of Constance is almost always discussed as a thing apart; it will be considered here within its medieval literary context.

[73] 'Improvisation in the Middle English Romance', *PAPS*, 103 (1959), 418–54.

The *King of Tars* is a romance full of the atmosphere of the crusades and the conflict of Christianity and heathendom. The opening of the story is similar to that of *Le Bone Florence of Rome*; both romances contain a heathen ruler who, having failed to win the hand of a Christian princess, invades her country and kills many knights. It has been suggested, first by Laura Hibbard[74] and later, by Robert Geist,[75] that the French original of *Le Bone Florence of Rome* supplied the introduction to the *King of Tars*. Very likely the influence did not move in the reverse direction, since the French chanson, *Florence de Rome*, dates from the first quarter of the thirteenth century, and the *King of Tars* was composed later (*c.* 1325).

The author of the *King of Tars* is less concerned with making his heroine a type of chastity (one of Florence's dominant virtues) than he is with emphasising her *pietas* and *fortitudo* (virtues which Florence also exemplifies). The heroine's trust in God and strength of belief make her an incarnation of Christian *pietas* and *fortitudo*, enabling her to become an instrument of the Christian God's might.

To summarise the romance's action briefly, the daughter of the King of Tars reluctantly marries the heathen sultan of Damascus and gives birth to a deformed child. Each parent claims the beliefs of the other to be responsible. Whereas the prayers of the Sultan to Mahoun are futile, the child immediately becomes handsome and well-formed when it is baptised at its mother's request. The power of the Christian God is thereby verified, and the Sultan adopts the faith of his wife.

The homiletic tendency of the romance is patent in the heroine's catechising of the convert-husband in Christian dogma. Although the Sultan decides to embrace Christianity after the occurrence of the miracle, it is clear that his conversion is not complete until his wife teaches him about the

---

[74] Laura Hibbard, *Medieval Romance in England: A Study of the Sources and Analogues of the Non-Cyclic Romances* (New York, 1924), 15.

[75] Robert Geist, 'On the Genesis of the *King of Tars*', *JEGP*, 42 (1943), 265.

principles of Christian belief—the Trinity, the death and resurrection of Christ, and the Last Judgement. The poet's probable intention is to make the point that *pietas* and *fortitudo* are not the result of faith alone, but must be informed by knowledge. It is not enough to be moved by miracles. The beautification of the monstrous child is made possible by the prayers of a Christian whose *pietas* and *fortitudo* are grounded in knowledge. Florence's miraculous healing power does not seem to be qualified in this way.

The *King of Tars* is more consistently religious in tone than *Le Bone Florence of Rome*. Indeed, it seems to have been regarded as a devotional tale rather than a romance by the compilers of the manuscripts in which it appears. It is separated from the romances in the Auchinleck MS, where it is placed between *Adam and Eve* and the legend of Gregory; and it is included as well in the Vernon MS, which is concerned almost completely with materials which are religious in character.

The romance of the sufferings of Emaré also seems to have been regarded as a devotional tale, placed as it is among religious works in MS Cotton Caligula A. II. Emaré is another learned heroine. She is not, like the daughter of the King of Tars, an instructress of Christian dogma, but she has learned courtesy and embroidery from a lady called Abbro and, in a more limited way than Florence, practises nursing. A late work, like *Le Bone Florence of Rome*, the *Emaré* was written within ten years of the *Man of Law's Tale*, of which it is a fairly close analogue. *Emaré* and the *Man of Law's Tale* belong to the Constance cycle, a somewhat separate branch of the family of romances dealing with persecuted women who are the victims of false accusation. In *Emaré*, as well as in Chaucer's Tale of Constance, the heroine suffers persecution and exile because her mother-in-law accuses her of giving birth to a monster; in *Le Bone Florence of Rome* the sorrowful fate of Florence is the result of her brother-in-law's charge of adultery.

Although Emaré is more distantly related to Florence than she is to Constance, there are striking resemblances between them. Florence's flawless beauty and gleaming garments, for example, merely the conventional attributes of a courtly lady in the first half of the romance, become by the midpoint of the story symbolic reflections of her virtues. Emaré's celestial beauty functions in the same way from the outset of the story. Her rich robe, described at length in 109 lines, seems to be an external reflection of her inner perfection. Each time she is cast adrift on the sea like a martyr, the poet emphasises that she is wearing the beautiful garment which sets her apart, indeed, above her dreary circumstances. For both Florence and Emaré, beauty, symbolic of moral perfection, is also the basic cause of suffering. As Florence is mistaken in her magnificent dress by the wicked Machary for a 'fende of helle', so Emaré's intriguing mother-in-law takes Emaré's beauty as a sign that the heroine is an offspring of hell. In both instances, the misapprehension flows from evil which cannot recognise beauty for what it is.

The heroine's sufferings are not educative, for her virtuous nature cannot be improved. An innocent sufferer, she places her trust in God, whose providence never forsakes her. An embodiment of *pietas* and *fortitudo* like Florence and the daughter of the King of Tars, she is rewarded, after having twice been cast adrift on the sea, through the agency of God's justice,

> She was dryven toward Rome,
> Thorow the grace of God yn trone,
> That all thyng may fulfylle.[76]
> [ll. 679–81]

It is the unfailing justice of God's providence which Emaré's fortunes exemplify.

The poet of *Emaré* frequently rises to a high level of artistry, making his version of the Constance story one of the more humanised renderings before Chaucer's unsurpassed *Man of Law's Tale*.

Whether the Man of Law was really intended to be the narrator of Chaucer's tale is not a question that is relevant for

[76] Joseph Ritson, ed., *Emaré*, *Ancient English Metrical Romances*, 3 vols. (London, 1802), II, 232.

the present discussion; there are, however, at least two reasons which make him seem appropriate. First, as an earthly representative of justice, it is somehow fitting that he should tell a tale about the working of Divine Justice; and second, as a representative type of middle-class tastes, it is reasonable that he might be attracted to so sentimental a tale as the story of Constance and her succession of miraculous preservations. These are generally characterised by critics as 'glaring improbabilities',[77] but, in point of fact, they are not so very different from the pageant of incredible disasters which intrigue thousands of housewives on television soap operas today.

The problems in the action of the story which Chaucer inherited from his sources are mitigated somewhat by his drawing attention away from the dramatic events of the narrative to the pathos of Constance's personal situation. He is sensitive to the heroine's emotions, for instance, as she leaves her family for a strange land,

> Allas! what wonder is it though she wepte,
> That shal be sent to straunge nacioun
> Fro friendes, that so tendrely hir kepte,
> And to be bounden under subjeccioun
> Of oon, she knoweth not his condicioun?
> [ll. 267–71]

We have, too, the nice human touch of brave Constance smiling through her tears as the ship sets sail:

> She peyneth hire to make good contenance.
> [l. 322]

Aside from Chaucer's superior sensibility in managing the emotional qualities in the story, he seems to present a more comprehensive view of the central theme of God's justice than is found in any of the other of the Eustace–Constance–Florence–Griselda romances which I have read. In a sense, Chaucer's Tale of Constance is more effectively didactic because the poet's insight into the idea of God's justice is more theo-

---

[77] George Kane, *Middle English Literature: A Critical Study of the Romances, the Religious Lyrics, Piers Plowman* (London, 1951), 62.

logically sound. Chaucer's understanding of the propelling idea behind the legend reminds us that Chaucer's poetry cannot be detached from medieval Christianity.

Chaucer presents a rounded view of God's justice by playing on the contrast between the Man of Law's self-indulgent, misguided understanding, and the deeper view of the order of things possessed by Constance, which functions as a corrective. Keeping his eye on the 'sentence' like the dedicated Robertsonian that he is, Chauncey Wood notes quite accurately that the Man of Law wrongly makes value judgements about God's ways.[78] Whereas he only praises God when Constance escapes from a tight spot, the heroine welcomes God's 'sonde' (lines 523 and 826) whether it means good or bad Fortune. Constance's prayers to God sound the same when she is cast adrift and when she is safe on shore. Her saintly attitude apprehends that if it comes from God it must be just.

Chaucer's use of the Man of Law's attitude as a counterweight is astute, if, perhaps, a little over-subtle. Few in Chaucer's audience, I suspect, who would have identified with the very natural reactions of the lawyer would then have realised they ought to be reacting to Fortune like the saintly Constance. Nevertheless, this tension exists, and it is important.

Professor Wood's intelligent if narrow view of the tale leads him to treat the Man of Law too harshly. Besides representing that of a Christian who has confounded personal comfort with an understanding of God's justice, the Man of Law's emotional involvement with Constance's fate is an artistic necessity. If the Man of Law were not intruding—however anti-intellectually—with sympathetic commentary and interpretation of the vicissitudes of the story, the audience would be much more aware of the 'glaring improbabilities' that George Kane complains of. The emotional involvement of the narrator with the plight of the heroine is also a major reason that Chaucer's narrative is a more human and moving story than *Le Bone Florence of Rome*, the *King of Tars*, and *Emaré*.

There are many romances about persecuted women in Middle English. Besides those discussed above, seven more are

[78] *Chaucer and the Country of the Stars* (Princeton, 1970), 197.

extant: *Sir Isumbras, Octavian, Sir Eglamour, Torrent of Portyngale, Sir Triamour,* Chaucer's *Clerk's Tale,* and *Lai le Freine.* Scores of similar tales are represented in the Continental literature of the Middle Ages as well. What motivated poets to write such stories? Why did they find such a ready audience?

An answer to these questions may be found in the general attitude towards women in the Middle Ages. As reflected in the literature of the period, this attitude is generally ambivalent. Among the works of individual writers like Chaucer, Lydgate, and Dunbar, misogynistic attacks on women occur as often as poems in fervent praise of women. This double vision reflects, in part, an obvious condition of human life: there are good and bad women. More significantly, it also reflects the two contradictory streams in medieval thought about women. The cult of courtly love and the chivalrous devotion inspired by the Virgin Mary tended to exalt women; on the other hand, anti-feminist clerical writing dwelt on the baneful influence of women. This negative strain in thinking about women seems to have out-weighed the positive. A reaction against courtly love (which exalted women to a level unprecedented in earlier periods) was implicit in the system. No doubt the unrequited courtly lover occasionally wondered whether he had, perhaps, over-idealised love, a reaction probably intensified by the fact that the courtly love object is an adulteress. Interestingly enough, Andreas Capallanus' manual, *The Art of Courtly Love,* includes a section entitled 'The Rejection of Love'. Despite the worship of the Virgin, clerical feeling in the Middle Ages inclined toward anti-feminism. Robert Brunne's *Handlyng Synne,* a manual of moral instruction, warns that even a chaste man alone with a woman will fall into lechery.[79] A striking example of the effect of clerical misogyny on romance writing occurs in *Gawain and the Green Knight*:

Bot hit is no ferly þaȝ a fole madde,
And þurȝ wyles of wymmen be wonen to sorȝe,
For so watz Adam in erde with one bygyled,

---

[79] Robert of Brunne, *Handlyng Synne,* ed. F. J. Furnevall, EETS, ES, 119 (London, 1901), 240.

And Salamon with fele sere, and Samson eftsonez—
Dalyda dalt hym hys wyrde—and Dauyth þerafter
Watz blended with Barsabe, þat much bale þoled.
Now þese were wrathed wyth her wyles, hit were a wynne huge
To luf hom wel, and leue hem not, a leude þat couþe.
For þes wer forne þe freest, þat folȝed alle þe sele
Exellently of alle þyse oþer, vnder heuenryche
    þat mused;
    And alle þay were biwyled
    With wymmen þat þay vsed.
    Þaȝ I be now bigyled,
    Me þink me burde be excused.[80]

                        [ll. 2414–28]

The Gawain poet launches this attack with the stock medieval
examples of men degraded by women.

The two streams of the ambivalent medieval attitudes
towards women seem to converge in the cycles of romances
about persecuted women. Although an allegorical reading of
the tales indicates that the heroines are types of one virtue or
another, a moment's consideration of the literal events of the
romances would lead one to suspect that their creators were
unconsciously stalking shadowy villains. In the light of the
essentially devotional nature of the Eustace–Constance–
Florence–Griselda cycle, it is likely that many of the romances
were written by clerics who believed that women, even the
best of them, were ensnaring creatures 'beautified with the
face of a noble lion, yet . . . blemished with the belly of a
reeking kid and . . . beweaponed with the virulent tail of a
viper',[81] threatening degradation of the soul. On an uncon-
scious level, at least, there must have been something con-
genial to clerical minds in a story about the persecution of a
woman, even a woman saint.

These stories involving ambivalent attitudes toward women
did not originate in the Middle Ages. As Margaret Schlauch has

[80] *Sir Gawain and the Green Knight*, ed. J. R. R. Tolkien and E. V.
Gordon, 2nd ed., rev. Norman Davis (Oxford, 1967), 66–7.

[81] From Walter Map's 'Letter from Valerius to Ruffinus', quoted
by Katharine M. Rogers, *The Troublesome Helpmate* (Seattle, 1966),
p. ix.

demonstrated, the motifs in the families of romances involving persecuted women have folklore backgrounds.[82] Moreover, the stories emerge in eastern as well as western literature, and they do not cease to evolve in the Middle Ages. The ambivalent attitude reflected in the medieval romances must, indeed, be archetypal, perhaps stemming from a boy's initial erotic attachment to his mother and his subsequent fear of female dominance, a phenomenon amply explored by Freud. Modern permutations of the theme are numerous. The eighteenth-century novel *Clarissa Harlowe* is commonly referred to as a derivative saint's legend about a woman who 'is pure . . . and yet to be violated'.[83] Hawthorne's *The Scarlet Letter*, which bears the sub-title 'A Romance', even contains some of the motifs found in the Eustace–Constance–Florence–Griselda cycle: a distasteful proposal of marriage from an old man (here marriage is not merely threatened, it occurs); the accusation of having borne a demon child; a heroine with a flair for embroidery (like Emaré);[84] a persecuted woman turned nurse. By the twentieth century the literary theme has been provided with an explicit theoretical frame of reference by Freud, who emphasises the great influence of the mother over her son. Writers dwelling on the negative aspects of maternal influence have emphasised the woman's capacity for destruction. D. H. Lawrence, in an eccentric discussion of the *Scarlet Letter*, sounds like a direct descendent of Walter Map:

> Even when she is most sweet and a salvationist, she is her most devilish, is woman. She gives her man the sugar-plum of her submissive sweetness. And when he's taken this sugar-plum in his mouth, a scorpion comes out of it.[85]

[82] Margaret Schlauch, *Chaucer's Constance and Accused Queens* (New York, 1927).

[83] Dorothy Van Ghent, 'Clarissa Harlowe', *The English Novel* (New York, 1961), 50.

[84] In both cases there may be a trace of the medieval, indeed ancient, view that women are frivolous and only care about clothes.

[85] D. H. Lawrence, *Studies in Classic American Literature* (New York, 1953), 104.

DIALECT AND DATE

The dialect is north Midland, but its northern character must be emphasised.

The phonology and the accidence of *Le Bone Florence of Rome* are characterised by a combination of northern and Midland elements such as we might expect to find in a north Midland dialect. There are many instances of the Midland rounded development of OE *ā* proved original by rhyme— *bloo: thertoo*, ll. 2022, 2025; *foys: goys: rose: lose*, ll. 744, 747, 750, 753; *stone: tone*, ll. 340–1; *thyckfolde: colde: bolde: holde*, ll. 873, 870, 867, 864. However, the northern preservation of unrounded *ā* is predominant—*sa: culpa*, ll. 1360–1; *blake: sake: wrake: take*, ll. 579, 576, 582, 585; *hale: tale*, ll. 1130, 1129; *are: fare*, ll. 1876–7; *hare: mare: sware: dare*, ll. 87, 84, 90, 93; *sare: care: mare: answare*, ll. 684, 687, 690, 693; *rase: face*, ll. 565–6; *goost: haste*, ll. 778–9. In the last case, the *oo* is probably a scribal error for *aa*.

The genitive singular of nouns is generally formed with the Midland ending—(*y*)*s* (*ther gatys gayne*, l. 149), but the northern uninflected form is also found (*Florence fadur*, l. 364).[86]

The third person feminine pronoun is characteristically the Midland form *s(c)he*; northern *scho(o)* also appears twice and is proved original by rhyme (ll. 1466, 1980).

The verbal inflections are similarly mixed. Northern (*-ys*) as well as Midland (*-yth*, *-eth*) forms of the third person singular present indicative appear. Also, the present participle ending has the form *-yng* as in the Midlands as well as *-ande* which is found in the north and north Midlands.

The manuscript contains a considerable number of exclusively northern features. These are:

1. the dropping of the *-n* in the infinitive (the exceptions in *Florence* tend to occur in northern texts).

2. the persistence of *-n* in the past participles of strong verbs (*tobrokyn*, l. 103).

3. the assimilation of the vowel of the plural to that of the

---

[86] In nouns which end in *-s* the uninflected genitive may appear for phonetic reasons (*a burges house*, l. 446).

singular, in the preterite of strong verbs. There are, however, exceptions among Class I and Class V verbs. In Class I verbs the preterite singular is $\bar{a}$ (*rase*, l. 565; *wrate*, l. 2173) and $\bar{\varrho}$ (*glode*, l. 1709; *rode*, l. 588) while the preterite plural is always $\bar{\varrho}$ (*abode*, l. 446; *rode*, l. 155; *schoon*, l. 156). The preterite singular of Class V verbs is $\bar{e}$ (*ete*, l. 1463) or *au* (*sawe*, l. 289), but the preterite plural is *ai* (*laye*, l. 1566).

4. the shortened stem of 'take', *ta* (l. 1107), which is proved original by rhyme.

5. the appearance of an important group of words found only in northern texts. My list of thirty-five northernisms agrees with that compiled by Dunlap[87] (*bigge, blome, busk, gayne, gere, lithe, min, nefe, raike, ser, site, thro, ware, lele, trayne, barmeteme, beld, brand, fax, helde, lende, sayne, spere, stith, strynde, swime, thikke, folde, tuggel, happe, irke, thertil, thir, brysse, strik*).[88]

On these grounds, I judge that the author of this romance lived in the northernmost part of the Midland area where both northern and Midland sounds and forms would be used, but where northern influences would be especially strong. The predominant unrounded development of OE. *a*, even before l+consonant and frequently before nasals (*lappe: happe*, ll. 113, 112; *alse: false*, ll. 752, 751; *halle: crystalle*, ll. 325–6; *walle: small*, ll. 160–1; *landys: standys*, ll. 220–1), points to an eastern part of the northern Midland area.

Professor Lillian H. Hornstein dates the manuscript between 1475 and 1500.[89] The palaeographical evidence and the relatively large number of forms not recorded with these meanings before the sixteenth century[90] in the vocabulary

[87] A. R. Dunlap, 'The Vocabulary of the Middle English Romances in Tail-Rhyme Stanzas', *Delaware Notes*, series 14 (1941), 39.

[88] *Bowrnes*, the southern variation of ME. *burn*, should also be noted. Since it is unique, I think it must be considered a curiosity.

[89] 'Le Bone Florence of Rome', *A Manual of the Writings in Middle English*, 131.

[90] These are *eyen*, 'young hawks' (l. 845), *forne*, 'on account of' (l. 67), *garson*, 'retainer' (l. 118), *gente*, 'courteously' (l. 2133), *hodur*, 'cuddle' (l. 112), *happe*, 'embrace' (l. 112), *hypping*, 'limping' (l. 1991), *knok*, 'attack' (l. 281), *meene*, 'intend' (l. 2182), *ryall*, 'noble' (l. 174), *rechyd*, 'launched' (l. 132), and *stekyth*, 'sticks' (l. 1472).

make 1500 seem nearer the fact than 1475. To be sure, the *terminus ad quem* would represent an unusually late date if this manuscript were the first written version of the English romance. I doubt, however, that it is the original. Very likely, it is a northern copy of a manuscript written about fifty years earlier in the north-east Midlands. It might be argued that the original could be northern and the copy from the north-east Midlands; however, by 1500, a scribe from the Midlands would be so conditioned by the London standard that he could not fail to note northern features and remove them. A northern scribe, on the other hand, less influenced by London, might still in 1500 retain and introduce into the text distinctly northern dialectal traits, especially if he were somewhat past middle age.

My assumption of a northern copy of a north-east Midland manuscript enables me to accept, in part, both Knobbe's assignment of the dialect area to the northern border of the Midlands and Wilda's[91] localisation in the southern part of the north.

[91] O. Wilda, *Ueber die örtliche Verbreitung der zwolfzeiligen Schweifreimstrophe in England* (Breslau, 1887).

SELECTIVE BIBLIOGRAPHY

MANUSCRIPT

MS Cambridge University Ff. 2.38 (More 690), ff. 239b–254a.

EDITIONS OF THE STORY OF FLORENCE

I. Middle English

Knobbe, W. Albert, *Über die Mittelenglische Dichtung Le Bone Florence of Rome*. Diss. Marburg, 1899, Marburg: N. G. Elwert'sche Verlagsbuchhandlung, 1899 (introduction).

Ritson, Joseph, ed. *Ancient English Metrical Romances*. 3 vols. London: W. Bulmer & Co., 1802. III, 1–92.

Vietor, Wilhelm, *Le Bone Florence of Rome*. Diss. Marburg, 1893, Marburg: N. G. Elwert'sche Verlagsbuchhandlung,1893 (text).

II. Continental

Dit de Flourence de Rome, ed. Achille Jubinal, *Nouveau Recueil de Contes, Dits, Fabliaux et Autres Pièces Inédits des XIIIe, XIVe, et XVe Siècles*, VI, 88–117. Paris: E. Pannier, 1839–42.

Florence de Rome: Chanson D'Aventure du Premier Quart du 13e Siècle, ed. A. Wallensköld. *SATF*. 2 vols. 1909; rpt. New York: Johnson Reprint Corp., 1968.

Historia Critica de la Litteratura Española, ed. Amador de los Ríos, 'Cuento Muy Famoso del Enperador Ottas de Roma', V, 391–468. Madrid: J. Muñoz, 1864.

REVIEWS OF VIETOR–KNOBBE EDITION

Heuser, W., *ES*, 29 (1899), 123–5.

Holthausen, Ferdinand, *Anglia*, 10 (September 1899), 129–30.

Stengel, E., *Kritische Jahresbucher*, 7, pt. 2 (1901), 72.

Wallensköld, A., *Deutsche Litteraturzeitung* (1900), 422–4.

Weyrauch, M., *Archivum*, 110 (1900), 446.

TEXTUAL

Holthausen, Ferdinand, 'Zu Mittelenglischen Romanzen', *Anglia*, 41 (1917), 497–512.

Kolbing, E., 'Kleine Beitrage zur Erklärung und Text-Kritik Englischer Dichter', *ES*, 3 (1880), 92–105.

LANGUAGE, DIALECT

A New English Dictionary on Historical Principles, ed. James A. H. Murray. 10 vols. Oxford: Clarendon Press, 1888.

Brandl, Alois H., 'Mittelenglische Literatur', in Paul, *Grundriss der Germanischen Philologie*, II, 2, 609–718. Strassburg, 1891–3.

Curtius, F. J., 'An Investigation of the Rimes and Phonology of the Middle-Scotch Romance Clariodus', *Anglia*, 16 (1894), 387–450.

Dunlap, A. R., 'The Vocabulary of the Middle English Romances in Tail-Rhyme Stanza', *Delaware Notes*, Ser. 14 (1941), 1–42.

Kurath, Hans and S. M. Kuhn, *Middle English Dictionary*. Ann Arbor: University of Michigan Press, 1952– .

Moore, Samuel, S. B. Meech, and Harold Whitehall, 'Middle English Dialect Characteristics and Dialect Boundaries', *Essays and Studies in English and Comparative Literature*, 13. Ann Arbor: University of Michigan Press, 1935, 1–60.

Mossé, Fernand, *A Handbook of Middle English*, trans. James Walker. Baltimore: Johns Hopkins Press, 1952.

Mustanoja, Tauno, *A Middle English Syntax, Memoires de la Société Neophilologique*, XXIII. Helsinki: Société Neophilologique, 1960.

Skeat, Walter W., *Principles of English Etymology*. Oxford: Oxford University Press, 1891.

Sweet, Henry, *History of English Sounds*. Oxford: Clarendon Press, 1888.

Trounce, A. McI., 'The English Tail-Rhyme Romances', *MÆ*, 1 (1932), 87–108; 2 (1933), 34–57; 3 (1934), 30–50.

Wilda, O., *Ueber die Örtliche Verbreitung die Zweizeiligen Schweifreimstrophe in England*. Breslau, 1887.

SOURCES AND ANALOGUES

I. General studies

Aebisher, Paul, 'Fragments de la Chanson de la Reine Sebile et du Roman de Florence de Rome', *Studi Medievali*, N.S., 16 (1943–50), 135–60.

Boyd, Beverly, *The Middle English Miracles of the Virgin*. San Marino: Huntington Library, 1964.

Chaytor, H. J., 'A Fragment of the Chanson D'Aventure, Florence de Rome', *Modern Humanities Research Bulletin*, 1 No. 2 (September 1927), 48.

Christophersen, Paul, *The Ballad of Sir Aldingar*. Oxford: Clarendon Press, 1952.

Geist, Robert, 'On the Genesis of the *King of Tars*', *JEGP*, 42 (1943), 260–8.

Gough, Alfred B., *The Constance-Saga*. Berlin: Mayer & Müller, 1902.

Hibbard, Laura, *Mediaeval Romance in England*. New York: Oxford University Press, 1924.

Hilka, Alfons, 'Zum Crescientiastoff', *Archiv*, 133 (1915), 135–41.

Hornstein, Lillian H., 'A Folklore Theme in the *King of Tars*', *PQ*, 20 (January 1941), 82-7.

——, 'The Historical Background of *The King of Tars*', *Spec.*, 16 (October 1941), 404–14.

——, 'New Analogues to the "King of Tars" ', *MLR*, 26 (October 1941), 432–42.

——, 'Trivet's Constance and the *King of Tars*', *MLN*, 55 (1940), 354–7.

Isaacs, Neal D., 'Constance in Fourteenth Century England', *Neuphilologische Mitteilungen*, 59 (1958), 260–77.

Karl, Louis, 'Florence de Rome et la Vie de Deux Saints de Hongrie', *Revue des Langues Romanes*, 52 (1909), 163–80.

Krappe, Alexander H., 'The Offa–Constance Legend', *Anglia*, 61 (1937), 361–9.

Lawrence, William W., 'The Banished Wife's Lament', *MP*, 5 (January 1908), 1–19.

Mussafia, Adolf, 'Über eine Italienische Metrische Darstellung der Crescentia Saga', *Sitzungsberichte der Phil.-Hist. Classe der Kais. Akad. der Wissenschaften*, 51 (Vienna, 1865), 589–692.

Rickert, Edith, 'The Old English Offa Saga', *MP*, 2 (January 1905), 1–56.

Schlauch, Margaret, *Chaucer's Constance and the Accused Queens*. New York: New York University Press, 1927.

Siefkin, Ortgies, *Das Geduldige Weib in der Englischen Literatur bis auf Shakspere: Der Konstanzetypus*. Diss. Leipzig, 1903. Rathenow: Buchdruckerei von Max Babenzien, 1903.

Stefanovic, S., 'Die Crescentia–Florence Sage: eine Kritische Studie ueber ihren Ursprung und ihre Entwicklung', *Romanische Forschung*, 29 (1908), 461–557.

Teubert, S., *Crescentia-Studien*. Diss. Halle, 1906.

Wallensköld, A., 'Le Conte de la Femme Chaste Convoitée par son Beau-frère', *Acta Societatis Scientiarum Fennicae*, 37 (Helsingfors, 1907), 1–172.

——, 'L'Origine et l'Evolution du Conte de la Femme Chaste', *Neophilologus Mitteilungen*, 14 (Helsingfors, 1912), 67–77.

Wenzel, Rudolph, *Die Fassungen der Sage von Florence de Rome*. Diss. Marburg, 1890. Marburg: Buchdruckerei Fr. Sommering, 1890.

Whiting, B. J., 'Proverbs in Certain Middle English Romances in Relation to Their French Sources', *Harvard Studies in Philology and Literature*, 15 (1933), 75–121.

Wickert, Maria, 'Chaucer's Konstanze und die Legende der Guten Frauen', *Anglia*, 69, pt. 1 (1950), 89–104.

II. Editions

Alfonso X el Sabio, *Cantigas de Santa Maria*, ed. Walter Mettman. 2 vols. Coimbra: Acta Universitatis Conimbrigensis, 1961.

Arabian Nights Entertainments, ed. Jonathan Scott, 'The Adventures of the Cauzee, His Wife . . .', VI, 396–408. London: Printed for Longman, Hurst, Rees, Orme and Brown, 1811.

Besançon, Etienne de, *Alphabetum Narrationum*, ed. M. M. Banks, EETS, OS, 126, 127. London: K. Paul, Trench, Trübner & Co., 1904–5.

Bonafadini, Antonio, *La Vita di Santa Guglielma*. Bologna: G. Ferrara, 1878.

The Book of the Thousand Nights and One, ed. John Payne, 'The Jewish Cadi and His Pious Wife', V, 9–13. London, 1883.

Bourbon, Etienne de, 'Liber de Septem Bonis', *Anecdotes Historiques, Legendes et Apologues Tirés du Recueil Inédit d'Etienne de Bourbon*, ed. A. Lecoy de la Marche, 115–17. Paris: Libraire Renouard, 1877.

Briccio, Giovanni, *La Historia di Flavia Imperatrice*. Venice, 1812.

Child, Francis J., ed. *The English and Scottish Popular Ballads*. 5 vols. Boston: Houghton, Mifflin & Co., 1882–98.

Coinci, Gautier de, 'De l'Emperirix qui garda sa Chastée', *Nouveau Recueil de Fabliaux et Contes Inédits*, ed. Dominique M. Méon, II, 1–128. Paris: Chasseriau, 1823.

Contes Inédits des Mille et une Nuits, ed. G. S. Trebutien, 'La Vertuese Israelite', III, 422–4. Paris: Dondey-Duprés, 1828.

Croix, Petis de la, trans., 'Histoire de Repsima', *Mille et un Jours*, V, 241–95. Paris: C. F. Lehoucq, 1840.

Dias, Balthasar. 'Historia da Imperatriz Porcina', *Floresta de Varios Romances*, ed. Theo. Braga, 104–49. Portugal: Typ. da Livaria Nacional, 1869.

Emaré, ed. Edith Rickert, EETS, OS, 99. London: K. Paul Trench, Trübner & Co., 1906.

Fabliaux ou Contes du XIIᵉ et du XIIIᵉ Siècle, ed. P. J. B. Le Grand, 'De La Bonne Imperatrice', v, 125–9. Paris: Jules Renouard, Libraire, 1829.

Garlande, Jean de, *The Stella Maris of John of Garland*, ed. Evelyn Faye Wilson. Cambridge, Mass.: published with Wellesley College by Medieval Academy of America, 1946.

Gesta Romanorum, ed. Hermann Oesterley, 'De Octavian qui Super Omnia Uxorem Dilexit', 648–53. Berlin: Weidmann, 1872.

Gesta Romanorum, trans. Charles Swan, rev. ed. E. A. Baker. London: G. Routledge & Sons, 1905.

Gobii, Johannes Junior, *Scala Celi*, copied by Luella Carter. Chicago: J. Zainer, 1928.

Grimms, Brüder, 'Hildegard', *Deutsche Sagen*, ii, 83–5. Leipzig, 1818.

Herold, Johannes, 'Discipulus Redivivus', *Promptuarium de Miraculis Beate Marie Virginis*, No. 635, ed. Bonaventura Elers. Nürnberg, 1728 [not seen].

Hoccleve, Thomas, 'Fabula de quadam Imperatrice Romana', *Hoccleve's Minor Poems*, ed. F. J. Furnivall and I. Gollancz, EETS, ES, 61, 140–73. London: K. Paul, Trench, Trübner & Co., 1892.

Die Kaiserchronik, ed. Edward Schröder, 'Crescentia', 289–314. Hannover: Hahn, 1892.

Macaire: Chanson de Geste, ed. M. Francis Guessard, *Les Anciens Poètes de la France*, ix. Paris: A. Franck, 1866.

La Manekine, ed. Hermann Suchier, *Oeuvres Poetiques de Philippe de Remi Sire de Beaumanoir*, *SATF*, xxvii. Paris: 1884–5.

Monmerqué, Louis and F. Michel, eds., *Théâtre Français au Moyen Age*, 'Mystère de l'Empereris de Rome', 365–416. Paris: Didot, 1840.

Nino, Antonio de, 'Favola Gentile', *Usi e Costumi Abruzzesi*, iii, 153–6. 1883: rpt. Firenze: L. S. Olschki, 1963–5.

Octavian, ed. G. Sarrazin, Altenglische Bibliothek, iii. Heilbronn: Gebr. Henniger, 1885.

Pulci, Antonio, 'Santa Guglielma', *Sacre Rappresentazione*, ed. Allesandro d'Ancona, iii, 208–34. Firenze: Successori Le Monnier, 1872.

Rosenblut, Hans, 'Ein Liepleich History Von Groszer Schone, Gedult und Kuscheiteiner Edeln Keyseryn', *Fastnachtspiele aus dem Funfzehnten Jahrhundert*, ed. Adelbert Keller, III, 139–49. Stuttgart: Litterarischer Verein, 1853.

Tales from the Arabic, ed. John Payne, 'Story of the Pious Woman Accused of Lewdness', III, 263–74. London: printed for the Villon Society, 1884

Timoneda, Juan, *El Patrañuelo*. Madrid: Espas-Calpe, S.A., 1958.

Tuti-Nameh, ed. Goerge Rosen, 'Geschichte der Merhuma', I, 89–108. Leipzig: F. V. Brodhaus, 1858.

RELATIONSHIP WITH FOLKTALES

Barry, P., 'Bells Rung Without Hands', MLN, 30 (1915), 28–9.

Child, Francis J., ed., *The English and Scottish Popular Ballads*. 5 vols. Boston: Houghton Mifflin & Co., 1882–98, II, 34; III, 235.

Dickson, Arthur, *Valentin and Orson: A Study*. New York: Columbia University Press, 1929, 72.

Fahlin, Carin, 'La Femme Innocente Exilée dans une Forêt: Motif Folklorique de la Litterature Médiévale", *Mélanges de Philologie Romane Offerts à M. K. Michaelsson*, 138–48. Göteborg, 1952.

Grundtvig, Svend., H. G. Nielsen, and A. Olrik, eds., *Gamle Folkeviser*, I, 195; III, 782; IV, 730. Copenhagen, 1853, 1862, 1883.

Stefanovic, S., 'Ein Beitrag zur Angelsachsischer Offa Sage', *Anglia*, 35 (1908–11), 483–525.

Tatlock, J. S. P., 'Notes on Chaucer', *MLN*, 29 (1914), 98.

Thompson, Stith, *Motif Index of Folk Literature*. 6 vols. in 4. Helsinki: Suomalainen Tredeakatemia Academia Scientiarum Fennica, 1932–6.

METRE

Baugh, Albert C., 'Improvisation in the Middle English Romance', *PAPS*, 103 (1959), 418–54.

Borroff, Marie, *Sir Gawain and the Green Knight: A Stylistic and Metrical Study*. New Haven: Yale University Press, 1962.

Curschmann, Michael, 'Oral Poetry in Medieval English, French, and German Literature, Some Notes on Recent Research', *Spec.*, 42 (January 1967), 35–52.

Oakden, J. P., *Alliterative Poetry in Middle English*. 1930–5; rpt. New York: Archon, 1968.

Sir Gawain and the Green Knight, trans. Marie Borroff. New York: W. W. Norton, 1967, 55 ff.

Waldron, Ronald A., 'Oral Formulaic Technique and Middle English Alliterative Poetry', *Spec.*, 32 (October 1957), 792–802.

PALAEOGRAPHY

Dawson, G. E. and L. Kennedy-Skipton, *Elizabethan Handwriting* 1500–1600. New York: Faber, 1968.

Jenkinson, Hilary, *The Later Court Hands in England from the Fifteenth to the Seventeenth Centuries*. 1927; rpt. New York: Frederick Unger Publishing Co., 1969.

——, *Palaeography and the Practical Study of Court Hand*. Cambridge: Cambridge University Press, 1915.

Johnson, Charles and Hilary Jenkinson, *English Court Hand A.D. 1066-1500*. 2 vols. 1915; rpt. New York: Frederick Unger Publishing Co., 1967.

Parkes, Malcolm B., *English Cursive Book Hands, 1250–1500*. Oxford: Clarendon Press, 1969.

Wright, C. E., *English Vernacular Hands: From the Twelfth to the Fifteenth Centuries*. Oxford: Clarendon Press, 1960.

BIBLIOGRAPHIES

Hornstein, Lillian H., 'Le Bone Florence of Rome' and 'Eustace–Constance–Florence–Griselda Legends', *A Manual of the Writings in Middle English 1050–1400*, ed. J. Burke Severs, Fasc. 1, I, 131–2, 278–92. New Haven: Connecticut Academy of Arts and Science, 1968.

Bossuat, R., ed., *Manuel Bibliographique de la Litterature Française du Moyen Age*. Paris: Libraire d'Argences, 1951 (1st supplement, Paris, 1955; 2nd supplement, Paris, 1961).

Brown, Carleton and Rossell H. Robbins, *An Index of Middle English Verse*. New York: Columbia University Press, 1943.

A Catalogue of the Manuscripts Preserved in the Library of the University of Cambridge, ed. H. R. Luard *et al.* 5 vols. Cambridge: Cambridge University Press, 1857.

Chauvin, Victor, *Bibliographie des Oeuvrages Arabes ou Relatifs aux Arabes*. Liege: H. Vaillant-Carmanne, 1892–1907.

Renwick, W. L. and H. Orton, *The Beginnings of English Literature to Skelton, 1509*. rev. ed. London: Cresset Press, 1952.

OTHER

The Catholic Encyclopedia, ed. Charles G. Hebermann *et al*. 16 vols. New York: Robert Appleton Co., 1909.

Clement of Rome, 'The First Epistle of Clement to the Corinthians', *The Ante-Nicene Fathers*, ed. Alexander Roberts and James Donaldson, I, 5–21. New York: Scribner's, 1926.

Gibbs, A. C., *Middle English Romances*. London: Edward Arnold and Evanston, Ill.: Northwestern University Press, 1966.

Graesse, J. G. Th., Friedrich Benedict, and Helmut Plechl, *Orbis Latinus: Lexikon lateinischer geographischer Namen des Mittel-alters und der Neuzeit*. 3 vols. Braunschweig: Klinkhardt & Biermann, 1972.

Hibbard, Laura, *Mediaeval Romance in England*. New York: Oxford University Press, 1924.

Hughes, Muriel J., *Women Healers in Medieval Life and Litera-ture*. New York: Columbia University Press, 1943.

Kane, George, *Middle English Literature: A Critical Study of the Romances, the Religious Lyrics, Piers Plowman*. London: Methuen, 1951.

Mehl, Dieter, *The Middle English Romances of the Thirteenth and Fourteenth Centuries*. London: Routledge & Kegan Paul, 1968.

Plato, *The Republic*, trans. Paul Shorey. 2 vols. London: William Heinemann Ltd., 1935.

Praz, Mario, *The Romantic Agony*. London: Oxford University Press, 1933.

Richmond, Velma B., *Laments for the Dead in Medieval Narrative*. Pittsburgh: Duquesne Studies (Philological Series), 1966.

Robert of Brunne, *Handlyng Synne*, ed. F. J. Furnivall. EETS, 19. London: K. Paul, Trench, Trübner & Co., 1901.

Rogers, Katharine, *The Troublesome Helpmate*. Seattle: University of Washington Press, 1966.

Schelp, Hanspeter, *Exemplarische Romanzen in Mittelenglischen*, *Palaestra*, 246. Göttingen: Vandenhoech & Ruprecht, 1967.

Schofield, William H., *English Literature from the Norman Con-quest to Chaucer*. New York: Macmillan Co., 1906.

Sir Gawain and the Green Knight, ed. J. R. R. Tolkien and E. V. Gordon. 2nd ed., rev. Norman Davis. Oxford: Clarendon Press, 1967.

Thomas Aquinas, St, *Summa Theologica: Latin Text and English Translation*, ed. and trans. by Blackfriars (*Virtues of Justice in the Human Community*, trans. T. C. O'Brien (vol. 41)). 60 vols.

London: Eyre & Spottiswoode and New York: McGraw-Hill, 1964– .

Van Ghent, Dorothy, *The English Novel: Form and Structure*. New York: Harper & Row, 1953.

Vergilius Maro, Publius, *Vergil*, trans. R. Rushton Fairclough. 2 vols. London: W. Heinemann and Cambridge, Mass.: Harvard University Press, 1954–6.

Weber, Henry, ed., *Metrical Romances of the Thirteenth, Fourteenth, and Fifteenth Centuries*. 3 vols. Edinburgh: A. Constable & Co., 1810.

Wood, Chauncey, *Chaucer and the Country of the Stars*. Princeton: Princeton University Press, 1970.

The Works of Geoffrey Chaucer, ed. Fred N. Robinson. 2nd ed. Boston: Houghton Mifflin Co., 1957.

NOTE ON THE TEXT

The text of the present edition was transcribed from a microfilm copy of the MS Cambridge Ff. 2.38 and afterwards compared with the original in the University Library, Cambridge.

Instead of reproducing the appearance of the manuscript with regard to column divisions, I have separated and numbered stanzas. Capitals and punctuation are modern. Words of which the prefixes and stems are separated in the manuscript are joined together in my edition. Contractions are expanded without notice. These are common and are indicated either by a superior letter or by a vertical line above or through the affected letter. The insertion of letter a over the line usually stands for 'ra' or just the letter a itself. Other superior letters which appear are t ($w^t = wyth$, $þ^t = þat$), e ($Boþ^e = Boþe$, $þ^e = þe$), u ($þ^u = þou$) and a special form of r which is used for ur. A horizontal line through h denotes omission of m ($ħy = hym$) or es ($Jħu = Jhesu$); a curved line over on signals the dropping of y; over w, the absence of m, and over yg, the elimination of n.

Abbreviation by 'special signs' is another common method. These signs may indicate suspensions (the omission of final letters) as well as contractions. Examples of the latter are the upward curve from the end of a letter which stands for re or er, and the p with a horizontal line through its limb which stands for er. Common signs for suspensions are the broken oblique stroke curving from the end of a letter which stands for yr and the flourish turning downwards after the end of a letter which usually stands for ys. Two special signs are noteworthy for appearing nearly always without connecting strokes to other letters. One is the Tironian sign for *and* and the other is a figure, rather like a long s with the lobe of a thorn superimposed on it, which means *syr*. One last unique use of a superior letter remains to be mentioned with these special signs, that is, l over Roman numeral M (M^l) representing one thousand.

The text is printed as I wish it to be read. Where emenda-

c

tions have been made, the state of the manuscript is shown
in footnotes. There is a minimum of emendations in the text.
In general, I have emended only in order to make sense of the
text or to remove certain obvious errors.

The spelling of the manuscript is reproduced. I have not
attempted to regularise the appearance of þ and *th*, ȝ and *gh*,
or *u* and *v*. The letter *i* is retained for vowels and *j* for con-
sonants in order to avoid forms like *jn*.

It has been thought expedient to give in the footnotes—
apart from manuscript readings for places in which I alter the
text and descriptions of deletions, holes, and interlinear
insertions which affect readability—the points at which
Ritson (*R.*) and Vietor (*V.*) differ from my interpretation of
the manuscript. Suggested emendations by Holthausen[1] which
I have adopted are signalled by *H.* in the textual footnotes.

[1] Ferdinand Holthausen, 'Zu Mittelenglischen Romanzen', *Anglia*,
41 (1917), 497–512.

LE BONE FLORENCE OF ROME

1

As ferre as men ryde or gone f. 239c
A more chyualrous town þen Troy was ⟨oon⟩
  In londe was neuyr seen;
Nor bettur knyȝtys þen came of hyt
In all thys worlde was neuyr ȝyt, 5
  For bothe hardy and kene.
Then came oon hyght Awdromoche,
The furste byger of Anteoche,
  And enhabyted cuntreys clene;
Antenowre was of þat barmeteme, 10
And was fownder of Jerusalem,
  That was wyght wythowtyn wene.

2

Helemytes hyght the thryd Troyon,
And was a stronge man of blode and bone,
  That fro Troye came to Awfryke; 15
Eneas be schyp gate to Rome,
The chefe cyte of crystendome,
  Then was ther none hyt lyke.
Vnto þe tyme þat þe emperowre Syr Garcy
Werryd on hyt, and herkenyth why, 20
  That many a oon sore can syke;
Of Costantyne þe nobull was he,
A doghtyar knyght þar not be
  In batell for to stryke.

3

Another emperowre reygned at Rome, 25
Syr Otes þe grawnt hyght þat gome,
  That wyght was vnder schylde;
A feyre lady he had to wyfe,

2 ⟨oon⟩, *inserted under* was *in bracket*   10 *H.* barneteme,
also possible   15 *R.* Troy   17 *R.* cytè   19 *R.* emperowr

That on a day loste hur lyfe,
    That worthy was to welde,   f. 239d
And dyed of a maydyn chylde,   31
That aftur waxe boþe meke and mylde,
    So fayre was seen but selde.

4

Whan þe emperys was dedd,
The emperowre was wylde of redd,   35
    He gart crysten thys chylde bryȝt,
And callyd hur Florens þys maydyn ⟨feyre⟩,
Boþe hys doȝtyr and hys heyre,
    In þys worlde was not soche a wyȝt.
Wolde ye lythe Y schoulde yow telle   40
Of þe wondurs þat there befelle
    Abowte in cuntreys ryght:
For þre dayes hyt reyned blode,
And bestys faght as þey were wode,
    Bothe wylde and tame wyth myght;   45

5

Fowlys in the fyrmament
Eyther odur in sondur rente,
    And felle dedd to þe grownde,
Hyt sygnyfyed þat aftur come,
Grete trybulacyons vnto Rome,   50
    Schulde many a man confownde;
As was for þat maydyn small,
Owtetakyn Troye and Rownsevall,
    Was neuyr in þys worlde rownde,
Syr Otes, þe nobull emperowre,   55
Gart norysch þe chylde wyth honowre,
    And kept hur hole and sownde.

6

He set to scole that damysell,
Tyll sche cowde of þe boke telle,

37 ⟨feyre⟩, *inserted interlinearly under* maydyn   53 *R.* Troy

And all thynge dyscrye, 60
Be þat she was xv yere olde,
Wel she cowde as men me tolde,
   Of harpe and sawtyre.
All hur bewteys for to neuyn
Myght no man vnder heuyn, 65
   For sothe nomore may I. f. 240a
To mykyll bale was sche borne,
And many a man slayn hur forne,
   And in grete batels can dye.

7

When Syr Garcy herde seye 70
That þe emperowre of Rome had soche a may
   To hys doghtur dere,
He waxe hasty as the fyre,
And gart sembyll þe lordys of hys empyre,
   That bolde and hardy were. 75
He seyde, 'Ofte haue ye blamed me,
For Y wolde not weddyd bee,
   Y have herde of a clere,
Florens þat ys feyre and bryght,
In all þys worlde ys not soche a wyȝt 80
   Y wyll hur haue to my fere.'

8

As þe Romans trewly tolde,
He was a hundurd yerys olde,
   And some boke seyth mare.
He was arayed in ryche parell, 85
Of sylke and golde wythowtyn fayle,
   All whyte was hys hare.
He seyde 'Syrs wendyþ ouyr þe see,
And bydd þe emperowre of Rome sende me
   Hys doghtur swete and sware. 90
And yf he any gruchyng make,
Many a crowne Y schall gare crake,
   And bodyes to drowpe and dare.'

61 *R.* sche fyftene   74 *R.* empyr

9

Hys flesche trembylde for grete elde,
Hys blode colde hys body vnwelde, 95
   Hys lyppes blo forthy;
He had more mystyr of a gode fyre,
Of bryght brondys brennyng schyre,
   To beyke hys boones by,
A softe bath a warme bedd, 100
Then any maydyn for to wedd,
   And gode encheson why,
For he was bresyd and all tobrokyn, f. 240b
Ferre trauelde in harnes and of warre wrokyn.
   He tolde them redylye: 105

10

'When ye haue þe maydyn broght,
That ys so feyre and worthely wroght,
   Sche schall lygg be my syde,
And taste my flankys wyth hur honde,
That ys so feyre Y vndurstonde, 110
   Yn bedde be me to byde.
Sche schall me boþe hodur and happe,
And in hur louely armes me lappe,
   Bothe euyn and mornetyde;
Byd hur fadur sende hur to me, 115
Or Y schall dystroye hym and hys cyte,
   And þorow hys remes ryde.'

11

A prowde garson þat hyght Acwrye,
He was borne in Vtalye,
   The emperowre aftur hym sende; 120
And forty lordys wryttes wythynne,
That were comyn of nobull kynne,
   In message for to wende;
And forty stedys wyth þem he sente,

116 *R.* cytè   124 *R.* stedes

Chargyd wyth golde for a presente, 125
   'And, say hym as my frende,
That Y grete wele Syr Otes þe graunt,
And byd hym sende me hys doghtur aveaunt,
   That ys curtes and hende.'

12

He cawsyd þem to hye as þey were wode, 130
Wyth schyppes soone in to þe flode,
   They rechyd ouyr the depe;
Spaynysch stedys wyth þem þey ledd,
And cloþys of golde for back and hedd,
   That men myght vndur slepe. 135
Aye the wynde was in the sayle,
Ouyr fomes þey flett wythowtyn fayle,
   The wethur þem forþe can swepe.
The furste hauyn þat euyr þey hente
Was a towne þey calde Awtrement, f. 240c
   That folke þem feyre can kepe. 141

13

Soon ther tresowre vp they drowe,
And ther stedys strong ynowe,
   And made ther schyppys tome;
They lefte a burges feyre and wheme, 145
All ther schyppys for to ȝeme,
   Vnto ther gayne come.
They passed þorow Pole and Chawmpayn,
Euyr speryng ther gatys gayne
   Vnto the cyte of Rome. 150
They entyrde yn at þe ȝatys wyde,
Full ryally þorow þe cyte þey ryde,
   And dredyd no wrangdome.

128 *R.* his   avenaunt   146 *R.* yeme
148 Chawmpayn: *MS. curved mark over* w = wm
149 *R.* gane   150 *R.* cytè   152 *R.* cytè

14

Thee xl^{ti} messengerys as Y yow say,
Euery oon rode in feyre array,   155
   Ther sadyls schone full bryght;
Ther brydyls glyteryng all of golde,
Ther was neuyr frescher vpon molde,
   Made be day nor nyght.
A stede of Spayne, Y vnderstande,   160
Euery lorde ledd in hys hande,
   Bothe full prest and wyght;
All was couyrde wyth redd sendell,
The caryage behynde, as Y yow tell,
   Cam wyth þe tresur ryght.   165

15

Thorow þe towne þe knyghtys sange,
And euyr þer bryght brydyls range,
   Makeyng swete mynstralcy;
Lordys and ladyes of grete astate,
And odur many, well Y wate,   170
   At wyndows owt can lye.
And euyr þe formast speryd þe wayes
Vnto þe emperowrs paleys,
   Full ryall was that crye;
Feyre þey were resseyuyd thore   f. 240d
Wyth hym þat was full wyse of lore,   176
   Hys doghtur sate hym bye.

16

In a robe ryght ryall bowne,
Of a redd syclatowne,
   Be hur fadur syde;   180
A coronell on hur hedd sett,
Hur cloþys wyth bestys and byrdys were bete,
   All abowte for pryde.
The lyghtnes of hur ryche perre,

And þe bryghtnes of hur blee,   185
   Schone full wondur wyde.
There were kyngys in that halle,
Erlys and dewkys who rekenyth all,
   Full a hundurd that tyde.

17

Thes xl^{ti} messengerys at ones   190
Entyrd into þes worthy wones,
   And came into the halle.
Syr Acvrye haylsyd þe emperowre,
And hys doghtyr whyte as flowre,
   That feyrest was of all.   195
He askyd of whens þat þey myght bee.
'Of Costantyne þe nobull are we.'
'Feyre, syrrys, mote yow befalle.'
'A present we haue broght in hye,
Fro owre emperowre Syr Garcy,   200
   Stedys into thy stalle.

18

'An xl horsys chargyd ryght,
Wyth cloþys of golde, and besawntys bryght,
   Into thy tresory.
He byddyth, wythowte avysement,   205
That þy doghtur be to hym sent,
   For to lygg hym by.
Hys body ys bresyd, hys bones are olde,
That sche may kepe hym fro þe colde,
   Haue done now hastelye.   210
In comely cloþyng sche shall be cledd,
I haue grete hope he wyll hur wedd,   f. 241a
   Sche ys a feyre lady.

190 *R.* fourti   191 *R.* Entyre   193 *R.* Acwrye haylsed
194 *R.* floure
202 *R.* fourty
211 *R.* schall

19

'And yf þou sende hur not soone,
Hastelye, wythowten wone,   215
   Then ryseth ther a stryfe;
Ellys wyll he nygh þe nere,
Wyth hys ryche powere,
   And feche hur as hys wyfe.
He wyll dystroye þy bygly landys,   220
And slee all þat before hym standys,
   And lose full many a lyfe.
Haue done', he seyde, 'hastelye in hye,
An answere muste we gyf Garcy,
   At home when we can ryve.'   225

20

The emperowre seyde, as a man hende,
'Ye schall haue an answere or ye wende',
   And calde þe steward hym tylle:
'The ȝonder knyghtys to chawmbur ye lede
Of all thynge that they haue nede   230
   Serve them at ther wylle;
They are Syr Garcys messengerys,
And go we to owre councell perys,
   And leue them bydyng stylle,
To loke what beste ys for to doo,   235
Soche typyngys ys comyn vs too,
   Loke whedur we wyll fulfylle.'

21

The emperowre hys doghtur be þe hande hent,
And to a chaumbur they wente,
   Hys councell aftur hym ȝede   240
And askyd yf sche wolde sent þertylle,
For to be at Syr Garcyes wylle.
   And sche seyde, 'Jhesu forbede!'
Sche seyde, 'Be God þat boght me dere,

229 *R.* yonder
231 *V.* Serue

Me had leuyr þe warste bachylere,   245
   In all my fadurs thede,
Then for to lye be hys bresyd boones,
When he coghyth and oldely grones,   f. 241b
   I can not on hys lede.'

22

Hur fadur lykyd hur wordys wele,   250
So dud hys cowncell euery dele,
   And blessyd hur for hur fame.
They seyde, 'Yf that Garcy come,
In euyll tyme he hedur nome
   Hedurward for to drawe.   255
The garsons be not so doghtye,
But mony of þem soone schall dye,
   Yf we togedur plawe;
Go we hens owre redd ys tane,
Odur cowncell kepe we nane,   260
   Be ryght nodur be lawe.'

23

The emperowre came into þe halle,
The messengerys had etyn all,
   And stode to byde an answare.
He seyde, 'Syrs, wendyth hame   265
For here schall ye haue no game,
   God forbede hyt so ware!
Take the tresowr þat ye broght,
But my doghtur gete ye noght,
   For all yowre bostefull fare;   270
We schall stonde owre chawnce vnto,
Whedur he come or not so do,
   Full mekyll we schall not care.'

24

Then Acurye can say,
'In the begynnyng of Maye,   275
   My lorde wyll buske hym to ryde,

252 *R.*, *V.* sawe   258 togedur: *MS.* togodur *V.* to gedur

And take the somer before hym clene,
And dystroye they londys all bedeene,
  Who ys he þat schall hym byde?'
Then answeryd Syr Egraveyne,   280
'We shall founde to knok ageyne,
  For all hys grete pryde.'
The emperowre comawndyd no man schulde do   f. 241c
Harme the messengerys vnto,
  They toke ther leue that tyde.   285

25

Then the messengerys all togedur,
Wyth þe tresowre þat þey broȝt thedur,
  Went home agayne.
Also tyte as Syr Garcy sawe,
Wyt ye well he lyste not to lawe,   290
  But mornyd in mode and mayne.
Altherfurste he toke hym tome
To spere the estyrs of Rome,
  To telle hym Acurye was fayne,
'Syr, hyt ys feyre bygged wyth halles and bowrys,   295
We tolde the vii hundurd towrys,
  So Cryste me saue and sayne;

26

'And ther lorde Syr Otes the graunt,
Wyth mekyll worschyp þey hym avaunt,
  Of curtesye he ys the welle,   300
And therto trewe as any stele,
Forþy, syr, men loue hym wele,
  Mony wyth hym do dwelle.
He ys bothe ware and wyse,
And geuyth þem gyftys of pryce,   305
  The certen sothe to telle;

286 *R.* Then
287 *R.* browght
292 *R.* come
296 *R.* Seven
303 *After H.*, do dwelle: *MS.* to dwelle *R.*, *V.* to dwelle

And hys doghtur þe feyrest þynge,
That euyr was seen wolde or ȝynge,
   Made of flesche and felle.

27

'Thogh a man sate on a wyght palfreye   310
All the longe somersday,
   Avysyd myght he be
For to ryde Rome abowte,
And come yn whereuyr he went owt,
   Hyt were a grete yurne.   315
Euery day in the yere
The feyre ys þere lyke playnere,
   Amonge the folke so free;
Syxty dewkys are calde hys perys,   f. 241d
And twenty þousande bachyleres,   320
   Longyth to that cyte.

28

'Of þe emperowrs pales Y wyll yow say,
Ther ys no soche in þe worlde today
   Stondyng vndur heuyn;
The pyllers þat stonde in þe halle,   325
Are dentyd wyth golde and clere crystalle
   And therto feyre and euyn.
They are fyllyd wyth syluyr as Cryste me couer,
And þere ys peyntyd wythynne and ouer,
   The dedly synnes sueyn;   330
There was peyntyd wyth þyngys sere
That men myȝt mewse on many a yere,
   Or he hyt scryed wyth steuyn.

310 *R.* palfraye
314 whereuyr: see Note to this line. *R.* wher *V.* where *R.* wente
315 *R.* yurne
321 *R.* cytè
328 Cryste: *MS.* cste
329 *R.* ther
332 *R.* yer
333 scryed: *MS.* stryed

29

'There comyth watur in a condyte,
Thorow a lyon rennyth hyt,   335
  That wroght ys all of golde,
And þat standyþ in þe myddys of þe halle;
A hundurd knyȝtys and ladyes smalle
  Myght wasche there and þey wolde
All at ones on that stone;   340
Many oþer waturs come þorow þe town,
  That fresche are vpon folde;
In myddys þe cyte ys oon rennande,
Tyber hyt hyght Y vnderstande,
  As men ther vs tolde,   345

30

'The effect of Rome Y haue yow tolde,
And of þe beste barons bolde,
  That lygge there wythynne;
But of þe feyrenes of þe maye
I can not telle mony a day,   350
  Ne noght Y wyll begynne,
But syr,' he seyde 'Also mote Y the
Thyn eyen mon sche neuyr see
  To welde ȝyt nodur to wynne.'
Full grete othys Garcy hath sworne,   f. 242a
'Many a þousand schall dye þerforne   356
  Or Y of my brethe blynne

31

'Or þre monythys and a halfe be gone,
I schall dystroye hys landys euerychon,
  And wynne hys doghtur wyth were.'   360
Then he made to sende owt wryttys wyde,
In hys londe on euery syde,
  Messengerys can them bere;

---

336 wroght: g *partly obliterated by hole*   343 *R*. cyté
344 *After H.*, Tyber: *MS*. Tyger *R.*, *V*. Tyger
347 *R*. best

And Florence fadur at hame
Ordeygned hys men on the same,   365
    Wyth armowre schylde and spere.
And þus begynneth a bale to brewe,
Many a man therfore myght rewe,
    And wemen hyt dud grete dere.

32

    370
Syxty þousand sembelde þen
Of garsons and of odur men
    To Garcy in that stownde,
They set vp seylys and forþe þey rode,
And ay hymselfe wythowten bode,
    The formaste forthe can fownde.   375
Syxty myle fro Rome ryved they,
Hyt went nere on þe thrydd day,
    Ther was not oon drowned.
They tyght þer pavylons in a stede,
The brode felde waxe all redd,   380
    So glemed golde on þe grownde.

33

The medowe was callyd Narumpy,
The water of Tyber rennyng by,
    There Garcyes pavylon stode.
All þe cloþys were of sylke,   385
The ryche ropys were ryȝt swylke,
    The boosys were redd as blode.
Ther was no beest þat yede on fote
But hyt was portreyed þere, Y wote,
    Nor fysches swymmyng in flode.   390
Fyftene pomels of golde þere schoon,   f. 242b
An egyll and a charbokull stone,
    Wyde the lyghtnes gode.

366 *R.* With
369 wemen: *MS.* wemon
386 *R.* ryght
393 *R.* yode *V.* ȝode

34

The emperowre of Rome lay on hys walle,
And hys doghtur gente and small,   395
   Florence the feyre sche hyght;
And sye the garsons assay þer stedys,
Sterne men in stele wedys,
   The medowe all can lyght.
He seyde, 'Y haue golde ynogh plente,   400
And sowdears wyll come to me,
   Bothe be day and nyght.
Now schall Y neuyr my golde spare,
But faste vpon þys warre hyt ware,
   God helpe me in my ryght.'   405

35

The kynge of Hungary þat tyme was dedd,
And lefte hys sonnes wylde of redd,
   Syr Mylys and Syr Emere.
Ther modur was weddyd to a stedd,
Agenste all the baronage redd,   410
   As ye schall further here,
To a lorde that wonnyd thereby,
Syr Justamownde of Surry,
   That sterne was to stere.
The kynge of Naverne toke þes chyldur two,   415
And made þem knyghtys bothe tho,
   And manhode can them lere;

36

Tyll hyt felle oones on a day
They wente to a medowe to playe,
   To lerne them for to ryde;   420
Syr Emere bare in hys schylde:
A whyte dowve who so behelde,
   A blakk lyon besyde.
The whyte dowve sygnyfyed

399 *R*. medow *R*. plentè   422 dowve: *MS*. dowbe
424 dowve: *MS*. dowbe

That he was full of knyghthedd,   425
   And mekenes at that tyde;
The lyon þat he was ferse and felle,   f. 242c
Amonge hys enmyes for to dwelle,
   And durste beste in batell byde.

37

A wery palmer came þem by,   430
And seyde, 'Syrrys Y haue ferly
   That ye wyll not fare
I haue bene at grete Rome,
To seke Seynt Petur, and thens Y come,
   Straunge tythyngys harde Y thare.   435
Ther ys an emperowre þat hyght Garcy,
Is logyd in the Narumpy,
   Wyth syxty thousande and mare,
He seyth þe emperowre of Rome schall not leue
But yf he to hym hys doghtur geue,   440
   That ys so swete of sware.'

38

Than Syr Mylys and Syr Emere
Toke wyth them forty in fere,
   That were comyn of gentyll kynne,
To grete Rome euyn they rode,   445
And at a burges hows abode,
   And there they toke ther ynne
They speryd of þer oste and þer ostes,
Of þer tythyngys more and lesse,
   Or euyr they wolde blynne.   450
They fownde hyt as þe palmer tolde,
They seyde wyth Otes dwelle þey wolde,
   Whedur hyt were to lose or wynne.

39

Fyve thousande on þe morne Garcy sent
Of hys men verament,   455
   Wele arayed in ther gere.

426 8¹, *written in same hand below line*   434 *R.* seynte
455 hys men: *MS.* hys xx men

As nere as þey durste for dowte,
Fyfty of them yssewed owte,
   For to juste in werre.
That sawe Syr Mylys and Emere,   460
Wyth þer ferys bothe in fere,
   They thoght them for to feere;
They passyd owt at a posterne,   f. 242d
Os men þat schoulde of batayle lerne,
   Wyth armowre schylde and spere.   465

40

Thes fyfty had forjusted soone,
And slewe þem down wythowten mone,
   All that wolde abyde;
Oon came prekyng owt of þe prees,
To Syr Emere euyn he chese,   470
   But soone was fellyd hys pryde.
Syr Emere reysyd hys spere on hyȝt,
Thorow þe body he bare þe knyght,
   And downe he felle that tyde.
Than þey faght hande ouyr heuydd,   475
Many oon þere þer lyuys leuydd,
   That came on Garcyes syde.

41

The emperowre of Rome lay on hys wall,
And hys doghtur gent and small,
   Florence feyre and free;   480
Sche seyde, 'Fadur, wyth mylde steuyn,
To vs ys comyn helpe fro heuyn,
   Fro God in mageste;
Yondur ys a nobull knyght,
That styrryth hym styfly in þe fyght,   485
   Beholde and ye may see.
Wyth þe whyte dowve and þe blak lyon,
The beste þat comeþ he strykeþ down,
   Helpe that he rescowde bee.'

475 *R.* hand   heuydd: *MS.* hedd *V.* hedd *R.* hevydd *H.* heuidd
483 *R.* magestè

42

The emperowre calde Syr Egravayne,   490
And Syr Sampson þat was hym gayne,
   Armed well and ryght,
A hundurd men wyth þem he toke,
Vp they lepe, so seyth þe boke,
   On stedys stronge and wyght.   495
All þat were left onslayne,
Fledd vnto þer strenkyþ agayne,
   Hyt was a semely fyght.
Then swere Garcy, in full grete yre,   f. 243a
That he wolde brenne all Rome wyth fyre,   500
   On the morne yf that he myght.

43

Then Syr Mylys and Syr Emere,
Wyth þer forty felows in fere,
   Come the emperowre beforne;
They salutyd hym full ⟨ryally⟩,   505
And hys doghtur þat stode hym by.
   He askyd where they were borne.
They answeryd hym full curteslye,
'We were þe kyngys sonnes of Hungary
   Owre fadur hys lyfe hath lorne,   510
And hedur are we come to the,
As sowdears, yf mystyr bee;
   We speke hyt not in skorne.'

44

'God and Seynt Petur of Rome,
ȝylde yow yowre hedurcome,'   515
   The emperowre can sey;
'So doghtely as ye haue begonne,
Was neuer men vnder þe sonne
   So lykyng to my paye.'
Then þe maydyn þankyd þem efte,   520

498 *R., V.* syght   505 ⟨ryally⟩, *written interlinearly above* hym
515 yowre, *hole in MS. above* e

He þem wythhelde wyth þem þey lefte,
  To mete then wente thay.
The emperowre set Syr Mylys hym by,
Emere cowde more of curtesye,
  And he ete wyth the maye.   525

45

Sche þoght hym a full curtes knyȝt,
Feyre, yonge, semely, and wyght,
  Hur harte to hym can ȝylde.
Syr Myles seyde þe emperowre too,
'And ye wolde at my councell doo,   530
  Ye schoulde not fyght in fylde,
But close þe ȝatys and þe bryggys vp drawe,
And kepe vs clene owt of þer awe,
  And owre wepons wyghtly welde.
And kepe þe town boþe nyght and day,   535
Tyl þey be wery and wende a way.'   f. 243b
  Syr Emere hym behelde.

46

Emere seyde Mylys vnto,
'So myght a sympull grome do,
  Kepe an holde wythynne;   540
But we wyll manly to þe felde,
And Syr Garcy batell ȝelde,
  To morne or þat we blynne.'
Then þey made crye þorow cyte
That no man schoulde so hardy bee,   545
  That waryson wolde wynne.
But folowe þe standarde whereuyr hyt goys,
And freschly fyght vpon owre foys,
  Bothe the more and the mynne.

47

Than Syr Garcy wyth mekyll pryde   550
Made to crye þe same on hys syde,
  Amonge the barons bolde;

544 *R.* cytè   547 *R.* standard whereuyr: see Note to line
314. *R.* wher *V.* where.

The kynge of Turkay he seyde than,
'Thou art a full madde man,
   And fayleste wyt for elde;   555
Syr Otes þe graunt hath noght gylte,
Let therfore no blode be spylte,
   For hym that all schall welde.'
'Nay he warnyd me hys doghtur schene,
And þat hath tymberde all my teene,   560
   Full dere hyt schall be selde.'

48

A Roman stode besyde and harde,
To þe towne full soone he farde,
   And tolde the emperowre;
The maydyn mylde vp sche rase,   565
Wyth knyghtys and ladyes feyre of face,
   And wente vnto a towre.
There sche sawe ryght in þe feldys,
Baners brode and bryght scheldys,
   Of cheualry the flowre.   570
They nowmberde þem xl M*l* men
And a hundurd moo þen hur fadur had þen,
   That were ryght styffe in stowre.

49

'Allas!' seyde that maydyn clere,   f. 243c
'Whedur all þe ȝonde folke and þere   575
   Schoulde dye for my sake,
And Y but a sympull woman.'
The terys on hur chekys ranne,
   Hur ble beganne to blake.
'Put me owt to olde Garcy,   580
Yf all þes men schulde for me dye,
   Hyt were a dolefull wrake.'
Hur fadur seyde hyt schulde not bee;
Hors and armowre askyd hee,
And soone hys swyrde can take.   585

571 M*l*: *MS.* M*l* *R.* forty thousand   573 8ii, *written in same*
hand below line

50

He lepe on hys stede Bandynere,
And in hys honde he hent a spere,
   And rode abowte all nyght.
To the lordys of the towne,
And bad þey schulde be redy bowne,   590
   Tymely to the fyght.
They set þer standard in a chare,
And feele folke wyth hyt can fare,
   That hardy were and wyght,
Syxe lordys and Syr Egravayne   595
To be all ther chefetayne,
   And kepe hyt well and ryght,

51

The standarde was of whyte yvore,
A dragon of golde ordeygned þerfore,
   That on the ouyrende stode;   600
That sygnyfyed that Otes ware
In the felde as bolde as any bare,
   And a sterne man of mode.
The vawewarde and þe myddyll soone,
And þe rerewarde owte of Rome   605
   The grete oost remouyd and ȝode;
Be then had Garcy takyn hys place,
And soone wythynne a lytyll space,
   Ranne bowrnes all on blode.

52

Than Syr Otes þe graunt can calle   610
On herawde and hys knyghtys all,
   In myddys of the prees,   f. 243d
'Who so beryth hym beste today
Ageyne Syr Garcy, as Y yow say,
   That wyrkyth me þys vnpees,   615
I schall geue hym a feyre flowre,
Of grete Rome to be emperowre,
   Aftur my dyssees,

598 *After R., H.,* yvore: *MS.* yvar *V.* yvar

And wedde Florens my doghtur bryȝt,
As Y am trewe crysten knyght,
 Certen wythowtyn lees.'

620

53

Syr Emere askyd hys lorde þe kynge,
Yf he myght haue þe furste rydynge,
 And he grauntyd hym tylle.
Owt of Garcyes oost came oon,
A prowde garson hyght Bresobon,
 A wykkyd man of wylle;
When Syr Emere wyth hym mett,
A stronge dynte on hym he sett,
 Thorow hys armowre stylle.
He fonde no socowre at hys schylde,
But dedd he felle downe in þe fylde,
 Hys harte blode can owte spylle.

625

630

54

Be þat þe grete oost began to sembyll,
Trumpes to blowe, and stedys to trembyll,
 Harde togedur they yede.
Ryche harburgens all torusched,
And stele helmes all todusched,
 And bodyes brake owt to blede;
Hedys hopped vndur hors fete,
As haylestones done in þe strete,
 Styckyd was many a stede.
For Florence loue, þat feyre maye,
Many a doghty dyed that day,
 In Romance as we rede.

635

640

645

55

Then Syr Garcy wyth mekyll pryde,
Made knyghtys on hys own syde,
 Syxty yonge and feyre;

626 Bresobon: *MS.* bresobon *R.* Bresebon *V.* bresebon
628 w^t: t *obliterated by a hole*

The warste of þer fadurs were barons,   f. 244a
And oght bothe towres and townes,   650
    And all were they ryght heyre.
When Emere and hys men wyth þem mett,
Stronge dyntys on them he sett,
    Among þem can they store;
At þe furste wynnyng of þer schone,   655
So tyte of lyuys were they done,
    That all deryd not a pere.

56

Then Garcy yede nere wode for yre,
And arayed hys batels in þat bere,
    And fared as he wolde wede;   660
He bad þer dyntys schulde be wele wared,
That no Roman on lyue be spared.
    Thowe þey wolde rawnsome bede.
Ageyne hym came Syr Otes þe graunt,
A doghty knyght and an aveaunt,   665
    On Bondenore hys stede;
When Garcy sye þat hyt was hee,
He seyde Syrrys, also mote Y the,
    We two muste do owre dede.

57

'Thou art wele strekyn in age, Y trowe,   670
But Y am ferre elder then thou,
    We two muste juste in werre;
Hyt ys sethyn Y armyd ware
Seuyn yere and somedele mare;'
    And eyther toke a spere.   675
So harde togedur can þey ryde,
Owt of þer sadyls þey felle besyde,
    And graspyd to odur gere;
Wyth scharpe swyrdys faght þey þen,
They had be two full doghty men,   680
    Gode olde fyghtyng was there.
    660 wede: *MS.* wode

58

Garcy hyt Otes on the helme,
That vpon hys hedd hyt can whelme,
   Hyt sate hym wondur sare.
'Syr, wyth þys dynte Y chalenge Rome,   f. 244b
And þy doghtur bryght as blome,   686
   That brewyd hath all thys care.
When þat Y haue leyn hur by,
And done hur schame and vylenye,
   Then wyll Y of hur no mare,   690
But geue hur to my chaumburlayne.'
Tho wordys made Otes vnfayne,
   And tyte he gaf an answare:

59

'God and Seynt Petur of thys towne,
Let neuyr Rome come in thy bandome,   695
   And saue my doghtur sownde;
Owre fyghtyng ys not endyd ȝyt.'
On the helme Garcy he hyt,
   That he felle to the grownde.
There had Syr Garcy bene tane,   700
But þer came garsons many oon,
   And rescowed hym in þat stownde.
Syr Emere horsyd hys lorde agayne,
And loouyd God he was not slayne,
   And faste to fyght they fownde.   705

60

Syr Emere lokyd a lytyll hym fro,
And sawe hys brodur suffur woo,
   In a stowre fyghtande.
The Grekys had fyred hym abowte,
That he myght on no syde owte,   710
   But styffely can he stande.

695 *R.* bandoune   700 *R.* misnumbers l. 700, 710   701 *R.* ane
702 *R.* rescowd   703 lorde: de *partly obscured by a smudge*
707 *R.* suffer

He rescowde hym full knyghtly;
Many a doghty made he to dye,
    That he abowte hym fande;
Euyll quytt he hym hys mede,   715
For Mylys was þe falsyst lede
    That euyr leuyd in lande.

61

When he had rescowde hys brodur Mylon,
Of hys fomen came thretty bowne,
    Stelyng on hym stylle;   720
All þer sperys on hym þey sett,
He drewe hys swyrde wythowten let,
    And Mylys fledde to an hylle.
He seyde, 'Brodur also mote Y the,
Thou schalt not be rescowde for me';   f. 244c
    Loke whedur that he dud ylle   726
But stryked yn at anodur stowre,
And mett hys lorde þe emperowre,
    Layeng on wyth gode wylle.

62

'Mylys,' he seyde, 'where ys þy brodur?'   730
    'At the deuyll,' quod the todur,
    'I trowe beste that he bee.
He ys belefte wyth Syr Garcy,
Ageyn yow, he tolde me why,
    He myght geve more then ye.   735
Be God, he seyde, þat all may
He ys false that dar Y lay,
    Trewly trowe ye me.'
The emperowre lykyd hyt ylle,
And leyde vpon wyth gode wylle,   740
    Tyll he myght the sothe see.

---

718 *R.* broder   719 *R.* camen   724 8ⁱⁱⁱ, *written in*
same hand below line   735 geve, v *is written over an* r
737 *R.* dare
740 And: d *written over erasure*   leyde: le *written over erasure*

63

Forthe then lokyed þe emperowre,
And sawe Syr Emere in a stowre,
   Fyghtyng agenste hys foys;
He stroke þe stede wyth þe spurrys,   745
He spared nodur rygge nor forows,
   But euyn to hym he goys;
All that he abowte hym fonde
He and hys men broght to grownde,
   That neuyr oon vp rose.   750
And there was Mylys preuyd false,
Wyth hym and odur lordys alse,
   And loste all hys gode lose.

64

Then Emere toke harte hym too;
Full doghtely then can he doo.   755
   Florence hym behelde,
And tolde hur maydyns bryght of ble,
'In the felde beste doyth he
   Wyth þe whyte dowve in hys schylde
And þerto the black lyon.'   760
Sche cryed to hym wyth grete sowne,
   'Thou be my fadurs belde,
And þou schalt haue all thy desyre,   f. 244d
Me and all þys ryche empyre,
   Aftur my fadur to welde.'   765

65

When he harde þe maydyn bryght,
Hys hedd he lyfte vpon hyght,
   The wedur waxe full hate.
Hur fadur nere hande can talme,
Soche a sweme hys harte can swalme,   770
   For hete he waxe nere mate.

742 *R.* lokyd   758 felde: *MS.* folde   759 *R.* yn
760 *R.* lyoun

When that þey had so done,
A quarell came fleyng soone,
   And thorow the hed hym smate,
They sende aftur þe pope, Symonde,   775
And he schrofe hym and hoselde on þat grounde,
   And assoyled hym well, Y wate.

66

As soone as þe emperowre ȝyldyd þe goost,
A prowde garson came in haste,
   Syr Synagote hyght hee;   780
And broght an hundurd helmes bryght
Of hardy men þat cowde well fyght,
   Of felde wolde neuyr oon flee.
Emere stroke into that stowre,
And many oon made he for to cowre,   785
   And slewe them be two and thre.
Soone thereaftur was he tane,
And knyghtys kene wolde hym haue slayne,
   But ther souereygn bad let bee.

67

'Vnto Syr Garcy haue hym seen,   790
I trowe hys lyfe he wyll hym leen,
   He ys so feyre a knyght.'
Leue we Syr Emere in the stowre,
And speke more of the emperowre,
   How they on a bere hym dyght,   795
And how þey broght hym to þe towne,
Wythowten belle or procescyon,
   Hyt was a drery syght.
They layned hyt fro þer enmyes whyll þey myȝt,
And fro Florence þat worþy wyght,   800
   Hys own dere doghtur bryght.   f. 245a

777 *R.* wel
778 *R.* gast
797 *R.* procescoun *V.* procescon

68

Soone þe standard yn þey dud lede,
And baners bryȝt þat brode dud sprede,
   The Romans lykyd ylle,
And seyde þey schulde vpon þe morne,   805
Fyght wyth Garcy yf he had sworne,
   That hyely was on hylle.
Florence lay in a cornell,
And hur maydyns, as Y yow telle,
   That was curtes of wylle;   810
They seyde men brynge yn a bere,
And þat wyth a full mornyng chere,
   But all was hoscht and stylle.

69

Then can feyre Florence sayne,
'ȝondur ys begonne an euyll bargayn,   815
   Y see men brynge a bere,
And a knyght in handys leede,
Bondynowre my fadurs stede';
   Then all chawngyd hur chere.
Sche and hur maystres Awdygon,   820
Went in to þe halle allone,
   Allone wythowten fere,
And caste vp þe cloþe þen was hyt so,
The lady swowned and was full woo,
   Ther myght no man hur stere.   825

70

'Allas,' sche seyde, 'þat Y was borne!
My fadur for me hys lyfe haþ lorne,
   Garcy may haue hys wylle,
All my brode landys and me,
That Y welde in crystyante,'   830
   Ther myght no man hur stylle.
Lordys and ladyes þat þere ware

816 men: *MS.* mon   817 in: n *obliterated by a hole*
830 *R.* yn

Tyll hur chaumbur can they fare,
   Lorde! That them lykyd ylle;
Knyghtys and squyers þat þere was   835
Wrange þer hondys and seyde, 'Allas!
   For drede sche schulde hur spylle.'

71

Dewkys and erles þer hondys wronge,
And lordys sorowe was full stronge,   f. 245b
   Barons myght haue no roo: 840
'Who schall vs now geue londys or lythe,
Hawkys, or howndys, or stedys stythe,
   As he was wonte to doo?'
Syr Garcy went crowlande for fayne,
As rampande eyen do in þe rayne,   845
   When tythyngys came hym too,
He bad hys men schulde make þem bowne,
And hastelye go stroye vp þe towne,
   'My byddyng that ye doo:

72

'Slo þem down where ye þem mete,   850
And fyre fasten in euery strete,
   Loke now that taste.
I schall wyrke as haue Y yoye,
As kynge Maynelay dud be Troye,
   And stroye hyt at the laste.'   855
When þey harde þat were wythynne,
To þe ʒatys can they wynne,
   And barryd them full faste,
And they wythowte yngynes bende,
And stones to þe walles þey sende,   860
   And quarels wyth arbalast.

73

They wythynne wolde haue gone owte,
her souereygn marred þem for dowte,
   And made þem to kepe ther holde,

843 *R.* wont   854 *R.* Kyng   861 arbalast: *MS.* alablaste
R., V. alablaste

They sygned to þe ʒatys of þe towne,   865
An hundurd men in armes bowne,
 That hardy were and bolde.
The pope came wythowten delyte,
And enteryd the emperowre tyte,
 They wepte bothe ʒonge and olde.   870
The boke seyþ God þat vs boght
Many myrakyls for hur he wroght,
 Many a oon and thyckfolde.

74

So longe logyd the sege there,
That þey wythynne nere famysched were,   875
 Euyll lyfe can they lede;   f. 245c
They were not ordeygned þerfore,
They had golde in warme store,
 But mete was þem full nede.
All þey cowncelde Florence to take   880
Oon of thes lordys to be hur make,
 That doghty were of dede;
For to mayntene and vpholde
Agayne Syr Garcy þat burne bolde,
 The towne leuyth all in drede.   885

75

And Awdegone hur cowncelde soo
Oon of thes lordys for to too,
 Syr Mylys or Syr Emere;
'And let hym wedde yow wyth a rynge
Ther fadur was a ryche kynge,   890
 Knowyn bothe farre and nere',
'Ye but now ys Syr Emere tane,
And Garcys men haue hym slayne,'
 Seyde that maydyn clere,
'Ye behove to haue anodur,   895

875 8ⁱⁱⁱⁱ, *written in same hand below line*
883 *After* R., H., For to mayntene: *MS.* For mayntene *V.* For
mayntene

Take Mylys þat ys hys eldyst brodur,
  Hyt ys my cowncell wythowten were.'

76

To Syr Mylys Awdegon went,
And askyd yf he wolde assent
  To wedde that maydyn free,   900
That ys whyte as lylly flowre,
And be lorde and emperowre,
  The grettyst in crystyante.
'But God forbede and Seynt Myghell,
That þou vndurtake hyt but þou do well,   905
  And trewe man thynke to bee.'
To hyr speche answeryd he noght,
But stylle he stode and hym beþoght,
  And seyde, 'Y schall avyse me.'

77

'Avyse þe,' seyde þat maydyn feyre,   910
  'For to be my fadurs heyre?
  Lyghtly may ye thynke.   f. 245d
Be hym þat suffurde woundys fyve,
I schall neuyr be thy wyfe,
  To suffur dethys dynte.   915
Kyngys and dewkys haue me askyd,
And all þer londys wolde haue geue me ⟨at þe laste⟩,
  And many a ryall thynke.'
Forþe he yede wyth syghyng and care
That he had geuyn þat fowle answare   920
  For sorowe nere wolde he synke.

78

Thys whyle had Synagot takyn Emere,
And broȝt hym before Syr Garcy in fere,
  And seyde, 'We haue tane a knyght

903 *R.* yn   904 But God forbede: *MS.* But for god for bede
V. considers first for *crossed out*   907 hyr: *MS.* hys *R.*, *V.* hys
910 *R.* thee   912 *After H.*, ye: *MS.* y *R.*, *V.* y
917 ⟨at þe laste⟩, *inside bracket in margin*

Agenste yow fyghtyng in þe stowre, 925
We refte hym hors and armowre,
    But he ys an hardy wyght.'
'Felowe,' he seyde, 'what dyd þou there?'
'Syr, wyth my lorde on þe to were,
    That now to dedd ys dyght; 930
As sowdears my brodur and Y,
We haue noght ellys to leue by,
    Owre fadur fordyd owre ryght.

79

'Syr Phelyp of Hungary owre fadur was,
Now ys he dedd, therefore, allas! 935
    Owre modur weddyd ys newe,
Into Surry to Syr Justamownde,
That ys abowte vs to confownde,
    And owre bytter bales to brewe.
He hath dysheryted vs wythowt lees, 940
That we had leuyr warre nor pees,
    Perchawnce þat may hym rewe.'
Syr Synagot cowncelde Syr Garcy soo,
'Syr, delyuyr hym qwyte, and let hym goo,
    He semyth couenawnt and trewe.' 945

80

Than answeryd Syr Garcy,
'When Y toke trewage of Turky f. 246a
    Thy fadur in stede stode me;
Therfore, Y schall let the goo,
And geue hym all ye toke hym fro.' 950
    Emere knelyd on hys knee,
'Syr, when Y come into þe towne,
I and my men muste be bowne
    To greue bothe thyn and the.
Ye godys forbode, that þou me spare, 955

949 *R.* schal   954 *R.* thee   955 *After H.*, þou me
spare: *MS.* þou spare *R., V.* þou spare   godys, *no longer fully legible*
because partly rubbed

D

But of þy warste wylle euyrmare.'
    Garcy, thus seyde he:

81

'What wenyst þou wyth þy bragg and boost
For to dystroye me and myn hoost?'
    He toke hys leue and yede;   960
Syr Synagot gaue hym all togedur,
Be þe leste þonge þat he bare þedur,
    Emere lepe on hys stede.
He ledd hym þorow þe pavylons all,
Tyll he came nere to Romes walle,   965
    And paste the moost drede.
Than þey wythynne were full fayne,
That þey had getyn þe gome agayne,
    Ther blysse beganne to brede.

82

And agayne Syr Emere they went,   970
And broght hym before þat lady gente,
    And askyd yf he wolde
Wedde the beste of hur elde,
And all hur londys for to welde,
    Ageyne Garcy to holde;   975
And helpe to venge hur fadurs dedd.
He dud ryght as the lady bedd,
    That hardy was and bolde.
He seyde preuely muste me do,
Tyll þe baronage be sworne vs to,   980
    Bothe the yonge and the olde.

83

Syr Sampson and Syr Egravayne,
Syr Clamadore and Syr Alayne,   f. 246b
    Wyste of that bargen newe.

957 *R.* sayde
962 þonge: on *obliterated by hole in MS.*, þonge *after V*.
975 *R.* Agayne

They went aftur Syr Geffrey of Pyse,   985
And Syr Barnarde of Mownt Devyse,
   Tho syxe were gode and trewe;
They made þem to swere þey schulde be lele,
And Syr Emers counsell heyle,
   And Florence feyre of hewe.   990
Thus he tylleþ þem be fowre and fyve,
All þey had sworne to hym be lyve,
   Then Mylys hymselfe can rewe.

84

The pope came as ye may here,
For to crowne Syr Emere,   995
   And wedd them wyth a rynge.
Sche seyde, 'Now are ye emperowre of Rome,
The grettyst lorde in crystendome,
   And hedd of euery kynge;
Ȝyt schall ye neuyr in bedde me by,   1000
Tyl ye haue broght me Syr Garcy,
   For no maner of thynge;
Or lefte hym in þe felde for dedd,
Be hym Y sawe in forme of bredd,
   When þe preest can synge.'   1005

85

Emere the emperowre can say,
'I schall do all that Y may,
   But charge me wyth no mare.'
Then þey wysche and to mete be gone,
'Of mynstralcy we kepe none,   1010
   We haue no space to spare;
Nodur harpe, fedyll, nor geest,
But ordeygn yow wyth moost and leest,
   That wyth me wyll fare;
And brynge my stede Bondynere,   1015
And feche me forþe boþe schylde and spere;'
   Full tyte þen were þey thare.

996 And wedd them: *MS*. And them, *after R.*
1007 that, a *partly rubbed*

86

Than was there no lenger bode,
But vp þey lepe and forthe þey rode,   f. 246c
   To preke aftur ther praye.   1020
When worde came to Syr Garcy
A sory man was he forthy,
   That weddyd was þat may,
That was whyte as lylly flowre,
And Syr Emere crowned emperowre,   1025
   'Allas!' then can he say,
'That euyr Y let þat traytur goo,
When he was in my bandome soo,
   Me dawyd a drery day!'

87

Ther was lefte no man in þat town   1030
To kepe the lady of renowne,
   That was of temporalte,
That myght wyth ony wepon wyrke,
Owttakyn men of holy kyrke,
   At home they let them bee.   1035
They beganne at þe nerre syde,
And slewe down all þat wolde abyde,
   Trewly trow ye me;
On felde þey faght as þey were wode,
Ouyr þe bentys ranne the blode,   1040
   All tho dyed that wolde not flee.

88

Then on the felde þey freschely faght,
Many oon ther dethe there caght,
   That came on Garcyes syde.
Syr Garcy toke hym to the fyght,   1045
Wyth an hundurd in harnes bryght,
   He durste no lenger byde;
Of all þe men he þedur broght,

1018 8ᵛ, *written in same hand below line*
1028 *R.* bandoune   1032 *R.* temporaltè

Many on lyue leuyd he noght,
   To schypp went they that tyde;   1050
They set vp sayle and forþe are gone,
To Costantyne þe nobull towne,
   Also faste as they myght glyde.

89

Also soone as Syr Emere wyste
Welnere for sorowe hys herte breste,   1055
   That he in schyppe can lende   f. 246d
He bad Syr Mylys turne agayne,
Syr Sampson and Syr Egravayne,
   'For Y wyll aftur wende.
Take an hundurd men of armes bryȝt,   1060
And kepe my lady day and nyght,
   That ys curtes and hende;
Say to hur Y am on the see;
Chasyng aftur myn olde enmye,
   That slewe hur derrest frende.'   1065

90

Syr Mylys seyde to þes hundurd all,
'Thys herytage to me wyll falle,
   My brodur comyþ neuyr agayne.
I wyll wedde the yonge bryde,
He slepyd neuyr be hur syde,   1070
   Nor hath hur not by layne.
All that wyll assent to me,
Grete lordys schall they bee;'
   To graunt hym þey were fayne.
Sampson seyde, 'þat wyll Y neuyr doo,   1075
Falsehedd my lorde vnto;'
   The same seyde Egravayne.

91

All þey assentyd but they two,
The todur parte was þe moo,
   And þat was þere well seen.   1080
   1069 *R.* wylle

Soche wordys among þem can falle,
They presyd abowte Syr Sampson all,
   And slewe hym in that tene.
They made Syr Egraveyne to swere soon,
Or þey wolde wyth hym þe same haue done,   1085
   To wote wythowten wene;
Sone a bere haue they ordeygned,
And the dedd corse þer on leyde,
   The sorte was false and kene;

92

And seþyn to Rome þey hym broght,   1090
And tolde Florence worthyly wroght,
   That Emere laye there dedd;
When þat sche had swowned twyes,   f. 247a
And thereaftur syghed thryes,
   Sche wepyd in that stedd.   1095
Mylys seyde, 'My lady fre,
Thy councell wyll þat Y wedde þe,
   Hyt was my brodurs redd.'
Sche seyde, 'Y wyll weddyd bee
To a lorde that neuyr schall dye,   1100
   That preestys schewe in forme of bredd.

93

'Furste þen was my fadur slayne,
And now my lorde ys fro me tane,
   Y wyll loue no ma,
But hym þat boght me on þe rode,   1105
Wyth hys swete precyus blode,
   To hym Y wyll me ta.'
Then Mylys made xii armed knyȝtys
To kepe the pales day and nyghtys,
   Sche myght not come them fra,   1110
And also swythe Syr Egravayne,

1086 *V.* wete
1108 *R.* seven   made: a *obliterated by a hole*
1111 as *erased after* swythe, *V. considers it crossed out*

Went to þe pope, þe soþe to sayne,
To telle he was full thra,

94

How that Emere was ouyr þe see,
Chasyng Garcy to hys cuntre,   1115
   And Mylys wolde haue hys wyfe;
He had a hundurd to hys assent,
And hyght þem londys, lyþys, and rente;
   But Sampson hath loste hys lyfe,
And broght hym home vpon a bere,   1120
And tolde Florence hyt was Emere,
   All Rome he hath made ryfe;
And certys Y am sworne þem too,
'Holy Fadur, what schall Y do,
   That turned were all thys stryfe?'   1125

95

Then þe pope was not lothe,
To assoyle hym of hys othe,
   For hyt to falsehed can clyne;
'Syr, Y schall telle þe a sekyr tale,   f. 247b
Hyt ys bettur brokyn then hale,   1130
   I set my sowle for thyne.'
Than he gart arme of þe spyrytualte,
And of the seculors hundurdys thre,
   Or euyr wolde he blynne;
To þe pales he made þem to brynge,   1135
For to dystroye that false weddyng,
   The matrymony was not fyne.

96

All þat they wyth false Mylys fonde
They bonde þem boþe fote and honde,
   But they wolde slee not oon,   1140
Mylys set hys back to a pyllere,

1121 Florence, *partly smudged*   1122 hath, *partly smudged*
1133 *V.* seculers   1140 *R.* ane   1141 *R.* backe
pyllere, *partly smudged*

And seyde all schulde dye þat came hym nere;
  But smartely was he tane,
And put in an hye towre,
Be þe reuerence of þe emperowre,   1145
  That was made of lyme and stane;
And twenty of þes odur ay in a pytt,
In stokkes and feturs for to sytt,
  Or euyr Pope Symonde blanne.

97

Than þe pope and Egravayne   1150
To telle þe lady were full fayne
  Hur lorde was on the see,
To Costantyne the nobull strekk;
All the lasse can sche recke,
  Tho all bryghtenyd hur blee.   1155
They went to þe bere wythowten wone,
And caste vp þe clothe and sye Sampson,
  That semely was to see;
They dud wyth hym as wyth þe dedd,
They beryed hym in a ryall stedd,   1160
  Wyth grete solempnyte.

98

All thys whyle was Syr Emere
Chasyng Garcy, as ye schall here,
  As the Romans tolde;
But Garcy had getyn hys pales before,   f. 247c
And vetaylyd hyt wyth warme store,   1166
  Hys wylys were full olde.
Syr Emere set hys sege þerto,
Full doghtely þere can he doo,
  That hardy was and bolde,   1170
Wyth men of armes all abowte,
That he myght on no syde owte,
  But hamperde hym in hys holde.

1142 þat, *partly smudged*
1164 8[vi], *written in same hand below line*

99

And þus þey segyd Garcy wyth strenkyth,
In hys pales large of lenkyth,   1175
   The Romaynce had ther wylle
Of Costantyne þe nobull cyte
In ther poscescyon for to bee,
   That many oon lykyd ylle.
Syr Emere comawndyd euery man   1180
To brooke wele þe tresur þat þey wan,
   So myght they þer cofurs fylle.
When Syr Garcy sawe all yede to schame,
He callyd to Emere be hys name,
   Downe at a wyndowe stylle: 1185

100

'Syr,' he seyde, 'also mote Y the,
Thou holdyst full wele þat þou hyghtyst me,
   When Y let the goo,
Ageyn to Rome as men may lythe,
Had Y wetyn what schulde haue be sythe,   1190
   Thou schuldyst not haue skapyd soo;
But syn Y qwyte claymed the þore,
Ȝyt muste þou be of mercy more,
   Thou graunt þat hyt be soo.
ix thousand pownde Y schall geue þe,   1195
To wende home to thy cuntre,
   And wyrke me no more woo.'

101

'Nay, be hym þat lorde ys beste,
Tyll Y haue þys londe conqueste,
   And efte be crowned newe;   1200
And yf my men wyll so als,   f. 247d
For Y trowe þer be noon fals,
   And yf þer be þemselfe schall rewe.'
Synagot seyde, 'Be Godys wayes,

1177 *R*. cytè   1189 *R*. Ayeyn   1190 haue, *R. omits*
1195 ix: *MS*. vx *R*. Nine thowsand

He wyll holde that he says,   1205
  He ys hardy and trewe.
I rede we do vs in hys wylle,
And ʒylde þys empyre hym tylle,
  Or he vs more bale brewe.

102

'Ther ys not, Y vndurstonde,   1210
An hundurd knyghtys in þy londe
  Moo then thou haste here,
Slewe he þem not vp at Rome?
In euyll tyme we thedur come,
  Or þat thy lore can lere.   1215
Whon þat þou went Florence to wowe,
Ouyr þe stremes þou madyste vs to rowe,
  And boght thy pryde full dere;
Many a chylde lefte þou thore
Fadurles for euyrmore,   1220
  And wedows in cuntreys sere.'

103

There þey openyd þer ʒatys wyde,
Syr Garcy came down þat tyde,
  Wyth a drawyn swyrde in hys hande,
And wyth a keye of golde clere,   1225
And ʒyldyd vnto Syr Emere,
  Hyt sygnyfyed all the lande.
They ledd yn hys baner wyth honowre,
And sett hyt on the hyest towre,
  That þey in castell fande;   1230
And soone vpon that odur day,
They crowned hym emperowre, Y saye,
  Ther durste no man agenste hym stande.

1210 vndurstonde: o *written over* a, *after* V.
1216 R., V., When
1218 R. pride   1219 R. left   1226 R. yeldyd
1230 *After* R., þey in castell: MS. þey castell V. þey castell

104

Then he gave londys to knyghtys kydde,
And newe men in offyce dydd,　　　　　　　　　1235
　　The lande to stabull and stere.
He seyde vnto Syr Garcye,　　　　　　　　　　f. 248a
'Syr, ye muste wende home wyth me,
　　Yf that yowre wylle were,
For to see Rome wythynne,　　　　　　　　　　1240
That ye wende sometyme to wynne,
　　And Florence þat ys to me dere;
Hyt schall turne yow to no grefe.'
Whether he were lothe or lefe,
　　Forthe they wente in fere.　　　　　　　　1245

105

Soche a nave as þere was oon
Was neuyr seen but þat allone,
　　When hyt was on the see;
Then Emere þoght on Mylys hys brodur,
And on Florence feyreste of odur,　　　　　　1250
　　At them then wolde he bee.
He seyde vnto Syr Garcy,
And to odyr lordys þat stode hym by,
　　'To Hungary soone wyll wee,
Justamownde for to forfare,　　　　　　　　　1255
And crowne Mylys my brodur þare,
　　For knydyst heyre ys hee.'

106

A messengere to londe wanne,
That some tyme rode and sometyme ranne,
　　Tyll he came Rome wythynne;　　　　　　　1260
He tolde Florence bryght of hewe,
How hys lorde was crownyd newe,
　　And the empyre can wynne;

1234 *R.* gaye　　　　1246 *After R.*, as þere: *MS.* or þere *V.* or þere
1253 lordys: y *partly obliterated by a hole*
1261 He: H *written over erasure*

And wyth hym bryngyth olde Garcy,
The lady fayne was sche forthy,   1265
   Sche was comyn of gentyll kynne.
Sche gafe hym for hys newe tythandys,
Worthe a baronry of landys,
   Or euyr wolde sche blynne.

107

Lorde that ys bothe God and man,   1270
Gyf þe emperowre had wetyn þan,
   The treson of hys brodur,
That he dud in hys absence;
To Sampson and to feyre Florence,   f. 248b
   And Egravayne the todur!   1275
The lady went vp to a towre,
Be reuerence of þe emperowre,
   And wyth hur many odur,
And toke hym downe þat cursyd thefe,
That afturward dud hur grete grefe,   1280
   Ther was neuyr no sawe sotheyr.

108

The lady preyed Syr Egravayne,
And odur lordys þat þey wolde layne
   The treson of the knyght,
And all that he hath done to me,   1285
All forgeuyn schall hyt bee,
   For Godys loue moste of myght.
Sche set hym on a gode palfray,
And bad hym wende vpon hys way,
   Agenste hys brodur ryght.   1290
When that he came to the see,
A false lesynge there made hee
   Of Florence feyre and bryght.

1268 *R.* barony
1269 Or, *partly smudged*
1270 Lorde, Lor *partly smudged*
1290 *V.* A genste

109

Syr Egravayne sadylde hys stede,
And hyed hym aftur a gode spede, 1295
 He hopyd that he wolde lye;
When Mylys sawe the emperowre,
He felle downe in a depe fowre,
 Fro hys hors so hye.
Emere seyde, 'Mylys, what eylyth the?' 1300
'Syr, thus thy wyfe hath dyght me,
 For Y seyde Y schulde hur bewrye,
When Y fonde Egravayne lygyng hur by,
In preson put sche me forthy,
 And sorowe hath made me to drye.' 1305

110

The emperowre smote down wyth hys hevydd,
All hys yoye was fro hym revydd
 Of Florence that he hadd,
All þe lykyng of hys longe trauayle
Was away wythowten fayle, 1310
 In sorowe was he stadde.   f. 248c
All the lordys that were hym by,
Recowmforde hym full kyndely,
 And bad hym not be adradd
'Tyll we the sothe haue enqueryd, 1315
Bothe of lewde and of lerydd';
 Thes wordys ȝyt made hym gladd.

111

Then came Egravayne wythowten lees,
Faste prekynge into the prees,
 The sothe he wolde haue tolde, 1320
But Mylys owte wyth a swyrde kene,
And wolde Egravayne tene,

1300 *R.* Emere, seyde Mylys
1304 *R.* yut   1306 hevydd: *MS.* hedd *V.* hedd
1310 8ᵛⁱⁱ, *written in same hand, appears an inch below* wythowten
1316 *After H.,* lerydd: *MS.* lernydd *R., V.,* lernydd

But he a mantell can folde
Ofte sythys abowte hys arme.
And kepyd hym wele fro any harme, 1325
    That hardy was and bolde.
The emperowre bad put þem insondur,
'Ane of yow schall bye þys blundur
    Whych hath the wronge in holde.'

112

Syr Egravayne seyde, 'Syr now Y schall 1330
Telle yow a full sekyr tale,
    And ye wyll here hyt wele.
Syr when ye went vnto þe see,
Ye lefte an hundurd men and vs thre,
    Armed in yron and stele, 1335
To kepe Florence tyll ye came agayne;
And þat made my brodur Sampson slayne,
    And wroght hath myn vnhele.

113

'Vnnethe were ye on the see,
When Mylys seyde, here standyth he, 1340
    That ye foreuyr were gone.
He seyde he wolde be emperowre,
And wedde yowre lady whyte as flowre,
    That worthy ys yn wone.
He had an hundurd at hys assente, 1345
And hyght þem londys and ryche rente,
    That made Syr Sampson slone.
And broght hym home on a bere tree,
And tolde Florence þat hyt was ye, f. 248d
    Then made sche full grete moone. 1350

114

'And when he wolde hur haue wedde,
Faste away fro hym sche fledde,
    And wolde haue stolyn awaye.

1328 Ane: *MS*. And *R*., *V*., And   1349 *V*. that   1350 *R*. Thon

Then Mylys made to arme xii knyghtys,
To kepe þe place day and nyghtys,   1355
   And wach abowte hur lay;
And certys Y was to them sworne,
And ellys had my lyfe be lorne,
   The certen sothe to saye.
I went to þe Pope and tolde hym sa   1360
And he assoyled me a pena et culpa
   Wythowtyn any delay.

115

'Then he gart arme an hundurd clerkys,
Doghty men and wyse of werkys,
   To þe pales he can þem brynge,   1365
They bonde þe false boþe honde and fote,
And in pryson caste þem, God hyt wote,
   And þeryn cam þem thrynge;
And Florence let owt Mylys nowe,
For to wende agenste yow,   1370
   Be Jhesu heuyn kynge.
Thys wyll wytnes pope Symond,
He wolde not for a þousand pownde,
   Telle yow a lesynge.

116

'Ye schall come home, as Y yow say,   1375
Be tomorne that hyt be day,
   And thys was at the none.'
The emperowre in þys whylys
Drewe a swyrde to Syr Mylys,
   But lordys helde hym soone,   1380
He badd, 'False traytur flee!
That þou neuyr þy brodur see,
   For wykkydly haste þou done.'

1360 *a word struck out above* hym sa
1363 *R.* ame   1365 can: an *partly obliterated by a hole*
1366 *R.* hond
1368 *R.* can

Euyn to Rome ageyne he rode,
Hastely wythowten bode,   1385
　　Or euyer he wolde awey gone.

117

To feyre Florence can he saye,
A lesyng þat hur wele can paye,   f. 249a
　　'My lorde byddyth that ye schall
Come agayne hym in þe mornynge.'   1390
Blythe þer of was þat maydyn ȝynge,
　　And trowed hys false tale.
Sche sente to the pope ouyr nyght,
And bad he schulde be tymely dyght,
　　Wyth mony a cardynale.   1395
And sche ordeygned hur meyne als,
And went wyth hym þat was false,
　　And passyd bothe downe and dale.

118

When þey came wythowte the cyte
Mylys seyde, 'My lady free,   1400
　　We two muste ryde faste,
And let the pope and hys meyne
Come behynde the and me,
　　For thus then ys my caste;
That þou may speke wyth my lorde þy fylle,   1405
And wyth Garcy wykkyd of wylle,
　　And be nothynge agaste.
For when þe emperowre þe Pope can see,
Mekyll speche wyll ther bee,
　　And þat full longe wyll laste.'   1410

119

'Mylys,' sche seyde, 'God ȝylde hyt the,
That Y soone my lorde may see,
　　Thou makyste me full fayne.'

1388 A lesyng: *MS.* Alesyng
1412 That: Th *written over an erasure*   1413 *R.* makyst

The ryght wey lay euyn este,
And he lad hur sowtheweste,   1415
   And thus he made hys trayne,
Tyll þey came downe in a depe gylle;
The lady seyde, 'We ryde ylle,
   Thes gatys þey are vngayne;
I rede we lyght vnto þe grownde,   1420
And byde owre fadur þe pope a stownde,'
   He seyde, 'Nay, be Goddys payne,

120

'Thou schalt hym see neuyrmare.'
Tho þe lady syghed wondur sare,
   And felle of on hur palfray.   f. 249b
He bete hur wyth hys nakyd swyrde,   1426
And sche caste vp many a rewfull rerde,
   And seyde ofte, 'Weleawaye
Schall Y neuyr my lorde see?'
'No, be God that dyed on tre,'   1430
   The false traytur can saye.
Vp he hur caste, and forþe þey rode,
Hastely wythowten any abode,
   Thys longe somersday.

121

They were nyghtyd in a wode thyck,   1435
A logge made that traytur wyck,
   Vndurnethe a tree.
There he wolde haue leyn hur by,
And sche made hur preyer specyally,
   To God and Mary feyre and free: 1440
'Let neuyr thys false fende
My body nodur schame nor schende,
   Myghtfull in mageste!'

1428 *After R.*, Weleawaye: *MS*. Wele a saye
1440 Mary feyre and free: *MS*. Mary and free *R*. Mary free *V*.
Mary and free

Hys lykyng vanysched all away.
On þe morne when hyt was day,   1445
  Ther horsys bothe dyght hee.

122

Vp he hur caste and forthe þey rode,
Thorow a foreste longe and brode,
  That was feyre and grene.
Tyll eyder odur mekyll care,   1450
The lady hungurd wondur sare,
  That was bryght and schene.
Sche had leuyr a lofe of bredd,
Then mekyll of þe golde redd,
  That sche before had seen;   1455
To hyt drewe to þe euenynge,
Then they herde a belle rynge,
  Thorow þe grace þat Godd can lene.

123

A holy Armyte fownde he there,
To greve God full loþe hym were,   1460
  For he had seruyd hym aye.
Thedur they wente to aske mete;
The Armyte seyde, 'Soche as Y ete   f. 249c
  Ye schall haue, dere damysell Y say.'
A barly lofe he broght hur too,   1465
And gode watur; full fayne was scho,
  That swete derworthe maye.
Therof the yonge lady ete,
Sche thoght neuyr noon so swete,
  Be nyght nodur be day.   1470

124

Mylys ete therof als;
He seyde, 'Hyt stekyth in my hals,
  I may not gete hyt downe.

1449 and: *MS.* n *crossed out*   1453 *R.* She
1459 *V.* mis-numbered 1460
1462 8^viii, *written in same hand below line*

Chorle, God, yf þe schames dedd,
Brynge vs of thy bettur bredd, 1475
 Or Y schall crake thy crowne.'
'Be God,' he seyde, 'þat boght me dere,
I had no bettur thys vii yere.'
 The wykkyd man þo made hym bowne,
In at the dore he hym bete, 1480
And sethyn fyre vpon hym sete,
 Ferre fro euery towne.

125

The holy Armyte brente he thare,
And lefte that bygly hows full bare,
 That semely was to see. 1485
The lady beganne to crye and ȝelle,
And seyde, 'Traytur þou schalt be in helle,
 There euyr to wonne and bee.'
He made þe lady to swere an othe,
That sche schulde not telle for lefe nor loþe, 1490
 Neuyr in no cuntre,
Fro whens þou came nor what þou ys,
Nor what man broght þe fro þy blysse,
 Or here Y schall brenne the.

126

To make þat othe þe lady was fayne, 1495
And þere he wolde by hur haue layne,
 But sche preyed God to be hur schylde;
And ryght as he was at assaye.
Hys lykyng vanyscht all awaye, f. 249d
 Thorow þe myght of Mary mylde. 1500
Tymely as the day can dawe,
He led hur thorow a feyre schawe,
 In wodes waste and wylde;
Euyn at vndurne lyghtyd he,
Downe vndur a chesten tre, 1505
 The feyrest in that fylde.

1502 *R.* her

127

He seyde, 'Þou haste wychyd me,
I may not haue to do wyth the,
   Vndo or thou schalt abye.'
Sche answeryd hym wyth mylde mode,   1510
'Thorow grace of Hym þat dyed on rode,
   False traytur thou schalt lye.'
He bonde hur be þe tresse of þe heere,
And hangyd hur on a tre there,
   That ylke feyre bodye;   1515
He bete hur wyth a ȝerde of byrke,
Hur nakyd flesche tyll he was yrke,
   Sche gaf many a rewfull crye.

128

There was a lorde þat hyght Tyrry
Wonned a lytyll thereby,   1520
   In a forest syde,
Thedur was he comyn þat day,
Wyth hawkys and howndys hym for to play,
   In that wode so wyde.
He harde the crye of þat lady free,   1525
Thedur he went and hys meyne,
   Also faste as þey myght ryde;
When Mylys was warre of þer comyng,
He lepe on hys hors and forthe can spryng,
   And durste no lenger byde.   1530

129

The feyrest palfrey lefte he there,
And hurselfe hangyd be the heere,
   And hur ryche wede;
Hur sadull and hur brydull schone,
Set wyth mony a precyus stone,   f. 250a
   The feyrest in that thede.   1536
Sche was the feyrest creature,
And therto whyte as lylly flowre,
   In romance as we rede;
   1514 hur: u *partly obliterated by a hole*

Hur feyre face hyt schone full bryght, 1540
To se hyt was a semely syght,
   Tyll hur full faste they yede.

130

Then þey lowsyd hur feyre faxe,
That was ȝelowe as the waxe,
   And schone also as golde redd. 1545
Sche myȝt not speke, þe romance seyde,
On a lyter they hur leyde,
   And to the castell hur ledd.
They bathyd hur in erbys ofte,
And made hur sore sydes softe, 1550
   For almoste was sche dedd.
They fed hur wyth full ryche fode,
And all þyng þat hur nede stode,
   They seruyd hur in that stedd.

131

The lorde comawndyd hys men euerychon 1555
That typyngys of hur þey shulde spere noon,
   Nor ones aske of whens sche were.
Vnto the stabull they ledd hur stede,
And all hur odur gere þey dud lede,
   Vnto a chaumbur dere. 1560
The lorde had a doghtur feyre
That hyght Betres, schulde be hys heyre,
   Of vysage feyre and clere;
To Florence they can hur kenne,
To lerne hur to behaue hur among men, 1565
   They lay togedur in fere,

132

In bedd togedur, wythowte lesynge.
Florence that was feyre and ȝynge,
   If any many hur besoght

1551 was: s *partly obliterated by a hole*   1556 *R.* sper

Of loue, sche gaf them soche answare   1570
That þey wolde neuyr aske hur mare,
 That was so worthely wroght.   f. 250b
Sche preyed to God þat boght hur dere
To sende hur sownde to Syr Emere,
 That hur full dere had boght;   1575
Be that he was comyn to Rome,
He thoght hyt a full carefull come,
 Where sche was he wyste noght.

133

Off Garcy Y wyll telle yow mare,
That was cawser of hur euyll fare,   1580
 And cawsyd hur fadur to be slayne,
Emere vengyd well hys dedd,
And broght hym fro hys strenkyþfull stedd,
 To grete Rome agayne.
There lykyd hym noght to bee,   1585
And soone thereaftur dyed he,
 The sothe ys not to layne;
Sche sawe hym neuyr wyth hur eye,
That cawsyd hur all þat sorowe to drye,
 Of hur haue we to sayne.   1590

134

Wyth Syr Tyrry dwellyd a knyght
That hardy was, and Machary he hyght,
 He was bolde as any bare.
To hys lemman he wolde haue had þat bryght,
And spyed hur bothe day and nyght,   1595
 Therof came mekyll care.
Tyll hyt befelle vpon a day,
In hur chaumbur stode that maye,
 To hur than can he fare;
He leyde hur downe on hur bedd,   1600
The lady wepyd sore for dredd,
 Sche had no socowre thare.

135

Before hur bedd lay a stone,
The lady toke hyt vp anon,
   And toke hyt yn a gethe,   1605
On þe mowþe sche hym hyt,
That hys fortethe owte he spytt,
   Above and also benethe.   f. 250c
Hys mowthe, hys nose, braste owt on blood,
Forthe at þe chaumbur dore he ȝode,   1610
   For drede of more wrethe;

136

And to hys chaumber he hyed hym ryȝt,
And dwellyd forthe a fowrtenyght,
   And then he came agayne,
And tolde hys lorde þat he was schent,   1615
Euyll betyn in a turnement,
   The sothe ys not to layne.
'The tethe be smetyn owt of my mowþe,
Therefore my sorowe ys full cowthe,
   Me had leuyr to be slayne.'   1620
He wolde haue be vengyd of þat dede,
Florence myght full sore hur drede,
   Had sche wetyn of hys trayne.

137

A scharpe knyfe he had hym boght,
Of yron and stele well ywroght,   1625
   That bytterly wolde byte.
And euyn to hur chaumbur he ȝode,
And vp behynde a curten he stode,
   Therof came sorowe and syte.
When he wyste they were on slope   1630
To Betres throte can he grope,
   In sonder he schare hyt tyte.
And ȝyt the thefe or he wolde leeue,
He put the hafte in Florence neeve,
   For sche schulde haue the wyte.   1635

   1607 8ix, *written in same hand below line*

138

Forthe at þe chaumber dore he ȝode,
And Betres lay burlyng in hur blode,
   And Florence slepyd faste.
Hur fadur thoght in a vysyon,
Hys doghtur schulde be strekyn downe,   1640
   Wyth a thonderblaste;
And as a þyck leyȝtenyng abowte hur ware.
Vp he starte wyth mekyll care,
   And a kyrtell on he caste;
A candyll at a lawmpe he lyght,   1645
And to hur chaumber reykyd he ryght,
   Thorowly on he thraste;   f. 250d

139

And fonde Betres hys doghtur dedd,
The bedd was full of blode redd,
   And a knyfe in Florence hande.   1650
He callyd on Eglantyne hys wyfe,
Knyghtys and ladyes came belyfe,
   Wondur sore wepeande:
Gentyll wemen sore dud wepe,
And euyr can feyre Florence slepe,   1655
   That was so feyre to fande.
Sche glyste vp wyth þe hedeows store,
A sorowfull wakenyng had sche þore,
   Soche anodur was neuyr in lande.

140

Abowte the bedd they presyd thyck,   1660
Among þem came þat traytur wyck,
   The whych had done that dede.
He seyde, 'Syr, Y schall set a stake
Wythowte þe towne a fyre to make,
   And Florence thedur lede.   1665
Ye myght see be hur feyre clothyng,
That sche was no erthely thynge,
   And be hur grete feyre hede.
   1664 a, *partly obliterated by a hole*

But some false fende of helle
Ys comyn þy doghtur for to qwelle,   1670
   Let me quyte hur hur mede.'

141

They dyȝt hur on þe morne in sympull atyre,
And led hur forthe vnto the fyre,
   Many a oon wyth hur ȝede;
Sche seyde, 'God of myghtys moost,   1675
Fadur and Sone and Holy Goost,
   As Y dud neuyr thys dede,
Yf Y gyltles be of thys,
Brynge me to þy bygly blys,
   For Thy grete godhede.'   1680
All that euyr on hur can see,
Wrange þer hondys for grete pyte
   And farde as they wolde wede.

142

The lorde that had þe doghtur dedd,
Hys herte turned in that stedd,   1685
   To wepe he can begynne.   f. 251a
He seyde, 'Florence, also mote Y the,
I may not on thy dethe see,
   For all the worlde to wynne.'
To hur chaumbur he can hur lede,   1690
And cled hur in hur own wede,
   And seyde, 'Y holde hyt synne.'
They set hur on hur own palfraye,
In all hur nobull ryche arraye,
   Or euyr wolde he blynne;   1695

143

And gaf hur þe brydull in hur hande,
And broght hur to þe wode þere he hur fande,
   And than he lefte hur thare.

1672 atyre, *compressed and difficult to read R.* atyr *V.* a tyre
1682 *R.* pytè   1692 *R.* hold   1697 *R.* ther

And betaght hur God and gode day,
And bad hur wende on hur way, 1700
   And then sche syghed sare;
'Syr,' sche seyde, 'for charyte,
Let none of þy men folowe me
   To worche me no more care.
'Nay for God,' he seyde, 'noon schulde 1705
For ix tymes thy weyght of golde';
   Home then can he fare.

144

Thorow þe foreste the lady rode,
All glemed there sche glode
   Tyll sche came in a felde. 1710
Sche sawe men vndur a galows stande,
Thedur þey ledd a thefe to hange,
   To them then sche helde;
And haylesed them full curteslye.
They askyd fro whens sche came in hye, 1715
   That worthy was to welde.
Sche seyde, 'Ye schall wete of me no mare
But as a woman dyscownfortyd sare
   Wythowten bote or belde;

145

'No leuyng lefe wyth me Y haue, 1720
Wolde ye graunt me to be my knaue,
   The thefe that ye thynke to hynge.
The more buxvm wyll he bee,
That he were borowyd fro þe galow tree,
   I hope be Heuyn Kynge.' f. 251b
Then ther councell toke thay, 1726
They were lothe to seye hur nay,
   Sche was so feyre a thynge.
They gaf hym to hur of þer gyfte,
He was full lothe to leeve hys thefte; 1730
   Sche thankyd þem olde and ȝynge.

1702 _R._ charytè   1706 _R._ nyne
1713 then sche: _MS._ can _crossed out before_ sche _V._ then can sche

146

Sche seyde, 'Wolde þou serue me wele,
I schulde the quyte euery dele.'
  He seyde to hur, 'Ȝaa,
Ellys were Y a grete fole, 1735
And worthy to be drowned in a pole,
  The galowse þou delyuyrd me fra.'
Sche thynkyth, 'Myȝt Y come ouyr þe see,
At Jerusalem wolde Y bee,
  Thedur to ryde or ga; 1740
Then myȝt Y spyr tythandys of Rome,
And of my lordys home come;'
  But now wakenyth hur waa.

147

A burges that was the thefys reyset,
At the townes ende he þem mett, 1745
  The lady rode ouyr an hylle,
'I wende þou hadyst be hangyd hye'
And he twynkylde wyth hys eye,
  As who seyth, 'Holde the stylle.'
'Thys gentyll woman hath borowed me 1750
For Y schulde hur knaue bee,
  And serue hur at hur wylle';
And sythyn he rowned in hys eere,
'I behete the all þys ryche gere,
  Thy hows Y wyll brynge hur tylle.' 1755

148

He led hur vp into the towne,
At þys burges hows he toke hur downe,
  There was hur harburgerye.
On the hye deyse he hur sett,
And mete and drynke he hur fett, 1760
  Of the wyne redd as cherye.

1745 *R*. end   1749 Hold: *MS*. holde
1751 schulde: *MS*. *letters after* l *illegible because rubbed*
1758 harburgerye: *MS*. harbuergerye

The burges wyfe welcomed hur ofte,
Wyth mylde wordys and wyth softe,
   And bad hur ofte be merye.
Tho two false wyth grete yre,   f. 251c
Stode and behelde hur ryche atyre,   1766
   And beganne to lagh and flyre.

149

The burges wyfe wyste ther þoght,
And seyde, 'In feythe ye do for noght
   Yf so be that Y may.'   1770
At nyght to chaumbur sche hur ledd,
And sparryd the dore and went to bedd,
   All nyght togedur they laye,
Sche calde on Clarebolde hur knaue,
'A lytyll errande for sothe Y haue   1775
   At the see so graye;
Yf any schepe wende ouyr þe streme
To the cyte of Jerusalem,
   Gode sone wytt me to saye.'

150

Clarebalde seyde the burges tylle,   1780
'Thys nyght had we not owre wylle,
   We muste caste anodur wyle.'
To the see they went in fere,
And solde hur to a marynere,
   Wythynne a lytyll whyle;   1785
'On covenawnt sche ys þe feyrest þynge,
That euyr ye sye olde or ȝynge,'
   And he at them can smyle.
So mekyll golde for hur he hyght,
That hyt passyd almoost hur weyght,   1790
   On eyther parte was gyle.

1764 8ˣ, *written in same hand below line*   1767 *R. flerye*
1769 *R.* we   1778 *R.* cyté   1779 *V. notes* w *in* wytt
written over t; t *could be a* c   saye, a *written over* l   1784 *R.* sold

151

'Take here the golde in a bagg,
I schall hyt hynge on a knagg,
   At the schyppborde ende.
When ye haue broght that clere, 1795
Put vp yowre hande and take hyt here;'
   Aftur hur can they wende.
They seyde a schypp ys hyred to þe,
That wyll to Jerusalem ouyr þe see,
   Sche þankyd þem as sche was hende, 1800
Sche gaf þe burges wyfe hur palfray,
Wyth sadyll and brydyll þe soþe to say,
   And kyste hur as hur frende.

152

Altherfurste to þe kyrke sche went, f. 251d
To here a masse verament, 1805
   And preyed God of hys grace,
That he wolde bryng hur to þat ryke,
That euyrmore ys yoye in lyke,
   Before hys worthy face;
And or sche dyed Emere to see, 1810
That hur own lorde schulde bee,
   In Rome that ryall place.
To þe schypp þey went in fere,
And betoke hur to þe marynere,
   That louely vndur lace. 1815

153

They toke þe bagg þey went hyt had be golde,
And had hyt home in to þer holde,
   They lokyd and þen hyt was ledd;
The burges seyde to Clarebalde,
'Thou haste made a sory frawde, 1820
   God gyf þe schames dedd;
For certenly wythowten wene,

1796 here: *MS. hole obliterates letters between* h *and* e

Thou haste begyled a lady schene,
   And made hur euyll of redd.'
To the see hyed they faste,   1825
The sayle was vp vnto þe maste,
   And remeuyd was fro þat stedd.

154

All men þat to þe schypp can longe,
They went Florence to leman haue fonge,
   Ylke oon aftur odur had done;   1830
But þey faylyd of ther praye,
Thorow grace of God þat myghtys maye,
   That schope bothe sonne and moone.
Sche calde on Clarebalde hur knave,
The marynere seyde, 'Y hope ye rave,'   1835
   And tolde how he had doone.
Sche prayde God schulde hym forgeue,
A dreryar woman myȝt noon leeue,
   Vndur heuyn trone.

155

The marynere set hur on hys bedd,   1840
Sche had soone aftur a byttur spredd,   f. 252a
   The schypp sayled belyve;
He seyde, 'Damysell Y haue þe boght,
For þou art so worþely wroght,
   To wedde the to my wyve.'   1845
Sche seyde, 'Nay that schall not bee
Thorow helpe of Hym in Trynyte
   That suffurde woundys fyve;'
In hys armes he can hur folde,
Hur rybbes crakyd as þey breke wolde,   1850
   In struglynge can they stryve.

1823 *R.* hast   1825 hyed, e *partly rubbed*
1832 Thorow, w *partly rubbed R.* may   1833 That: *MS. last* t
crossed out   1835 *R.* marynar   1836 *R.* hade
1838 *R.* dreryer   1840 *R.* maryner
1841 *R.* hadd   1847 *R.* trynytè

156

Sche seyde, 'Lady Mary free,
Now thou haue mercy on me,
   Thou faylyst me neuyr at nede.
Here my errande as þou well may,   1855
That Y take no schame today,
   Nor lose my maydynhede.'
Then beganne þe storme to ryse,
And that vpon a dolefull wyse,
   The marynere rose and yede.   1860
He hyed to the toppe of þe maste,
They stroke þe sayle þe gabuls braste,
   They hyed them a bettur spede.

157

He seyde, 'But yf þys storme blynne,
All mvn be drowned þat be hereynne,'   1865
   Then was that lady fayne.
Sche had leuyr to haue be dedd,
Then þere to haue loaste hur maydynhedd,
   Or he had hur by layne.
Then þe schypp claue insondur,   1870
All þat was yn hyt soone went vndur,
   And drowned boþe man and swayne.
The yonge lady in that tyde,
Fleytd forþe on þe schyppes syde,
   Vnto a roche vngayne.   1875

158

The marynere sate vpon an are,
But nodur wyste of odur fare,
   The todur were drowned perde.
The lady steppyd to a ston,   f. 252b
Sche fonde a tredd and forþe ys gon,   1880
   Loudyng the Trynyte.
To a noonre men calle Beuerfayre,

1874 *After H.*, schyppes: *MS.* schyp *R., V.* schyp
1875 Vnto: t *written over an* o   1878 *R.* perdè
1882 Beuerfayre: *MS.* Benerfayre, *V. notes same*

That stondyþ on þe watur of Botayre,
   That rennyth in to þe grekys see,
A stepull then the lady sye,   1885
Sche þoght þe wey þedur full drye,
   And therat wolde sche bee.

159

Syr Lucyus Jbarnyus was fownder þere,
An hundurd nonnes þeryn were,
   Of ladyes wele lykeande.   1890
When that sche came nere þe place,
The bellys range þorow Godys grace,
   Wythowten helpe of hande.
Of Seynt Hyllary þe churche ys,
The twenty day of ʒowle Y wys,   1895
   As ye may vnderstande.
They lokyd and sawe no leuyng wyght,
But the lady feyre and bryght,
   Can in the cloystur stande.

160

The abbas be þe honde hur toke,   1900
And ladd hur forthe so seyth þe boke,
   Sche was redd forronne.
Sche knelyd downe before þe crosse,
And looueyd God wyth mylde voyce,
   That sche was thedur wonne.   1905
They askyd hur yf sche had ony fere;
Sche seyde, 'Nay now noon here
   Leueyng vnder the soone.'
Sche askyd an hows for charyte,
They broght an habyte to þat fre,   1910
   And þere sche was made nonne.

161

The lady þat was boþe gode and feyre,
Dwellyd as nonne in Beuerfayre,
   Loueyng God of hys loone.

1887 *R.* thereat   1901 *R.* Annd *V.* forþe   1909 *R.* charytè

And Hys modur, Mary bryght,   1915
That safe and sownde broght hur ryght
   Vnto the roche of stone.   f. 252c
A systur of þe hows was seke,
Of the gowte and odur euyls eke,
   Sche myȝt not speke nor goon;   1920
Florence vysyted hur on a day,
And helyd hur or sche went away,
   Sche wolde þer had wytten þerof none.

162

The abbas, and odur nonnes by,
Tolde hyt full openlye,   1925
   That hyt was so verraye,
Ther was noon syke nor sare,
That come þere þe lady ware,
   But they went sownde away.
The worde sprang in mony a cuntre,   1930
And into Rome the ryche cyte,
   There hur lorde in laye,
Whych had an euyll in hys hevedd,
That all hys yoye was fro hym revedd,
   Bothe be nyght and daye.   1935

163

He was so tuggelde in a toyle,
For he werryd on the kyng of Poyle,
   And he on hym agayne;
And as he schulde hys helme avente,
A quarell smote hym verament,   1940
   Thorow owt bothe bonne and brayne.
The leche had helyd hyt ouyr tyte,
And hyt was festurd wythowte delyte,
   Theryn he had grete payne;

1924 abbas: *first* b *written over an indecipherable letter*
  1927 *V.* There   1930 sprang: *MS.* sprang[a] cuntre: *MS.* cun
crossed out R. cuntrè   1931 the ryche cyte, *partly obscured by*
brownish ink R. cytè   1933 *After R.*, hevedd: *MS.* hedd *V.* hedd

E

He had leuyr then all hys golde,   1945
That he had ben vndur þe molde,
   Or slyly had ben slayne.

164

He calde Egravayne hym too,
And seyde, 'What ys beste to do?
   Myn euyll encresyth ȝerne.'   1950
'Syr, at Beuerfayre dwellyþ a nonne,
The weyes thedur we ne conne,
   But we schall spyr and lerne.'
Mekyll golde wyth them they toke,
And went forthe, so seyth þe boke.   f. 252d
   Preuely and derne;   1956
And ȝyt for all þer mekyll fare,
Hyt was a grete whyle or þey came þare,
   Thogh all they hastyd ȝerne.

165

The emperowre toke hys ynne þereby,   1960
Althernext the nonnery,
   For þere then wolde he dwelle;
And Mylys hys brodur, þat graceles fole,
Dwellyd wyth oon Gyllam of Pole
   And was woxyn a fowle meselle.   1965
He harde telle of that lady lele,
And þedur was comyn to seeke hys hele,
   The certen sothe to telle;
He harberde hym far therfro
All behynde men, Y telle yow soo,   1970
   Hys sekenes was so felle.

166

And Machary was comyn alse,
Agenste the lady þat was so false,
   That slewe Betres and put hyt hur too.

1947 ben: *MS*. be *R*., *V*. be
1951 Beuerfayre: *MS*: Benerfayre *V*. Beuerfeyre

God had sende on hym a wrake, 1975
That in the palsye can he schake,
   And was crompylde and crokyd þerto.
He had getyn Syr Tyrry thedur,
And hys wyfe bothe togedur,
   Dame Eglantyne hyght schoo, 1980
The holy nonne for to praye,
For to hele hym and sche maye,
   That oght sche euyll to doo.

167

Syr Tyrrye the chastlayne
Harbarde the emperowre full gayne, 1985
   On the todur syde of þe strete;
And þe marynere þat had hur boght,
That wolde haue had hur hys leman to a ⟨wroȝt⟩,
   That on the ore can flete,
He came thedur wyth an euyll 1990
Hyppyng on two stavys lyke þe deuyll,
   Wyth woundys wanne and wete;
And Clarebalde þat was the thefe, f. 253a
Came wyth an euyll þat dud hym grefe,
   Thes iiii there all can meete. 1995

168

The emperowre to the church went,
To here a masse in gode entent,
   Hende as ye may here;
When þat the masse was done,
The abbas came and haylesyd hym soone, 2000
   On hur beste manere,
The emperowre seyde, 'Well þou bee,
The holy nonne wolde Y see,
   That makyth þe syke thus fere;
An euyll in my hedd smetyn ys, 2005
That Y haue loste all odur blys';
   They sente aftur that clere.

1978 *R.* geten   1987 *R. omits* had
1988 ⟨wroȝt⟩, *written interlinearly under* to a *and bracketed*

169

At hur preyers þere as sche ware,
When sche sawe hur own lorde þare,
   Sche knewe hym wele ynogh.   2010
So dud he hur he wolde not so saye,
Abowte þe cloystur goon are thay,
   Spekynge of hys woghe
Then was sche warre of þe iiii þare,
That had kyndylde all hur care,   2015
   Nere to them sche droghe.
They knewe hur not be no kyns thynge,
Therof thankyd sche Heuyn Kynge,
   And lyghtly at them loghe.

170

Mylys that hur aweye ledd,   2020
He was the fowlest mesell bredd,
   Of pokkys and bleynes bloo.
And Machary þat wolde hur haue slayne,
He stode schakyng the sothe to sayne,
   Crokyd and crachyd thertoo.   2025
The marynere þat wolde haue layne hur by,
Hys yen stode owte a strote forthy,
   Hys lymmes were roton hym froo.
They put Clarebalde in a whelebarowe,
That strong thefe be stretys narowe,   2030
   Had no fote on to goo.

171

Sche seyde, 'Ye that wyll be hale,   f. 253b
And holly broght owt of yowre bale
   Of that ye are ynne,
Ye muste schryue yow openlye,   2035
And that wyth a full lowde crye,
   To all þat be here boþe more and mynne.'

2010 hym: y *partly obliterated by a hole*   2013 *R.* Spekyng
2014 *R.* four   2017 *R.* knew   2026 *R.* maryner
2032 *After V.,* th *crossed out before* Ye   2035 *R.* must

That they þoght full lothe to doo,
Mylys seyde, 'Syth hyt muste be soo,
 Soone schall Y begynne.   2040
I lykyd neuyr wele, day nor nyght,
Syth Y ledd awey a lady bryght,
 From kythe and all hur kynne.'

172

Than he seyde to them verament,
How he þe lady wolde haue schent,   2045
 And tolde them to the laste;
And þat he wolde haue be emperowre,
And weddyd þe lady whyte as flowre,
 And all hys false caste;
And sythe awey he can hur lede,   2050
'For Y wolde haue refte hur maydynhede,
 That sche defendyd faste,
I had neuyr wyth hur to doo,
For Y myght not wynne hur to,
 But clene fro me sche paste.'   2055

173

And sythyn he tolde þem of þe barley bredd,
And how he brent þe armyte to dedd,
 And hangyd hur vp be the hare;
'Then Y sye men and howndys bathe,
And to the wode Y went for wrathe'; 2060
 There Tyrry gaf answare,
'Then came Y and toke hur downe,
And had hur wyth me vnto þe towne,
 And that rewyd me full sare;
Sche slewe Betres my doghtur schene, 2065
That schulde my ryght heyre haue bene,
 And ȝyt let Y hur fare.

2051 *After H*. refte hur maydynhede: *MS*. refte fro hur hur maydyn
hede *R*. refte fro hur hur maydynhede *V*. refte fro hur hur maydyn
hede

174

'For sche was so bryght of blee,
And so semely on to see,
  Therfore let Y hur goo.'   f. 253c
Then Machary, for he muste nede,   2071
'Sche dyd me oonys an euyll dede,
  My harte was wondur throo.
When Y wolde haue leyn hur by,
My fortethe smote sche owt forþy,   2075
  That wakenyd all my woo;
I slewe Betres wyth a knyfe,
For Y wolde sche had loste hur lyfe,
  Trewly hyt was soo.'

175

Then Tyrry farde as he wolde wede,   2080
And seyde, 'False traytur dyd þou þat dede?'
  Then wepyd dame Eglantyne,
And seyde, 'Allas þat we came here,
Thys false traytur for to fere,
  That wroght vs all þys pyne.   2085
Ʒyt Y am warse for þat feyre maye,
That was so vnfrendely flemed away,
  And was gyltles therynne.
Clarebalde seyde, "Sche came be me,
I stode vndur a galowe tree,   2090
  And a rope abowte hals myne;

176

'Fro þe galowse sche borowed me,
For Y schulde hur knave haue bee,
  And serue hur to hur paye.
We were togedur but oon nyʒt,   2095
At the see Y solde that bryght,
  On the seconde day.'
Then spake þe marynere þat hur boʒt,
'When Y wolde hur to wyfe haue wroʒt
  Soone sche seyde me naye;   2100
2098 R. maryner

Sche brake my schypp wyth a tempeste,
Sche fletyd sowþe and Y northweste,
   And syth sawe Y neuyr that maye.

177

'Vpon an ore to londe Y wanne,
And euyrsyth haue be a drery man,   2105
   And neuyr had happe to hele.
And syth Y haue be in sorowe and syte,
Me þynkyth we iii be in febull plyte,
   That cawsyd hur to wante hur wylle.'   f. 253d
Sche handylde þem wyth hur hande,   2110
Then were þey hoole, Y vnderstande,
   And odur folke full feele.
Hur own lorde, altherlaste
The venome owt of hys hedd braste,
   Thus can sche wyth them dele.   2115

178

The venome braste owt of hys ere,
He seyde, 'Y fynde yow iiii in fere,'
   Hys herte was full throo.
He made to make a grete fyre,
And caste þem yn wyth all þer tyre,   2120
   Then was the lady woo.
The emperowre toke dame Eglantyne,
Tyrrye, and Florence, feyre and fyne,
   And to the halle can goo.
They looueyd God lesse and more,   2125
That þey had fownde þe lady þore,
   That longe had be them froo.

179

Soche a feste as þere was oon,
In þat lande was neuyr noon,
   They gaf the nonnes rente,   2130

2104 Vpon: *MS.* po *illegible because blotted out in black ink*
2108 *R.* four   2114 *R.* venom   2117 *R.* fynd

And all þer golde, wythowt lesynge,
But vnnethys þat þat myȝt þem home brynge,
   And þankyd þem for that gente.
Florence seyde, 'Syr, wyth yowre leeve,
Tyrrye some þynge muste yow geue,   2135
   That me my lyfe hath lente.
He gaf hym þe cyte of Florawnce.
And bad hym holde hyt wythowt dystawnce;
   They toke ther leue and wente.

180

Tyrrye wente home to hys cuntre,   2140
And þe emperowre to Rome hys ryche cyte,
   As faste as euyr they maye.
When þe pope harde telle of þer comyng,
He went agayne þem wythowt lesynge,
   In full ryall arraye.   2145
Cardynals were somned be þer names,
And come syngyng Te deum laudamus,
   The certen sothe to saye;   f. 254a
They loouyd God boþe more and lesse,
That they had getyn þe emperes,   2150
   That longe had bene awaye.

181

Soche a brydale as þere was oon
In that lande was neuyr noon,
   To wytt wythowten wene.
There was grete myrþe of mynstrals steuyn,   2155
And nobull gyftys also geuyn,
   Bothe golde and robys schene;
Soone aftur on þe fowretenyth day,
They toke þer leue and went þer way,
   And thankyd kynge and quene.   2160
They loouyd God wyth myȝt and mayne
That þe lady was comyn agayne,
   And kept hur chaste and clene.

    2137 *R.* cytè   2140 *R.* cuntrè   2141 *R.* emperowr cytè

182

They gate a chylde the furste nyght,
A sone that Syr Otes hyght, 2165
   As the boke makyth mynde.
A nobull knyȝt and a stronge in stowre,
That aftur hym was emperowre,
   As hyt was full gode kynde.
Then the emperowre and hys wyfe, 2170
In yoye and blysse þey lad þer lyfe,
   That were comyn of gentyl strynde.
Pope Symonde thys story wrate,
In þe cronykyls of Rome ys þe date,
   Who sekyth þere he may hyt fynde. 2175

183

Forþy schulde men and women als,
Them bethynke or þey be false,
   Hyt makyth so fowle an ende.
Be hyt neuyr so slylye caste,
Ȝyt hyt schamyþ þe maystyr at þe laste, 2180
   In what londe þat euyr þey lende.
I meene be thes iiii fekyll,
That harmed feyre Florence so mykyll,
   The trewest that men kende.
And þus endyth þys romance gode 2185
Jhesu that boght vs on the rode   f. 254b
   Vnto hys blysse vs send

Amen

Explicit Le Bone Florence of Rome

2164 chylde: y *completely obliterated by a hole*
2179 *After R.*, slylye: *MS.* slylylye *V.* slylylye   2182 *R.* four
2188 *R. omits* Amen *R., V. omit* Explicit Le Bone Florence of Rome

NOTES

1 ff. The opening of the poem utilises the conventional Troy
material of chronicle and romance. It sets the story of
Florence in the framework of history. Trojans are founders
of great cities, the poet announces: Andromoche built
Antioch; Antenor, Jerusalem; Helemytes, Africa; and most
important, Aeneas founded Rome, the second Troy, which
was the capital of the Christian world. The historical back-
ground of Rome is intended to give more weight to the moral
aspects of the story of Florence, a story so closely allied to
the near destruction of Rome.

gone. Infinitives are, for the most part, uninflected in the
manuscript. This is one of the few *-n* forms among mono-
syllabic verbs. Cf. also l. 1386 and *goon*, l. 1920.

2 **more chyualrous town.** There is occasional use in the poem
of the periphrastic comparison using *more*. Cf. also *more
buxom*, l. 1723. The comparative, however, is generally
formed in the text by means of *-re* or *-ar*.

10 **barmeteme.** Holthausen (*Zu Mittelenglischen Romanzen*, p.
498) suggests *barneteme*. There is no need to change the
MS reading, as both forms are used in medieval writing.
Holthausen, perhaps, prefers the spelling with *n* because
it is closer to the OE. etymon, *bearn-team*.

Antenowre. In Greek legend, one of the wisest of the
Trojan elders. According to Dares and Dictys, he was said
to have treacherously opened the gates of Troy to the
enemy; in return for which, at the general sack of the city,
his house, distinguished by a panther's skin at the door,
was spared by the victors. Afterwards, according to various
versions of the legend, he either rebuilt a city on the site
of Troy, or settled at Cyrene, or became the founder of
Patavium (Padua). The poet's source for attributing the
founding of Jerusalem to Antenor is unclear.

The Roman historian, Livy, born at Patavium, was
proud of the ancient connection between his native city and
Rome. Padua, like Rome, claimed a Trojan origin and
Livy is careful to place its founder Antenor side by side
with Aeneas.

16 **Eneas be schyp gate.** This syntactic pattern, subject +

object + verb, is a basic ME. sentence variation. See Mossé (*A Handbook of Middle English*, trans. J. Walker (1952), 122).

18 **none.** This form, as well as *nane* (l. 260), displaces OE. *nāwiht* which, however, remains in the form *noght* (l. 907), of similar meaning.

21 The verb *can* is frequently used in combination with an infinitive to form a simple preterite as here: *can syke* = sought. *Can* as an auxiliary verb is evidently confused with ME. *gan*, did.

22 **Costantyne þe nobull.** Almost certainly a play on *Constantinople*.

25 ff. The third stanza is incomplete; it consists of three groups of three lines instead of four. The regular stanzaic pattern is composed of twelve lines of which every third line rhymes. Cf. stanza 112, also incomplete.

28 **had.** Class II weak verbs in the first and third persons preterite indicative end in -*d(e)*. Cf. *tolde*, l. 346; *seyde*, l. 76.

40–51 The description of the horrendous phenomena surrounding the birth of Florence and the death of her mother has one source, at least, in the *Apocalypse*. Among the details of the last days of the world is a direct parallel for the poem's rain of blood: '. . . . there was a storm of hail and fire mingled with blood, that fell on earth . . .' (ch. VIII, 7–8).

40–41 *Willan* is one of the common OE. modal auxiliaries which retained its original meaning in ME. Where in MnE. *want* is preferred, the poet has used *wolde*.

41 **befelle.** The stem vowel of the past plural of OE. Class VII (Reduplicating) strong verbs has become *e*. Note also the shifts in the past singular to *ę̄* (*behelde*, l. 422) and *i* (*hyght*, l. 7).

47 **Eyther odur.** The combination stands for the indefinite pronoun *each other*.

49 The pronoun *hyt* is used as a subject referring to the preceding lines describing the strange portents.

51 **man.** The usual method of expressing the sense of 'one' is by means of *man* or *men* (l. 62). In the frequent expression *many a oon*, *oon* is an indefinite pronoun meaning 'person' (l. 873).

58–63 The extent and variety of education for noble ladies in the fifteenth century were more restricted than that for noblemen brought up in their fathers' households. Women were instructed in religion, courtesy, and letters. Florence, at fifteen, seems to be getting the equivalent of a fifteenth-century grammar-school education. She is probably learning to read and write simple Latin. Although the 'harpe' and 'sawtrye' are common medieval stringed instruments, Florence's ability to play them indicates musical training well beyond the usual in singing.

60 **all thynge.** The uninflected plural is used in this expression as well as in one which appears later in the text. *some boke seyth* (l. 84). It should be noted that the form *þyngs* (l. 331) also occurs.

68 **hur forne.** The pronoun is a subjective gen.; and the sense of the phrase is 'on account of her'.

　forne. The *MED* (*s.v. forn* prep. c) finds the earliest appearance of the sense 'on account of' in *Florence*.

78 **a clere.** The adjective meaning 'fair', 'bright', is used as a noun with reference to the fair lady herself. Cf. ll. 1795, 2007.

85 **parell.** Palatal *l* in OFr. *apareil* became *il* and then the *i* combined with the preceding vowel to form a diphthong (*parell: fayle*).

92 **Many a crowne Y schall gare crake.** The syntactic pattern of this line, object + subject + verb, is a basic ME. sentence variation. See Mossé (*A Handbook of Middle English,* trans. J. Walker (1952), 122).

93 Both *drowpe* and *dare* depend on *gare* 'to cause' (something to be done), in the preceding line.

103 **tobrokyn.** The past participle stem vowel of OE. Class IV strong verbs has become $\bar{\rho}$.

106 ff. Garcy, the eager but aged suitor, is a type of the *amans senex*, recalling January of Chaucer's *Merchant's Tale* and Agape's senile husband in Boccaccio's *Ameto*. Other examples of the general type in both European and Oriental literature are cited by L. C. Stern in *Zeitschrift für Celtische Philologie,* v, 200, 310n.

112 **hodur.** The sense of 'cuddle' makes its earliest appearance in *Florence*. See *MED s.v. hoderen,* a.

　happe. The word with the sense 'embrace' is first recorded in a manuscript dated *c.* 1450. The *MED* (*s.v. happen* v., 2, 1C) also cites its use in *Florence*.

118 **garson.** The *MED* (*s.v. garsoun,* b.) lists the sense 'retainer, follower' as having made its first appearance in *Florence*.

128 Ritson's emendation of *aveaunt* to *avenaunt* seems to be quite unjustified. The sense of *aveaunt* ('forward') suits the line as does its rhyming with *graunt*. Moreover, the metre does not require the extra syllable

132 **rechyd.** This appears to be the nautical sense of *reaching* which is illustrated in the *OED* (*s.v. reach*, v.¹, II, 15c) entirely by nineteenth-century quotations! For example, 'A rattling breeze ... got up ... and she reached along like a schooner' (*Hunt's Yachting Magazine*, April 1884).

138 See note to line 21.

140 **Awtrement.** Not all the place-names in the poem are easy to identify and the geography may at times seem fanciful. Garcy's emissaries seem to be taking ship to a seaport named Awtrement (or Autrement—certainly a French town) and proceeding thence (l. 148) through Poland and Champagne in northern France on to Rome. This is about the most grotesque itinerary imaginable. There is an Autremencourt (from the German, Ostremund) in the department of Aisne in northern France, and the Roman name for Chartres was Autricum, but neither of these places was a seaport or anywhere near a logical route from Constantinople to Rome. If we are to read line 148 as indicating that the party passed through Poland and Northern France, we can only attribute the route to the poet's caprice or ignorance. If, however, we are willing to credit some rather plausible corruptions in spelling, we can vindicate the poet's sound geographical sense: the party took ship from Constantinople to Awtrement (Otranto), proceeded through Pole (Apulia) and Chawmpayn (Campania) to Rome. In other words, under the leadership of Italian-born Acwrye (who would very likely be aware that Otranto was a hospitable port), they took the most direct route to Rome possible.

141 The syntax of this line is problematical. It is unlikely that the clause introduced by 'That' is a purpose clause: 'In order that the people treated them well.' The line should probably be loosely translated, 'Where people treated them well.'

145 **wheme.** The usual spelling for OE. *hw* in ME, is *wh*, but in this instance *cw* (OE. *cweme*) has shifted to *wh*.

148 See note line to 140.

155 **rode.** The past plural stem vowel of OE. Class I strong verbs has become *ǭ*. Cf. *abode*, l. 446; *schone*, l. 156.

172 **formast.** An ordinal numeral, 'first'.

174 **Full ryall was that crye.** The sense is: 'The clamour was splendid.' *Ryall* is used colloquially to mean *splendid* or *first-rate*, a sense which *OED* (*s.v. royal*, A, I, 4) indicates first appeared in 1583.

188 There are only a few occurrences of relative **who** in the poem.

    rekenyth. The intransitive sense of 'number, amount to' is illustrated in *OED* (*s.v. reckon*, II, 15) by a single nineteenth-century quotation: 'He marched [them] into the camp before his own troop, which did not reckon nearly so many' (1877).

198 **Feyre, syrrys, mote yow befalle.** Ritson rightly observes that this interruption of the ambassador's address is a compliment on the king's part. Afterwards, the ambassador proceeds with his speech (III, 341).

    mote yow befalle. In Old English the modal auxiliary most commonly used to express permitting was *motan*. The verb does not exactly have the sense of permitting in this instance but rather that of wishing or commanding. The construction is an exact counterpart of the Latin jussive subjunctive.

212 The word 'hope' is puzzling. Everything which went before in the poem contributes to the impression that it is Garcy's intention to marry Florence once she is brought to him. Possibly the poet's inspiration was not equal to the metrical necessities of his line and he simply settled for an inaccurate phrase just to complete the line. Otherwise, 'hope' suggests an abduction of Florence with just a possibility of marrying Garcy. Stanza 19, which follows, however, makes clear Garcy's intention to wed Florence.

216 ff. The poet uses inexact rhymes of voiced and voiceless *f* (*stryfe: wyfe: lyfe: ryve*, ll. 216, 219, 222, 225).

228 **calde þe steward hym tylle.** The sense is 'called the steward to himself'.

229 The rare OE. demonstrative ȝeon 'yon' appears as ȝonder. Cf. also *Yondur* (l. 484.).

235 **what.** In strictly relative use *what* occurs without the antecedent having been expressed. Cf. ll. 1190, 1492.

244 **dere.** There is no formal distinction here between the adjective and the adverb. Cf. *all*, l. 87.

245 **Me had leuyr.** 'I would rather have.'

249 A puzzle. Loosely, perhaps something like 'I don't want to be near his direction.'

251 **euery dele.** 'In every detail,' a common phrase indicating multiplication. Cf. also *Many a þousand* (l. 356) and *Ofte sythys* (l. 1324).

252 The MS reading seems to be *fame* not *sawe*, as transcribed by Ritson and Vietor. Indeed, *f* and long *s* in which the stem descends below the line of writing are not well differentiated, and internal *w* and *m* are easily confused. Both *sawe*, in the sense of 'speech', 'discourse' and 'fame', meaning 'honour', are reasonable within the context.

254 **nome.** The past singular stem vowel of OE. Class IV strong verbs has become $\bar{\varrho}$.

258 Only a slight alteration of MS *togodur* is needed for the emendation *togedur*. Vietor's original transcription of *e* rather than *o* seems in error; the lobe of the letter is so rounded as to resemble most nearly the scribe's *o*'s.

275 **begynnyng.** The present participle has the ending *-yng* and *-ande* in the manuscript. Only *-yng* forms, as here, appear as the verbal noun.

279 **he þat.** The third person singular masculine pronoun used indefinitely: 'he who', 'the one who'.

281 **knok.** The sense of 'hit' or 'strike', as here, does not appear until about 1450 (see *MED s.v. knokken*, 3b).

283 An illegible letter followed by *gc* is written over *emperowre* in the same hand, and an illegible word scrawled over *no man schulde do* in a different hand.

289 **tyte.** The sense 'alert, smart' is used figuratively to describe the messengers (l. 286). The earliest use of the adjective itself cited in the *OED* is from Shakespeare (1606): 'Thou fumblest Eros, and my Queenes a Squire More tight at this then thou' (*Antony and Cleopatra*, IV, iv. 16). See *OED s.v. tight*, a., adv., 3.

   sawe. The past singular stem vowel of OE. Class V strong verbs has become *au*.

291 There are several erased letters followed by *lenyd* beside *But* in a similar but possibly different hand.

292 **altherfurste.** Adjectives have no ending or *-e* in the manuscript except that the genitive plural *alther* remains as an intensive prefix in words such as this, meaning 'first of all'. Cf. *althernext*, l. 1961 and *altherlaste*, l. 2113.

   Ritson's transcription of *come* instead of *tome* is an understandable error. The scribe does not always take care to differentiate *c* and *t* by continuing the shaft of *t* well above the headstroke. In any event, *tome* 'opportunity' makes more sense in the context.

296 **vii hundurd towrys.** So many 'towers' might seem better to typify an eastern city like Constantinople than Rome, the centre of western civilisation. The word 'tower', however, from the twelfth century, extended to include the whole fortress or stronghold of which a tower was the original nucleus. Hence, Acurye is referring to seven hundred well-fortified buildings.

303 **do dwelle.** The emendation follows Holthausen's suggestion (*Zu Mittelenglischen Romanzen*, 500). The alteration clarifies the meaning of ll. 302–3: 'On that account, sir, men love him, / And many people live with him.' MS *to dwelle* produces incoherent lines which translate roughly: 'On that account, sir, people like to live with him', leaving the phrase *Mony wyth hym* to float superfluously.

304–5 OE. *s* between vowels remains voiced (*wyse: pryce;* cf. *rase: face*, ll. 565–6). In both examples the letter *c* is used for *s* in OFr.

314 The final curl at the end of *wher* should probably be expanded to *whereuyr* by analogy to *euyr* (in MS, *eu*).

319 In a different hand, the word *haue* is written in the margin beside *Syxty* and *helyre** above. Also above the line, *Fernde* is written twice, *Fer* once, and a series of *r*'s and *e*'s appear.

321 In a similar but possibly different hand, the word *Fen* and four *n*'s in a series are written in the centre margin.

324 The word *Full* is written in the centre margin in a similar hand.

325 **The pyllers þat stonde in þe halle** suggest detached columns, a motif derived from Roman triumphal arches. Old Somerset House in the Strand (1546–9), influenced by the Italian style, contains such columns in its centre triple entrance.

The letters *gc* are written in the centre margin in a similar hand; also at 327.

328 **Cryste.** MS *cste* must signify *Cryste* even though there is no special sign to indicate the omission of *ry*.

329 ff. The painting of the seven deadly sins and 'þyngys sere' are most likely on the palace walls and not pillar decorations. As Gothic architecture is characterised by the almost total disappearance of wall-space and the introduction of stained glass, the wall painting would indicate that the palace is

built in the Romanesque style with its vast surfaces of walls and vaulting. There are almost no Romanesque buildings in England but numerous examples in provincial France—Tavant, Old Pouzauges, St Chef in Dauphiné, etc.

330 **The dedly synnes seuyn** are the seven capital sins: pride, envy, wrath, sloth, avarice, gluttony, and lust. They are distinguished from other sins because they are focal points of sins—sins which stand at the root of other sins. The conception of the seven deadly sins permeated medieval and Renaissance literature as well as art. A few examples of the idea in English literature occur in Chaucer's *Parson's Tale*, Gower's *Confessio Amantis*, and Spenser's *Fairie Queene* (Book I, Canto IV).

333 **scryed.** The sense of the line leaves no doubt that the poet intended *scryed*; however, the scribe wrote *stryed*. Comparison of the questionable letter with other *c*'s and *t*'s in the manuscript indicates that the shaft protrudes well above the headstroke which is quite broad, the case with most *t*'s.

334–41 The description of the fountain suggests that the poet had in mind the celebrated Fountain of Lions in the Alhambra, the oldest well-preserved Islamic palace in the world. It was built in Granada between 1248 and 1354. The Court of the Lions itself dates from the fourteenth century and is formed by the buildings of the Palacio del Harem, which was the private residence of the Nazarite kings. The fountain is fed by a remarkable conduit five miles long, and the water does run through the mouths of the supporting lions. Although the fountain's large alabaster basin could not support a 'hundurd knyʒtys and ladyes', many people could wash in it. The poet's reference to the 'oþer waturs' recalls the four streams and innumerable springs which flow to the central fountain. Indeed, it is impossible to escape the sound of water anywhere in the Alhambra.

344 The emendation of MS *Tyger* to *Tyber* yields the name of the familiar Roman river. Note that the manuscript does read *Tyber* at l. 383.

354 In a similar hand, *full grete othys* is written inside a box in the bottom margin. The word *Full* is also written over the box.

355 In a hand different from that which wrote the text as well

as the other marginalia, four illegible words are written vertically in the centre top margin.

363 bere. The infinitive indicates that were the present tense form of the OE. Class IV strong verb used in the text, it would have become *ę̄*.

364 Florence fadur. The uninflected genitive is occasionally used as in this instance. However, the genitive singular and plural of nouns is generally formed with the ending -(*y*)*s* (*ther gatys gayne*, l. 149; *þe emperowrs paleys*, l. 173).

365 'Ordered his men in the same way.'

Same, preceded by the definite article, is used as a demonstrative which indicates identity. Cf. l. 551.

369 wemen. MS *wemon* is an unlikely plural and is easily altered to the more familiar form. Although letter *e* in which the stem and lobe of the letter is formed in a single circular movement resembles *o*, the *o* in question is too rounded to have been intended as *e*.

374 hymselfe. The intensive pronoun is used as the subject of the sentence. It refers to *Garcy*.

382 Narumpy. The city of Narnia (present-day Narni) is, as l. 376 indicates, just about sixty miles north of Rome. The water of the Tiber is more or less 'running by' (l. 383), Narni being about seven miles up the river Nera (the Roman Nar) from the confluence of the Nera and the Tiber. The form of the name, Narumpy, is rather unusual; it is not clear whether there was a meadow near Narnia so named or whether the poet took the name from the name of the city.

The movement of the forces from Constantinople is not hard to follow, but one must assume that the troops were put ashore at some place like modern Civitavecchia. To arrive at 'Narumpy' they would have had to move some fifty miles inland.

385–90 The red 'boosys' appear to be round decorative embossed ornaments affixed to the rich ropes described which apparently control the silk cloths, holding them back, perhaps, when desired. These cloths are very likely tapestries with representations of fishes and a variety of animals. Thus, *þere* (l. 389) is taken to refer not to *boosys* but to *cloþys* (l. 385).

393 gode. The lobe of *g* is rounded and completely closed in the manuscript; the letter cannot be read as *y* (Ritson) or *ȝ* (Vietor). *Wyde the lytghnes gode* (roughly, 'as wide as the beautiful brightness') modifies *charbokull stone*. This stone evidently spans the length of the 'brightness' created by the fifteen 'pomels of golde'.

394 **lay on hys walle** 'watches from the ramparts'.

403–4 The sense of the lines is 'Now I shall not refrain from spending my gold, provided that it be spent on this war.' This translation, however, does not retain *hyt* as an indefinite subject in an impersonal construction.

408 Mylys and Emere are related to the many contrasted and quarrelling brothers, whether twins or no, in folklore and literature, who seem to reflect a sense of what we know as sibling rivalry. Cain and Abel, Jacob and Esau, Amphion and Zethus (in Euripides) are ancient instances; *Valentine and Orson* is an example from medieval romance.

422, 424 Ritson's transcription of the word *dowve*, without any indication of his alteration of the manuscript is in error. Even Vietor, whose text is strenuously diplomatic, notes his correction of MS *dowbe*. The pronounced hooks on the ascenders of the letter *b* preclude confusion with *v*.

443 **in fere**. Probably 'in company', i.e. with a company of fighting men. At ll. 922–3, there is what seems at first to be an unusual application of the phrase to a single knight: *Thys whyle had Synagot takyn Emere, / And broȝt hym before Syr Garcy in fere.* Such a use would not be unique; the phrase is applied to a lone knight fighting in *Rauf Coilȝear* (l. 702). However, Synagot's subsequent words, '*We haue tane a knyght . . .*', indicate that *in fere* applies not to Emere alone but to Synagot's martial company with which Emere has very likely fallen in.

446 **a burges hows**. In nouns which end in -*s*, the uninflected genitive may appear for phonetic reasons.

447 **they toke ther ynne** 'they took up their quarters'.

449 **more and lesse** 'all without exception'. Cf. l. 2149 where the phrase refers to persons of all ranks, high and low.

455 **hys men** is also recorded by Ritson and Vietor. The MS reading is *hys xx men*. The *x*'s do not appear to be crossouts, and the roman numeral, 'twenty', makes no sense as 'Fyve thousande' men cannot be taken from twenty.

461–2 Play on *fere* (military men in a company) and *feere* (verb, fear).

475 **heuydd**. See note to line 1306.

480 **feyre and free** is a commonly used alliterative pair.

498 Unless a very sloping short leg on the letter *y* is deceptive, the preceding letter appears to have a quite clear headstroke. Therefore, a *fyght* not a *syght* was *semely*.

522 **thay.** A common spelling for the personal pronoun from the fourteenth to the seventeenth century. The form appears three times in *Florence* (cf. also ll. 1726, 2012).

539 **grome.** In late Middle English the word became confused with *gome* 'man', which it eventually replaced. Cf. modern *bridegroom*, OE. *brȳdguma*. Here *grome* means 'man'.

547 Cf. note to line 314.

549 **the more and the mynne.** 'Those of high rank and those of low.' Adjectives are sometimes used in the text with the definite article as nouns signifying a person or persons.

559 **nay.** Used as an introductory word, without any direct negation. This usage first appears *c.* 1460 (see *OED s.v. nay*, A. adv.,1 d).

560 **teene.** This word for 'rage' contains a certain coloration of 'vexation' proper to Garcy's situation. Cf. the Pardon Scene of *Piers Plowman*. After a priest translates the pardon and declares, in effect, 'This is no pardon!', Piers tears it up for 'pure tene' (B. VII, 116).

571 **They nowmberde þem.** The reflexive relation is expressed by means of the simple personal pronoun, *þem*.

     nomberde. This sense, 'amounted to', is cited by the *OED* (*s.v. number*, v.,2 b) as appearing first in a fifteenth-century MS of uncertain date. The pronoun 'þem' is a redundant filler which re-emphasises the subject 'They', referring to the knights in the field. Vietor's diplomatic text neglects to note the bar running through the superscript *l*.

598 The emendation of *yvar* to *yvore* involves very little alteration of the manuscript reading and provides an improved rhyme word for *þerfore*.

599 **A dragon of golde.** According to folklore, dragons can be both benevolent and malevolent. In the east, where snakes are large and deadly, the serpent was symbolic of the principle of evil. In Greece and Rome, on the other hand, while the Oriental idea of the serpent as an evil power gave birth to a plentiful brood of terrors, dragons were also conceived as beneficent powers.

     The qualities of dragons being protective and terror-inspiring, and their effigies highly decorative, they were early used as warlike emblems. From the conquered Dacians the Romans in Trajan's time borrowed the dragon ensign. Under the late east Roman emperors the dragon ensign became the ceremonial standard of the emperors. The imperial fashion spread. In England before the conquest the dragon was chief among royal ensigns of war.

603 **mode.** An appropriate word for 'temperament' or 'disposition' in this military context, as the Old English senses of *mōd* are felt as overtones: 'courage', 'arrogance', 'pride', 'power', 'violence'.

604–5 The consonants *m* and *n* are rhymed together: *soone* with *Rome*.

611 **herawde.** The sense 'king's messenger' does not appear in manuscripts until *c.* 1440. See *MED s.v. heraud,* 2.

613 **Who so.** Simple interrogative pronouns are used as generalising relatives in the manuscript, as here, usually reinforced by *so.*

618 **dyssees.** Although OFr. *s* in loanwords tended to retain the French quality, the *ss* in this word represents voiceless *s* (: *prees: vnpees: lees,* ll. 612, 615, 621).

628 **mett.** In the first and third persons preterite indicative, Class III weak verbs end in *t(e).* Cf. also *lefte,* l. 1219; *boght,* l. 244).

637–8 **torusched** and **todusched.** The prefix *to* is a particle expressing separation, 'asunder, in pieces'. In OE. as well as ME. there are well over a hundred compound verbs formed with *to-.* Only a few such verbs are found after 1500. See *OED s.v. to, prefix*[2].

645 **In Romance as we rede.** The romance referred to is probably the original French text (see also ll. 1164, 1539), sometimes called the 'boke' (ll. 84, 494). At one point, the poet suggests that he has consulted more than one version of the story (l. 84).

649 **The warste** 'most inferior' (in terms of rank).

651 'And all of them were rightful heirs' (i.e., to the aforementioned properties).

654 'They [i.e., Emere and his men] all furnished [them].' The reader must supply the object 'them' which refers back to 'dyntys'.

655–7 A difficult group of lines: 'At the first winning of their shoes, they [i.e., Garcy's new knights] killed so many straightway that they lost nothing.'

655 **wynnyng of þer schone.** Ritson notes (III, 341) a similar
phrase in *The Squyre of Low Degre:*

> For, and ye my love should wynne,
> With chyvalry ye must begynne,
> And other dedes of armes to done,
> Through which ye may *wynne your shone.*

When a knight accomplished some noble deed, he was said
'to win his spurs'. 'To win his shoes' is a similar but less
elegant expression.

    schone. An *-en* plural. Most nouns form the plural by
adding *s*, *es*, or *ys*.

657 **deryd not a pere** 'risked not a thing', 'lost nothing'.

660 **wede.** There is no doubt that the poet intended the verb
wede, 'to become mad'. Note, in fact, that a form of the
expression, *fared as he wolde wede* ('behaved as if he would
become mad'), is used at l. 1683. Nevertheless, the scribe
wrote *wode*. Each letter of the word is shaped exactly like
that in the adjective *wode*, written two lines above. Evi-
dently, the similarity of the spelling, as well as the meaning
of the words, together with their proximity, caused the scribe
to write *wode* twice.

668 **mote Y the.** In Old English the modal auxiliary most often
used to express permitting was *motan*. The verb continues
to be used for permission in this instance. *So moot I thee* ('So
may I prosper') is a frequent adjuration in Chaucer.

670 **strekyn in age.** The past participle in this phrase, meaning
advanced in years, is a special use of the verb *stryke* in the
intransitive sense 'to go'. See *OED s.v. stricken*, pa. pple.
and ppl. a., A.

671 **elder.** Several adjectives retain the Old English mutated
comparatives and superlatives. Cf. also *nerre*, l. 1036; *eldyst*,
l. 896; *grettyst*, l. 903.

695 It is not necessary to follow Ritson in emending MS *bandome*
to *bandoune*. *Bandome* sounds close enough to *towne* to
constitute a tolerable off-rhyme. *Bandoune*, however, is a
phonologically possible derivative of OFr. *bandon*.

701 Ritson's emendation of MS *oon* to *ane* improves the rhyme
scheme and is phonologically possible as a derivative of OE.
ān. However, it is unjustifiable for two reasons: (i) *oon*
always, in this MS, follows the adjective *many* in the ex-

pression (abbreviated here), *many a oon*; (ii) the usual MS form of the pronoun 'one' used to refer to a person is *oon*.

702 **rescowed**. Ritson transcribes *rescowd*; usually when he drops *e*, it is in the final position.

707 Why Ritson should have changed MS *suffur* to *suffer* is unclear. Certainly the letter *u* is too distinct to misread, but Ritson seems to prefer the *er* ending to *ur*. For example, he invariably prints *er* for the abbreviation indicating *ur* whenever it appears, even though unabbreviated words, like MS *suffur*, with analogous suffixes are consistently written *ur* in the manuscript. Ritson's practice is not consistent. At l. 915, he does print MS *suffur* as *suffur*.

745 **spurrys**. Knobbe considers *spurrys: forows* a rhyme (see p. 30). It is an off-rhyme between *ŭ: ū*.

758 It is probably best to emend *folde* to *felde*. This emendation involves very little alteration of the manuscript reading and gives a word which is more appropriate in the context since *folde* refers to an enclosure for domestic animals and Florence is speaking of a plain which is the scene of military operations, i.e., a field of battle.

762 Proper understanding of this line may call for a reading like: 'Thou be of my father's courage.' If the line is read in the most literal way, it is difficult to tell what Florence means.

770 **sweme . . . swalme**. The emphasis given these words by the *sw* alliteration tends to underscore the sense of dizziness conveyed by the meaning of both words.

775 **þe pope, Symonde**. 'Pope Symonde' might have occurred to the poet as being the original name of St Peter, the first Pope.

778 Ritson evidently emends MS *goost* to *gast* because *goost* does not rhyme with *haste*. The emendation, nevertheless, alters the clear *oo* manuscript reading too much. An alteration to *aa* might be more justifiable, particularly since the evidence in the manuscript is that OE. ā tends to waver between *ā* and long open *ǭ*.

787 **tane**. The stem vowel of the pp. of OE. Class VI strong verbs has become *ā*. Note also *slayne*, l. 788 and the shifts to *ai* (*onslayne*, l. 496) and *o* (*sworne*, l. 355).

789 Who the 'souereygn' is seems unclear. In the broadest sense, this must be Garcy; however, as the sovereign tells the knights to send Emere to Garcy (ll. 790 ff.) he must be something like a field commander.

797 **procescyon.** Vietor prints *procescon* as if it were not an
abbreviation. However, the curved line in the MS over *on*
signals the dropping of *y*.

814 **sayne.** Infinitives in the text are mostly uninflected. This is
one of the few *-n* forms among monosyllabic verbs.

820 **maystres Awdygon.** As a title of courtesy prefixed to the
surname (in early use also to the Christian name), 'mistress'
first appears in the *Paston Letters*, 1471. See *OED s.v.
mistress*, sb., III 14.

834 Unless *Lorde* is regarded as an exclamation, this line is
puzzling.

835 **þat þere was.** The singular verb, *was*, is used after the
plural subject, 'Knyghtys and squyers'.

841-2 The lament of the barons gains particular emotional effect
by the addition of alliteration. Note a similar use of allitera-
tion in a passage from *Emaré* describing the heroine's plight,
cast adrift on the open sea:

> She was so dryven fro wawe to wawe,
> She byd her hede and lay full lawe,
> For watyr she was full woo.
>
> [ll. 322-4]

845-6 The comparison seems to have a proverbial quality.
Although Whiting (*Proverbs in Certain Middle English
Romances*, 120) considers the comparison original to the
English version, he does not feel it is inspired by a proverb
—native or otherwise.

845 **eyen.** An *-en* plural form, here meaning 'young hawks'.
The form appears again at l. 353 where the word, however,
has the meaning 'eyes'. Cf. Glossary.

According to the *MED* (see *s.v. eie* n. 3b), the sense of
'young hawks' appears first in *Florence*, of which the MS
is dated by the *MED* about 1500.

851 **fasten.** Best understood in the sense of 'land, cast' (*MED
s.v. fasten*, v. (1), 3b). This meaning first appears in a manu-
script dated about 1400.

861 **quarels wyth arbalast.** The manuscript reading, 'alablaste',
is probably a mis-spelling for 'arbalast', a cross-bow
furnished with a special mechanism for discharging arrows,
bolts or stones. The *OED* cites a contemporary reference

from Caxton: *A quarel . . . shotte out of Arbalaste* (1483).

875 **famysched.** The meaning 'starved' first appears in a manuscript dated *c.* 1450. See *MED s.v. famishen.*

878 **store.** This sense of 'abundant supply' does not appear until 1471. See *OED s.v. store,* sb., 4.

879 **þem.** A usage paralleling the Latin dative of reference, as may be seen by the literal translation: 'Food was most required by them'.

883 The addition of *to* to MS *For mayntene* provides an extra syllable which improves the rhythm of the line. Moreover, parallel infinitives seem likely since the preposition *for* is so often paired with infinitives (cf. l. 24, *for to stryke;* l. 64, *for to newyn*).

903 **grettyst.** An adjective with umlaut in the superlative. In the comparative, when the Old English ending *-ra* is added after final *-e*, a long stem-vowel is lost and a parasitic vowel develops from syllabic *r*. The short vowel is transferred to the superlative, hence ME. *grettyst.*

907 **hyr.** Mylys hesitates to reply to the preceding statement made by Awdegon (Florence's maid). Clearly the pronoun before *speche* should be *hyr.*

910 There seems to be a shift here that could be explained by part of the action being omitted or being assumed by the reader. In the preceding stanza we have the visit of Awdegon and Mylys and their conversation about a possible wedding with Florence. But there is a shift from line 909 to line 910; in the latter it is Florence herself who seems to be speaking. This would imply that Awdegon had returned to Florence with Mylys's message and that we are now hearing Florence's reaction. There is a problem with this assumption. It seems that Mylys and Florence are face to face when she says '*Avyse þe. . . .*' She is not just uttering an exclamation but is actually addressing Mylys.

The author must have forgotten that in stanza **76** he had Awdegon and Mylys talking. In any event, there is a fault in the narration here.

912 The emendation of MS *y* to *ye* improves our understanding of the situation. *y* means that Florence is the one who is thinking 'lyghtly', but there is no reason to think that if Mylys expects to inherit her father's wealth she should feel cheerful or foolish. Quite the reverse. No, she must be

warning him that if such is his expectation, *he* is thinking foolishly. Hence *ye*.

913 **woundys fyve.** An allusion to the five wounds of Christ's crucifixion.

916 **askyd.** Knobbe considers the rhyme *askyd*: *laste* an illustration of long *ā* (see p. 37). More likely, the sound is *ă*.

922–3 See note to line 443.

930 'That' seems to refer back to Emere himself, but the reference is an implicit one as Emere does not mention himself. The line means 'I who am now prepared to die.'

933 **Owre fadur owre ryght.** 'Our father refused us our inheritance.'

940–1 The sense is roughly, 'Since he has left us without protection, we don't care if there is war or peace.'

948 **in stede stode me.** 'was of service to me.'

955–6 In the preceding lines Emere explains that if he were left free and came into town, he would be obliged to do grief to Garcy and his people. He goes on here to say, in effect, that there would be no sound reason for Garcy's letting him go: 'The gods forbid that you spare me; it would be the worst decision you ever made.'

955 The addition of *me* introduces an unstressed syllable which avoids the awkwardness of two successive heavy stresses, *thăt pŏu spáre*.

Also, *me* reminds us of what is being spared. Note another example of the object of *spare* appearing immediately before the verb: *my golde spare*, l. 403.

959 **myn.** The first person singular adjectival possessive pronoun used to qualify the following noun, *hoost*. Cf. 1064, 1338.

991–2 Final *f* is sometimes voiced and sometimes not (*fyve*: *lyve*, but cf. *fyve*: *wyfe*, ll. 913–14).

992 **be lyve.** Ritson lists *be lyve* as an error which should be corrected to *belyve* (III, 440). The words should, however, remain separate as the noun *lyve* is often used in the phrase *sworne . . . be lyve*, meaning 'sworn . . . with one's life'.

993 **Mylys himselfe.** The pronoun 'hymselfe' is an intensifier. As Mylys is the subject rather than the object of 'rewe', he is not ruing himself but rather he himself is ruing.

1000 It is difficult to assess Florence's motivation here. She says she will not sleep with her husband Emere until he has brought her Garcy or left him in the field for dead. Then she affirms this with the strongest oath she can summon. Saintly heroine or not, she strikes one as somewhat vindictive.

1022 The instrumental of the simple demonstrative, OE. *þy*, remains in *forthy*, 'on that account'.

1028 Probably by analogy to his emendation of MS *bandome* to *bandoune* at the end of l. 695, Ritson again emends the word used within the line at 1028. The second, internal MS *bandome* ratifies the contention that a shift of OFr. *bandon* to ME. *bandoune* is not a feature of the spelling in this manuscript.

1036 **nerre.** The sense 'nearest' appears in a manuscript dated *c.* 1470. (See *OED s.v. nar*, a., 1 b.)

1049 The sense is that Garcy didn't leave many of them alive.

1050 Probably *tyde* here has the sense of time or occasion, but it could also refer to a literal tide. That is, they went to the ship when the tide was there.

1084 **Egraveyne.** The insertion of letter *a* over the line stands for *ra*. Cf. *trauelde*, l. 104; *prayde*, l. 1837; *grace*, ll. 1511, 1832).

1086 **To wote** appears to have the sense of present-day 'To wit'. The line means that they would do the same thing with Egraveyne: 'To wit without any misery', if he did not swear. It is not until ll. 1126 ff. that it is clear that Egraveyne did, indeed, swear.

1090 ff. The dead body which is presented to Florence as Emere's is Sampson's. Cf. l. 1157.

1093–4 **swowned twyes . . . syghed thryes.** It is common for medieval writers to be specific about numbers as there was a great deal of interest in numerology. Dante, for example, in the *Inferno*, Canto XXVI, ll. 130 ff., has Ulysses note that he had seen the moon wax and wane *five* times before a storm blew up, causing his ship to be whirled about *three* times and at the beginning of the *fourth* revolution, to be cast into the sea. Keats imitates this medieval penchant for specific numbers in *La Belle Dame sans Merci*: 'And there I shut her wild, wild eyes / With kisses four.'

1101 **forme of bredd.** The Eucharistic bread which, in the Mass, becomes the body of Christ. The priest does 'schewe' the Host when he raises it after the consecration for the congregation to see.

1107 **ta.** The voiceless velar stop, spelt *c* in OE. and *k* in ME., is entirely dropped at times when in final position (Note *ma: fra: thra*, ll. 1104, 1110, 1113). Sometimes it is silent (*askyd: laste*, ll. 916–17).

1140 Ritson's emendation of MS *oon* to *ane* improves the rhyme
scheme and is phonologically possible as a derivative of
OE. *ān*. Nevertheless, it is an unjustifiable alteration, as
the usual manuscript form of the pronoun *one* used to
refer to a person is *oon* (Cf. ll. 7, 343, 378, etc.).

1145 Who the emperor is is unclear, as the old emperor was
slain and the poet has not indicated that someone else took
his place. Later, lines 1297–1300 indicate that the emperor
is Emere.

1148 **stokkes.** Both Ritson and Vietor read the manuscript at
this point as *strokkes*, and then finding it in error, correct
to *stokkes*. Examination of the original manuscript reveals
not the slightest trace of a letter *r*.

1154 **All the lasse can sche recke.** Confusion of feeling and joy
prevent Florence from comprehending the good news.

1174–5 The voiceless stop appears instead of the voiced finally
before voiceless consonants in the group *ng*, as in the rhyme
strenkyth: *lenkyth*.

1179 **many oon lykyd ylle.** That is, many a resident of Con-
stantinople 'lykyd ylle'.

1203 **þemselfe schall rewe.** The personal pronoun with the
adjective *self* is used alone as the subject of a sentence.

1246–7 The emendation of MS *or þere* improves the sense of the
line which is roughly: 'A ship such as was there / Was
never seen.' The preposition *or* creates a pointlessly obvious
statement: 'Such a ship before there was one / Was never
seen.'

1281 **sotheyr.** The *th* in this noun is written for OFr. *d* in *soudier*
and thus is rhymed with *odur* (l. 1278).

1300 The punctuation indicating that Mylys is asking the
question of Emere is in error. It must be Emere who has
asked the question of Mylys, he who has just fallen off a
horse and 'eylyth'. The question allows Mylys to lie at
length about Florence's honour. Vietor's diplomatic text is
entirely unpunctuated and therefore offers no guidance.

1306 The rhyme with *revydd* makes *hevydd* preferable to MS *hedd*.
Also *hevydd* is phonologically probable as it can be derived
from OE. *hēafod*. Cf. the emendation at ll. 475, 1933.

1316 Only a slight alteration of MS *lernydd* is required to give
lerydd, a word which improves the rhyme with *enqueryd* and
which has the same meaning as *lernydd*, though derived
from a different Old English verb: *læran*.

1328 ms *And* must be emended to *Ane* in order to provide a subject for the clause.

1329 **Whych** is used in the manuscript with reference to persons as well as things. Cf. l. 1933.

1330 ff. Stanza 112 lacks a concluding group of three lines. Cf. stanza 3.

1348 **bere tree** 'wooden coffin'. The word *tree* in ME. often refers to something made of wood rather than the tree itself. In this ms note also l. 1430 where **tre** is a reference to Christ's cross.

1361 **a pena et culpa** 'From punishment and guilt'. Cf. B. vii, l. 3 of *Piers Plowman*. There a mere Pardon, which normally remits the *punishment* due to sins and does not forgive their guilt, absolves the Plowman. Properly only the sacrament of Penance offered total absolution, while pardons and indulgences remitted only the temporal punishment.

Here Egravayne receives absolution *a pena et culpa* in the true sense as his confession involves him in the judicial process by which the penitent is at once the accuser and the person accused, while the priest pronounces judgement and sentence. The grace conferred is deliverance from the guilt of sin and in the case of mortal sin from its eternal punishment (cf. *Catholic Encyclopedia*, xi, 619 ff., *s.v. Penance*).

But what is Egravayne guilty of and why does he make his confession to the Pope, Bishop of Rome?

Technically, he is an accomplice in the sin of *Raptus Violentiæ* (abduction by violence). This sin is committed when a reluctant woman is forcibly transferred with a matrimonial intent from a secure and free place to a morally different one and there held by threats, great fear, or fraud equivalent to force (cf. *Catholic Encyclopedia*, i, 32 ff. *s.v. Abduction*). It is not necessary that actual change of locality occur. Some jurists claim 'virtual change' from a state of freedom to that of subjection to be sufficient to constitute 'abduction'.

Christian law in the time of Innocent III with respect to abduction was the ecclesiastical discipline up to the sixteenth century, and it was vague. Not only does it not specify what the punishment of an accomplice should be, but Innocent III's decree let the abductor himself off easily. His decree practically made abduction worth trying, since marriage could occur as long as the woman's prior reluctance changed to willingness—even while in the power of the captor. It may have been the laxity of this decree which led Mylys, the clear-cut abductor, to commit an even more audacious abduction of Florence later in the poem.

As for Egravayne's confession to the Pope, it seems to anticipate the entirely new discipline introduced by the Council of Trent (1545–63), for according to the Council, whether the abduction ended with marriage or not, 'the abductor with all of his advisers, accomplices, and abettors' was to be 'excommunicated and declared forever infamous, incapable of acquiring dignities'.

The right to absolve in a case of excommunication belongs to him who can excommunicate and who has imposed the law. In Egravayne's case, the power would be the Pope's, as he is Bishop of Rome and the crime was committed in his jurisdiction. Hence the confession to Pope Symond.

1363 The misreading of *ame* for *arme* is an understandable error. Long-tailed *r* has lost its shoulder stroke and so is not easily distinguished from the minim strokes which make up the letter *m*. Nevertheless, the prominent descender and connecting stroke make the *r* sufficiently distinctive.

1377 **at the none** 'the hour of nones', a daily office said at the ninth hour of the day (about 3 p.m.) but in late Middle English use sometimes earlier; hence MnE. *noon*.

1384 The 'he' referred to is evidently Mylys.

1401 ff. Knobbe, having concluded that the *a* in *laste* (l. 1410) is long, incorrectly considers the Old Norse *a* in the closed syllable lengthened on the basis of rhyme (*caste* (ON. *kast*): *faste: agaste: laste*).

1428 **Weleawaye** is an emendation of MS *wele a saye* to the common interjection.

1430 **dyed on tre** 'died on the cross'. See note to line 1348.

1435 **were nyghtyd** 'were overtaken by night.' The *OED* cites this appearance in *Florence* as the earliest occurrence of this special use of the verb *nyghte* (see *s.v. night*, v.). A similar verb in OHG. is *nahten* (G. *nachten*).

1438–44 The chastity of the heroine is saved by her prayer to the Virgin Mary who makes the persecutor forget his passion. This miracle and others which occur under the influence of the Virgin Mary's power (cf. ll. 1499–500, 1852

ff.) underscore the ties that *Florence* has to Tales of the
Virgin. The pattern in nearly all these tales is the same:
some mortal, either saint or sinner, is in difficulty and prays
to the Virgin, who grants him deliverance as a reward for
either his sanctity or his repentance, as the case may be.

1440 The emendation of MS *Mary and free* to *Mary free* suggests
that the scribe, having just written *and* before the word
Mary, carelessly wrote it again. More likely, the scribe's
eyes moved faster than his hand when he came to the
common alliterative pair 'feyre and free' (cf. 1. 480), and
he dropped the word *feyre*.

1466 **scho.** This form of the feminine nominative pronoun is
found typically in the north and is first seen in literary
records towards the end of the thirteenth century. Cf. 1.
1980.

1472 **stekyth in.** When the verb *sticks* is used intransitively and
paired with *on*, *to*, *unto*, or *in*, it may have this sense of
'cleaves, adheres'. The *OED* (*s.v. stick*, v¹., II, 8) indicates
the earliest appearance of the usage in a manuscript dated
1558.

1478 **yere.** An uninflected noun expressing measurement. Cf.
pownde, 1. 1373 and *myle*, 1. 376. It should be observed that
the *-ys* form of *yere* occurs along with the uninflected form
(*yerys*, 1. 83).

1489 The narrator passes from indirect discourse (*He made þe
lady . . .*) to the direct discourse of ll. 1492–4. When we
read *From whens þou came . . .*, we are aware of an incon-
sistency in the recounting of these remarks. The absence
of a clear transition in the narrative testifies to the poet's
lack of perfect craft.

1498 The scribe practised writing *w* in the centre margin.

1516–17 OE. voiceless palatal stop *c* is represented by *k* rather
than the usual *ch* in the rhyme *byrke: yrke*, probably as a
result of Scandinavian influence. Cf. *swylke: sylke*, ll. 386,
385; *lyke: ryke*, ll. 1808, 1807.

1532 **hurselfe.** For metrical reasons the reflexive form is (illogic-
ally) used here rather than the simple object *hur*.

1534–47 The beauty of Florence, like that of Emaré, has some-
thing celestial about it. Florence's beauty, which in the
first part of the romance is the conventional attribute of
the courtly tale, is here raised to a visible symbol of her
virtue. Florence, as Emaré, is surrounded by an aura of

light and brightness. Cf. ll. 1708–9; when she rides through the forest it begins to shine.

1566 **lay.** The past plural stem vowel of OE. Class V strong verbs has become *ai*.

1567 **wythowte lesynge.** Why should Florence and Betres lie? The phrase makes somewhat more sense if taken as an implicit reference to the narrator's storytelling. The phrase may be an assurance that the poet is telling us the truth.

1569 **any many.** This unusual expression seems to be a plural form of *anyone*.

1583 **strenkþfull stedd.** Ritson's transcription reads *strenkth full stedd*. The manuscript indicates, however, a clear connecting stroke between þ and *f* which creates the adjective meaning 'full of strength'.

1592 **Machary.** This name occurs as Macaire in the Sibilla group of stories about the persecuted queen who is Charlemagne's wife. Macaire, the king's steward, is a villain who tries to make love to Sibilla and, having been thwarted, accuses her of adultery. He furnishes proof by smuggling someone into the queen's bed. In the respect that Macaire is the only persecutor, the Sibilla group is distinct from Florence. Also in contrast with Florence, Sibilla bears a son in exile, who plays a part in bringing about the reunion of his parents. Several notable resemblances to the story of Florence are that the queen is sent out into a wood for punishment and lives in exile for many years before her honour is vindicated. The story of Sibilla was the subject of an early French *chanson de geste*, but that poem is now preserved only in an Italianised version in which the queen's name is Blanchefleur. F. Guessard (ed., *Macaire*) has tried to restore the poem to its original French form. A second version of the story occurs in *La Reine Sibille*.

1605 **yn a gethe.** The word *gethe* is used only in this expression meaning 'spiritedly, hastily'. Cp. OI. *geð* 'mind, spirit'; OE. *ge(h)þu*.

1617 The line is best understood as the narrator's explanation of Machary's lie about the tournament. He lies because 'The truth is unpardonable'.

1618–20 As at line 1489, the narrator passes from indirect discourse to direct discourse without clear transition.

1624 ff. The motif of the bloody knife is also introduced into Gower's legend of Constance and Chaucer's *Man of Law's*

Tale. It does not, however, occur in *Emaré*, another related tale.

1639 ff. A masterly, dramatic description of Sir Tyrry's prophetic dream and his anxious candlelit walk to his murdered daughter's chamber.

1647 **thorowly.** The sense 'fully' does not appear in manuscripts until 1473. See *OED s.v. thoroughly*, 2.

1657 **glyste.** Referring to eyes: 'glared', 'stared'. The first appearance of this usage is in a manuscript dated *c.* 1450 (MED. *s.v. glisnen*, 2 b).

1662 **The whych.** The combination is used as a relative pronoun. Mustanoja (*A Middle English Syntax, Mémoires De la Société Neophilologique*, XXIII (1960), p. 198) suggests that the combination may be an imitation of OFr. *liquels.*

1666-9 The villainous Machary takes Florence's beautiful clothing and appearance as a sign that she is a devil. The implication is that evil cannot comprehend beauty. His view of evil in the guise of female beauty is also a common motif of medieval anti-feminist literature.

1692 It is unclear what Syr Tyrry holds to be sin. The pronoun *hyt* may refer either to Florence's presumed murder of Betres or to the act of putting Florence to death.

1708-9 See note to lines 1534-47.

1730 A strange idea. From what the thief says later in the following stanza, it is evident that he would not prefer hanging to giving up his life of thievery.

1756 ff. Although there seem to be no proverbs in the romance, B. J. Whiting feels that one incident, occurring in other stories belonging to the Florence-Constance cycle, 'was almost certainly inspired by a proverb' (*Proverbs in Certain Middle English Romances*, 119). That is the betrayal of Florence by the thief whom she had saved from the gallows. Whiting, however, neglects to supply the proverb he was thinking of.

1758 Vietor, not distinguishing the overlapping curls from *b* and *h* of *he*, l. 1759, concludes that the second *r* in *harburgerye* is written over a letter *g.*

1767 **flyre.** The sense is 'to mock', and according to the *MED* (see *s.v. flerien*) this meaning first appears in a manuscript dated *c.* 1440. The line from *Florence* is also cited. The sense of the word accords well with the situation described in which the thief and burgess flash knowing glances at one another as they hatch an evil scheme.

F

The emendation of MS *flyre* to *flerye* is not needed. The workmanlike poet who wrote *Florence* may have been content enough with the slight alteration of his usual tail rhyme scheme: *yre: atyre: flyre*.

1769 The misreading *we* for MS *ye* is puzzling, as the letter *y* is quite distinct.

1828–30 The lines mean 'all the men who departed for the ship tried to make love to Florence'.

1875 **roche.** In the twelfth-century Latin Miracle version of the tale the empress is exposed on a rock in the middle of a river (Bibliothèque Nationale, MS 14463).

1882 **Beuerfayre.** The MS reading *Benerfayre* must be in error. The English poet evidently means to Anglicise the French name for the convent, Beau-Repaire. Hence he needs the vowel *u*, not a consonant.

1888 **Lucyus Jbarnyus.** The reference to him as the founder of 'Beuerfayre'—in the French versions Beau-Repaire, a convent said to have been founded by Julius Caesar—has been taken as an indication that the poet had in mind the Lucius Iberius of the alliterative *Morte Arthure*, l. 86 (Knobbe, 9).

1892–3 Bells ringing of their own accord are common in hagiographic literature. The bells of Madrid are said to have rung spontaneously when the body of St Isidore was removed from the churchyard into the church. Bells also were supposed to have rung out miraculously to announce the murder of St Landry, *curé* of Lanslevillard. In the romance *Cheuelere Assigne* there is an unequal duel in which a twelve-year-old defeats a practised warrior. The religious, almost ritual character of the duel is underlined by the miraculous ringing of all the bells (ll. 272–4). Other examples are cited by Tatlock, *MLN*, 29 (1914), 98 and Barry, *MLN*, 30 (1915), 28–9.

1894 **Seynt Hyllary.** Bishop of Poitiers, one of the greatest religious luminaries of France in the fourth century. His feast day is in January, but it is celebrated on the 14th not the *twenty day of ʒowle*.

1910 **þat fre.** An adjective meaning 'noble or gracious in character', preceded by the demonstrative pronoun, takes on the force of a noun. Hence the sense, 'that noble lady'.

1927 ff. Nuns occasionally play the role of healer in medieval romances. The writings of Hildegarde, in fact, demonstrate the knowledge of herbs and medicine which an abbess might actually acquire (see M. Hughes, *Women Healers in Medieval Life and Literature*, 4).

1930 The superscript *a* above the *g* in MS *sprang* is puzzling, as no *a* has been omitted.

1933 **hevedd.** Cf. note to line 1306.

1947 MS *be* is emended to *ben* as the sentence structure, paralleling l. 1946, is improved by the repetition of the past participle *ben* rather than the infinitive form *be*. In other parts of the manuscript as well, the past participle appears either as *ben* or *bene*.

1976 **schake.** This infinitive of the OE. Class VI strong verb indicates that, were the present form used in the text, the present tense stem vowel would be *ā*. Cf. also *fare*, l. 593. Other infinitives of Class VI verbs indicate shifts to *a* (*stande*, l. 711), and *au* (*drawe*, l. 255).

1991 **hyppyng.** The word with this meaning, 'limping', is first recorded in a manuscript dated *c.* 1450 (see *MED s.v. hippen*, 2). Its appearance in *Florence* is also cited. Ritson claims *deuyll* as a 'corrected' reading for MS *deyll*. While the handwriting in the manuscript is somewhat compressed, *deuyll* is clearly discernible as the original reading.

Hyppyng on two stavys lyke þe deuyll. The phrase is a curious one, the earliest instance of which appears here in *Florence* (see B. J. Whiting, *Proverbs in Certain Middle English Romances*, 121).

2027 Although *standen . . . astrote* ('to bulge') is a common phrase (see *MED s.v. astrote*), it is not necessary to follow Ritson in 'correcting' MS *a strote* (III, 441). The poet may not have intended the adverb *astrote* but rather the noun *strote* ('projection, bulge') which stands in apposition to *yen*.

2037 **the more and mynne.** See note to line 549.

2051 Omitting *fro hur* improves the rhythm of the line. A stronger, more clear four-stress line emerges by reducing the number of unstressed syllables, and no damage is done to the meaning. In fact, redundancy is eliminated.

2072 **oonys.** 'At one time'. There are some common adverbs consisting of inflected forms of nouns and adjectives used independently, such as the genitives *oonys* and analogically *twyes* (l. 1093) and *thryes* (l. 1094).

2091 **myne.** The first person singular adjectival possessive pronoun used to qualify the preceding noun, *hals*.

2107–8 Knobbe theorises that the guttural spirant, spelt *gh*, *ȝ*, remains in Middle English, in the consonant group *ht* (p. 45). It is impossible to conclude anything with certainty from a study of the rhymes; however, the loss of [χ] is possibly indicated by the spellings *syte* (for *syght* or *syȝt*) and *plyte* (for *plyght* or *plyȝt*).

2133 gente. The word seems to be used as an adv. meaning 'courteously' and is cited by the *MED.* (see *s.v. gent* adj., 2) as having made its first appearance in *Florence*.

2147 Te deum laudamus. The famous hymn of thanksgiving whose composition is sometimes ascribed to St Ambrose.

2149 more and lesse. See note to line 449.

2175 Who is employed as an indefinite pronoun. The principal use made of *who* in the text, however, is as the interrogative pronoun (l. 279).

2176 ff. In the didactic closing stanza, the poet draws a universal moral from the events in the spirit of the exemplary tale. Attention is called to the unhappy fates of the four evildoers and to the vengeful decree of God against them. The poet calls his work 'þys Romance gode', that is, a meaningful romance for those who hear the call to follow the model of the saintly Florence.

2179 MS *slylylye* obviously needs to be corrected by dropping one *ly*.

2182 meene be. The sense here is 'to intend to refer to'. The *OED* (*s.v. mean,* v¹, 1 e) lists the first appearance of this construction as occurring in Mores, *Edward V* (1513): 'That ment he by the lordes of the quenes kindred. . . .'

Explicit Le Bone Florence . . . The poet seems to have been careless about gender. *La Bonne Florence* would be more correct unless it was to be understood that there was an ellipsis of 'Le Livre de la Bon[n]e Florence . . .'

GLOSSARY

This glossary is designed to record every form of every word which occurs in the manuscript except for words in Latin. References are limited to the first three consecutive appearances of a word. Idiomatic phrases, especially those constructed on a few fundamentally important verbs such as *do*, *make*, *take*, are fully recorded as well. Words subject to variation in form because of inflexion are set out according to a fixed order. Verbs, for example, are listed under the infinitive if it appears, followed by the imperative (which has the same form as the infinitive), the present tense (in order of person in the singular, then the plural), the past tense (singular, representing first or third person, second person singular, then plural), the subjunctive, present preceding past (singular, then plural), and the present and past participles. Less affected are nouns and adjectives. Plural and genitive forms (in that order) of the noun are given under the singular when it is recorded, and, likewise, the comparative and superlative forms of the adjective are entered under the uninflected form when it also appears. Where a single word occurs in several parts of speech, the arrangement of entries is noun, adjective, adverb, verb, etc. Cross-references are as full as possible. Parentheses enclose letters which may appear as alternative spellings.

In the etymologies, each etymon cited is given in the dialectal form that best accounts for the form in the manuscript. Therefore, the native Old English forms are Anglian, the Old French forms Anglo-French. The marking of long vowels has not been attempted in Old French. In Old English stable long vowels are marked with a macron as in *ān*; those which were shortened or of uncertain quantity are marked as in *ofdrĕdd*, except that æ when long is printed as *ǣ* and when shortened or of uncertain quality as *œ*, vowels lengthened in Old English (e.g. before *ld*) are marked as in *báld*. Long vowels in Old Norse are shown as in *ár*. Cross-references in bold type refer to entries in this glossary.

Entries are arranged so that ʒ has a separate place after *g*, and þ, *th*, a separate place after *t*. *i* and *y* (except as a consonant) are treated as the same letter and take the order of *i*. *u* and *v* are alternative forms of the same letter; when representing a vowel they come in the position of modern *u*, when a consonant in that of *v*. The same principles are observed for medial *u*.

ABBREVIATIONS

a.	adoption of	ad.	adaption of
abbrev.	abbreviation	adj.	adjective
absol.	absolute	adv.	adverb
acc.	accusative	aphet.	aphetic

app.	apparently	nom.	nominative
art.	article	num.	numeral
assoc.	association	obj.	object, objective
attrib.	attributive	*OED*	*The Oxford English*
auxil.	auxiliary		*Dictionary*
card.	cardinal	ord.	ordinal
coll.	collective	orig.	originally
comb.	combinations	pass.	passive
comp.	comparative	phr.	(in) phrase(s)
cond.	conditional	pl.	plural
conj.	conjunction	poss.	possessive
const.	construed with	pp.	past participle
cont.	contraction	pr.	present
cp.	compare	prec.	preceding (word)
dat.	dative	prep.	preposition
demons.	demonstrative	prob.	probably
dial.	dialect, dialectal	pron.	pronoun
dim.	diminutive	pr. p.	present participle
esp.	especially	pt.	past
f.	formed on	refl.	reflexive
fem.	feminine	rel.	relative
fig.	figurative	sg.	singular
gen.	genitive	subj.	subjunctive
imper.	imperative	suff.	suffix
impers.	impersonal	sup.	superlative
indef.	indefinite	temp.	temporal
infin.	infinitive	tr.	transitive
infl.	influenced	v.	verb
interj.	interjection	var.	variant
intr.	intransitive	vbl. n.	verbal noun
masc.	masculine	=	corresponding to
MED	*Middle English Dic-*	+	combined with
	tionary (Michigan)	*	theoretically recon-
n.	noun		structed
neut.	neuter		

LANGUAGES AND DIALECTS

A.	Anglian dialects of Old English	L.	Latin
		LG.	Low German
AF.	Anglo-French	Merc.	Mercian
CF.	Central (Old) French	MDu.	Middle Dutch
Dan.	Danish	ME.	Middle English
E.Fris.	East Frisian	ML.	Medieval Latin
Fr.	French	MLG.	Middle Low German
G.	German	MnE.	Modern English
Icel.	Icelandic	Norw.	Norwegian

Nth.	Northumbrian	ON.	Old Norse
ODan.	Old Danish	ONth.	Old Northumbrian
OE.	Old English	ONFr.	Northern dialects of Old French
OFr.	Old French		
OHG.	Old High German	OS.	Old Saxon
OI.	Old Icelandic	OSw.	Old Swedish
OIr.	Old Irish	SW.	Swedish

A

a *indef. art.* a 2, 14, 23, etc.; (*with num.*) 189, 338, 356, etc.; **an** (*before vowels*) 224, 227, 264, etc.; **an** *adj.* one 781, 866; **ane** *as subject:* one 1328; *many a oon*, many a one 873, 1674; *weleawaye*, weleawaye 1428. [OE. *ān.*]

abbas *n.* abbess 1900, 1924, 2000. [OFr. *ab(e)esse.*]

abyde *pr. subj. sg.* remain 468, 1037; **abode** *pt. pl.* remained, stayed 446. [OE. *abīdan.*]

abye *v.* pay for, atone for 1509. [OE. *abycgan.*]

abode *n.* stop, stay 1433. [rel. to *abide.*]

aboute *adv.* about, on all sides, here and there 42, 183, 588, etc.; round about 313, 708, 714, etc.; ready to 938. [OE. *abūtan.*]

absence *n.* absence 1273. [OFr. *absence.*]

adradd *pp.* afraid 1314. [OE. *ofdrĕdd.*]

aftur *prep.* in pursuit of 120, 1020, 1064, etc.; behind 240, 985, 1797; after, for 618, 775; according to 1295; *temp.* after 32, 49, 1059, etc.; *oon aftur odur*, one after another; *adv.* afterwards 765. [OE. *æfter.*]

afturward *adv.* afterwards 1280. [OE. *æfterweard.*]

agayne, ageyn(e) *adv.* again, back 281, 288, 497, etc. [ON. *i gegn*, OE. *ongegn.*]

agaste *pp.* astonished 1407. [*a* + OE. *gæsted*, afflicted.]

age *n.* age, time of life 670. [OFr. *age.*]

agenste, *prep.* against 410, 1233; in pursuit of 1233, 1290. [Extended from OE. *ongegn* + adv. *-es.*]

ay(e) *adv.* always, ever 136, 374, 1147, etc. [ON. *ei.*]

all *adj.* all 5, 64, 80, etc.; a whole 588; *pron.* all, everything 60, 163, 221, etc.; all (the people), everyone 195, 468, 496, etc.; *all thyng*, everything 1553. (OE. *al(l).*]

all *adv.* all, entirely, altogether 87, 103, 157, etc.; everywhere 183; *all on blode*, entirely with blood 609; *all in myddys*, amidst 611; *all tyll*, until 964; *all away*, completely (away) 1444. [OE. *al(l).*]

allas *interj.* alas! 574, 826, 836, etc. [OFr. *alas.*]

allone *adj.* alone, only 821, 822, 1247. [Orig. *all adv.* + *one.* Aphet. in northern dial. to *lone.*]

almoost, almoste *adv.* almost, nearly 1551, 1790. [OE. *eall e mæst*, nearly all.]

als *adv.* also, as well 1201, 1396, 1471, etc. [Reduced form of *also.*]

also, alse *adv.* as 289; also, as well 352, 668, 724, etc.; *also swithe*, as quickly (as possible), straightway; *also ... as*, as ... as 289, 1053, 1054, etc. [OE. *al-swā.*]

alther *intensive prefix in* **altherfurste**, first of all 292, 1804; **althernext**, next of all 1961; **altherlaste**, last of all 2113. [OE. *alra gen. pl.*]

altherfurste, altherlaste, althernext. See **alther.**

am *1 sg. pr.* am 620, 671, 1063, etc. [OE. *eam, am.*]

among(e) *prep.* among 428, 654, 552, etc.; in the midst of 318. [OE. *on mong.*]

an. See **a.**

and *conj.* and 6, 9, 11, etc. [OE. *and.*]

ane. See **a.**

any *adj.* any, some 91, 101, 301, etc.; *any many,* pl. of anyone 1876. [OE. *ǣnig.*]

anodur *adj.* another 25, 727, 1659. [OE. *ān + ōþer.*]

anon *adv.* at once, straightway 1604. [OE. *on ān.*]

answare, answere *n.* reply 224, 264, 693, etc. [OE. *andswaru.*]

answeryd *pt. sg.* answered 280, 907, 946, etc.; *pt. pl.* 508. [OE. *an(d)swarian.*]

arayed *pp.* dressed 85, 456; *pt. sg.* prepared 659. [OFr. *areier.*]

arbalast *n.* cross-bow 861. [OFr. *arbaleste.*]

are *n.* oar 1876. [OE. *ār.*]

are *pr. pl.* are 197, 208, 232, etc. [OE. (Nth.) *aron.*] See **art, be(e).**

arme *n.* arm 1324; **armes** *n. pl.* arms 113, 1849. [OE. *earm.*]

arme *v.* arm 1132, 1354, 1363; **armyd, -ed** *pp.* 492, 673, 1108, etc. [OFr. *armer.*]

armes *n. pl.* arms, weapons 866; *men of armes,* fighting men 1060, 1171. [OFr. *armes.*]

armyte *n.* hermit 1459, 1463, 1483, etc. [OFr. *(h)ermite.*]

armowre *n.* armour 366, 465, 584, etc. [OFr. *armeüre.*]

arraye *n.* array, dress 155, 1694, 2145. [OFr. *arei.*]

art *2 pr. sg.* art 554, 670, 1844. OE. *eart.*]

as *adv.* (just) as 52, 62, 73, etc. [As prec.]

as *conj.* (even) as, like 82, 126, 154, etc.; as if, as though 44, 130, 660, etc.; as (one who) 219; *with oaths,* so 328, 620; *(as)* ... *as, also* ... *as (followed by acc.)* 1, 194, 289, etc.; **ays,** while, when 136. [Reduced from *als.*]

aske *v.* inquire 1557, 1571; re-

quest 1462; **askyd** *pt. sg.* asked, inquired 507, 584, 622, etc.; *pt. pl.* 916, 1715, 1906; *pp.* 196, 241. [OE. *ǎxian.*]

assay(e) *v.* make trial of, put to the proof 397, 1498. [OFr. *essayer.*]

assent(e) *n.* service, disposal 1117, 1345. [OFr. *asente.*]

assent *v.* agree 899; support 1072; **assentyd** *pt. pl.* agreed 1078. [OFr. *asentir.*]

assoyle *v.* absolve 1127; **assoyled** *pt. sg.* 777, 1361. [OFr. *assoillir.*]

astate *n.* estate, rank 169. [OFr. *estat.*]

at *prep.* at 25, 190, 225, etc.; from 171, 364, 631; according to 231, 530, 1752, etc.; to 433; with 731, 1251; by 1185; *at the (þe) last,* finally 855, 917. [OE. *æt.*]

avaunt *v.* praise 299. [OFr. *avanter.*]

aveaunt *adj.* of a person, worthy, honourable 665 [OFr. *avena-(u)nt.*]

aveuant *adv.* forward 128. [OFr. *avant.*]

avente *v.* remove (one's helmet) 1939. [OFr. *esventer.*]

avyse *v.* deliberate 909, 910; **avysyd** *pp.* advised. [OFr. *aviser.*]

avysement *n.* the process of advising 205. [OFr. *a(d)visement.*]

away(e), awey *adv.* away 536, 1298, 1352, etc. [OE. *on-weg.*]

awe *n.* dread, fierceness, rage. [ON. *agi;* OE. *eȝe.*]

B

bachylere *n.* young knight 245
bachylers *n. pl.* 320. [OFr. *bacheler.*]

back *n.* back 134, 1141. [OE. *bæc.*]

bad(d) *pt. sg.* bade, asked, requested 590, 661, 789, etc.; ordered 1381; *pt. pl.* 1314. [OE. *biddan.*] See **bedd.**

bagg *n.* bag (money-bag) 1792, 1816. [ON. *baggi.*]

bale *n.* trouble, misery, sorrow 67, 367, 1209, etc.; **bales** *n. pl.* 939. [OE. *balu.*]

bandome *n.* power, rule 1028. [OFr. *bandon.*]

baner *n.* banner 1228; **baners** *n. pl.* 569, 803. [OFr. *ban(i)ere.*]

bare *n.* boar 602, 1593. [OE. *bār.*]

bare *adj.* only 421, empty 1484. [OE. *bær.*]

bare *pt. sg.* laid open, bore open 473; carried 962. [OE. *beran;* cf. OE. *beran ūp.*]

bargayn, bargen *n.* bad or unfortunate business 815, 984. [OFr. *bargaine.*]

bargen. See **bargayn.**

barley, barly *n.* barely 1465, 2056. [OE. *bærlīc.*]

barmeteme *n.* people, tribe 10. [OE *bearn-team; barm-* by assoc. with OE. *barm,* lap.]

baronage *n.* barons collectively, nobles, lords 410, 980. [OFr. *barnage.*]

baronry *n.* the domain of a baron 1268. [OFr. *baronie.*]

barons *n. pl.* barons 347, 552, 649, etc. [OFr. *barun.*]

barryd *pt. pl.* fastened with bars 858. [OFr. *barrer.*]

batayle, batell *n.* battle, fight 24, 429, 464; **batels** *n. pl.* 69, 659. [OFr. *bataille.*]

batell. See **batayle.**

bath *n.* bath 100. [OE. *baþ.*]

bathe. See **both, boþe.**

bathyd *pt. pl.* bathed 1549. [OE. *baðian.*]

be *prep.* by, beside 108, 111, 159, etc.; by means of 16; according to 261, 2146; (*in oaths*) 244, 736, 913; etc.; *be that adv.* by the time 61, 634; *conj.* since, because 1576. [OE. *be.*] See **by(e).**

be(e) *v.* be 77, 206, 211, etc.; *3 pr. sg.* 23, 278, 732, etc.; *pl.* 358, 1618; *pr. subj. sg.* 196, 312; *jussive subj.* 557, 789; *finite verb with pp. forms pass.* 122, 163, 211, etc.; **ben(e)** *pp.* 433, 700, 1947. [OE. *bēon.*]

bedd, *pt. sg.* requested 977. [OE. *biddan.*] See **bad(d).**

bedd(e) *n.* bed 100, 111, 1000, etc. [OE. *bedd.*]

bede *pt. pl.* offered 663. [OE. *bēodan,* already confused with *biddan.*]

bedeene *adv.* forthwith, withal 278. [See *MED.*]

befalle *v.* happen, chance 198; **befelle** *pt. sg.* 41. [OE. *be-fallen.*]

beest *n.* animal, creature 388; **bestys** *n. pl.* 44, 182. [OFr. *beste.*]

before, beforne *prep.* in front of, ahead of 221, 277, 971, etc.; *adv.* earlier 1165, 1455. [OE. *beforan.*]

began, beganne. See **begynne.**

begynne *v.* begin 351; *3 pr. sg.* 367; **began, beganne** *pt. sg.* 579, 639, 815; *pt. pl.* 1036; *pp.* 517, 815, 1009. [OE. *beginnan.*]

begynnyng *vbl. n.* beginning 275. [f. prec. v. + *yng.*]

begonne. See **begynne.**

behelde, *pt. sg.* beheld, looked 422, 537, 756, etc. [OE. *be-háldan.*]

behete *1 pr. sg.* promise 1754. [OE. *be + hátah.*]

beholde *imper.* behold 486. [OE. *be-háldan.*]

behynde *prep.* behind, 164; *adv.* 1403. [OE. *behindan.*]

beholde. See behelde.

behove v. impers. must needs, ought 895. [OE. be-hōfian.]

beyke v. bake 99. [OE. bacan.]

belde n. courage 762, 1719. [OE. béldo.]

belyfe, -lyve adv. eagerly 1652; rapidly 1842. [From ME. phr. bi live.]

belyve. See belyfe, -lyve.

belle n. bell 797, 1457; bellys n. pl. 1892. [OE. belle.]

bende pr. pl. bend 859. [OE. béndan.]

ben(e). See be(e).

bentys n. pl. grassy grounds, fields 1040. [A special use of ME. bent, grass; OE. beonet.]

bere n. clamour, outcry 659. [OE. ge-bēre.]

bere n. bier 795, 811, 816, etc. [OE. bēr.]

bere v. bear, carry 363; beryth 3 pr. sg. behaves, comports himself (with arms); borne pp. born 67, 119, 507, etc. [OE. beran.]

beryed pt. pl. buried 1160. [OE. byrgan.]

beryth. See bere.

besawntys n. pl. gold coins 203. [OFr. besan, pl. besanz.]

besyde prep. beside 423, 562, 677. [OE. be-sīdan, at the side.]

beste n. the best (men) 488; best (thing) 1949; adj. sup. best 347, 973, 2001; adv. 235, 429, 613, etc. [OE. betst.]

bete pt. sg. beat 1426, 1480, 1516; pp. embroidered 182. [OE. bēatan.]

bettur adj. comp. better 1475, 1478, 1863; more valiant 4; adv. 1130. [OE. betera, bet(t)ra, adj.]

bewteys n. pl. beautiful features 64. [OFr. beauté.]

bethoght pt. sg. reflected, thought 908. [OE. biþencan.]

bewrye v. distort 1302. [OE bewrēon.]

byd(d) imper. ask 89, 115, 128. [OE. biddan.]

byddyng n. bidding, commands 849. [f. byd(d).]

byddyth 3 pr. sg. ordered 205, 1389. [OE. biddan.]

byde v. tr. withstand 279; stand (and face) 429; intr. stay, await 111, 264, 1047; pr. pl. 1421; bydyng pr. p. 234. [OE. bīdan.]

by(e) prep. beside, by, along 99, 177, 207, etc.; by means of 932; near 412. [OE. bī.]. See be.

byger n. builder 8. [From ME. biggen.]

bygged pt. sg. built 295. [ON. byggva.]

bygly adj. strong, mighty 220, 1484, 1679. [Obscure].

byrdys n. pl. birds 182. [OE. bridd, young bird (late Nth. pl. birdas).]

byrke n. birch 1516. [Northern. OE. bierce, byrce.]

byte v. pierce 1626. [OE. bītan.]

bytter, -ur adj. bitter, hard 939, 1841; bytterly adv. 1626. [OE. bitter.]

black, blak(k) adj. black 423, 487, 760. [OE. blæc.]

blake v. to become pale 579. [Prob. OE. blāc, pale.]

blamed pt. pl. blamed, rebuked 76. [OFr. bla(s)mer.]

blanne. See blynne.

blaste n. blast (thunder) 1641. [OE. blæst.]

ble(e) n. hue, complexion 185, 579, 757, etc. [OE. blēo.]

blede v. bleed 639. [OE. blēdan.]

bleynes n. pl. sores 2022. [OE. blegen.]

blessyd *pp.* blessed 252. [OE. *blĕtsian.*]

blynne *v.* cease 357, 450, 543; *pr. subj. sg.* 1864; blanne *pt. sg.* put an end to 1149. [OE. *blinnan.*]

blys, blysse *n.* happiness, joy 969, 1679, 2006, etc. [OE. *bliss.*]

blo *adj.* blue 96. [OFr. *bleu.*]

blode *n.* blood 14, 43, 95, etc. [OE. *blōd.*]

blome *n.* flower 686. [ON. *blóm, blómi.*]

bloo *adj.* black and blue 2022. [ON. *blá-r.*]

blowe *v.* blow 635. [OE. *blāwan.*]

blundur *n.* trouble, confusion 1328, [Obscure.]

blythe *adj.* happy, glad 1391. [OE. *blīþe.*]

bode *n.* delay 374, 1018, 1385. [Aphet. f. *abode.*]

body(e) *n.* body 95, 208, 473, etc.; bodyes *n. pl.* 93, 639. [OE. *bodig.*]

boght, boȝt *pt. sg.* bought, ransomed 244, 871, 1105, etc.; *pp.* 1575, 1843, 1987. [OE. *bycgan.*]

boke *n.* book 59, 84, 494, etc. [OE. *bōc.*]

bolde *adj.* bold, valiant 75, 347, 552, etc. [OE. *báld.*]

bonde *pt. sg.* bound 1139, 1366, 1513. [OE. *bindan.*]

bone, bonne *n.* bone 14, 1941; bones, boones *n. pl.* 99, 208, 247. [OE. *bān.*]

bonne. See bone.

Boones. See bone.

boosys *n. pl.* bosses (raised ornaments) 387. [OFr. *boce.*]

boost *n.* boast 958. [Obscure].

borne. See bere.

borowed, -yd *pt. sg.* rescued 2092; *pp.* 1724, 1750. [OE. *borgian.*]

bostefull *adj.* proud 270. [Obscure.]

bote *n.* cure, redress, salvation 1719. [OE. *bōt.*]

bothe, boþe *adj.* both 114, 402, 461, etc.; each 416; *adv.* 6, 32, 45, etc.; as well 162. [ON. *baðir.*]

bowne *adj.* prepared, dressed 178, 866; ready 719, 847, 953, etc.; bound, setting out for 590. [ON. *búinn.*]

bowrys *n. pl.* bowers, chambers 295. [OE. *būr.*]

bowrnes *n. pl.* A small stream, brook 609. [Southern variation of ME. *burn*, OE. *búrne.*]

bragg *n.* arrogant or boastful language 958. [Obscure.]

brayne *n.* brain 1941. [OE. *brægn.*]

brake. See breke.

braste. See breste.

bredd *n.* bread 1004, 1101, 1453, etc. [OE. *brēad.*]

brede *v. intr.* spread, grow 969. [OE. *brēdan.*]

breke *v.* break 1850; brake *pt. sg.* 2101; *pt. pl.* 639; brokyn *pp.* 1130. [OE. *brecan.*]

brenne *v.* burn 500, 1494; brent(e) *pt. sg.* 2057, 1483; brennyng *pr. p.* 98. [ON. *brenna.*]

brennyng. See brenne.

brent(e). See brenne.

bresyd *adj.* bristling 103, 208, 247. [Obscure.]

breste *v.* burst 1055; braste *pt. sg.* 1609, 1862, 2114, etc. [OE. *berstan*; ON. *bresta.*]

brethe *n.* breath 357. [OE *bréþ.*]

brewe *v.* ferment 367, 939, 1209; brewyd *pt. sg.* 687. [OE. *breowan.*]

brydale *n.* wedding feast 2152. [OE. *bryd-eale.*]

bryde *n.* bride 1069. [OE. *brȳd.*]

brydull, brydyll *n.* bridle 1534, 1696, 1802; brydyls *n. pl.* 157, 167. [OE. *brīdel.*]

bryggys *n. pl.* (draw-)bridges 532. [OE. *brycg*.]

bryght, bryȝt *n.* fair one 1594, 2096; *adj.* bright, splendid, fair 79, 98, 156, etc. [OE. *berht*.]

bryghtenyd *pp.* brightened 1155. [OE. *berhtnian*.]

bryghtnes *n.* splendour, 185. [OE. *berht-nes*.]

brynge *v.* bring 811, 816, 1135, etc.; *imp.* 1015, 1475; *pt. subj. pl.* 2132; bryngyth *3 pers. sg.* 1264; broght, broȝt *pt. sg.* 781, 923, 1048, etc.; *pt. pl.* 268, 287, 749, etc.; *pp.* 106, 199, 1001, etc. [OE. *bringan*.]

bryngyth. See bryng(e).

brode *adj.* broad, wide 380, 569, 803, etc. [OE. *brād*.]

brodur *n.* brother 707, 718, 724, etc.; brodurs *n. gen.* 1098. [OE. *brōþor*.]

broght, broȝt. See bryng(e).

brokyn. See breke.

brondys *n. pl.* pieces of burnt wood 98. [OE. *bránd, brónd*.]

brooke *v.* enjoy, use. 1181. [OE. *brūcan*.]

burges *n.* townsman 1744, 1780, 1819; *gen.* 446, 1757, 1762, etc.; *n. pl.* 145. [OFr. *burgeis*.]

burlyng *pr. p.* wallowing (in blood) 1637. [OFr. *bourler* (beside *bouler*), roll.]

burne *n.* warrior, knight, man 884. [OE. *béorn*.]

buske *v.* to prepare oneself, make haste 276. [ON. *búask*, refl.]

but *adj.* except 1078, 1105. [OE. *būtan*.]

but *adv.* only 33, 577, 1192. [OE. *būtan*.]

but *conj.* but 257, 291, 352, etc.; however 269, 349, 789; unless 389, 956; *but yf* unless 440. [OE. *būtan*.]

buxvm *adj.* obedient, willing 1723. [OE. stem of *būgan* + -*sum*.]

C

caght *pt. pl.* received, got 1043. (ONFr. *cach(i)er*, infl. by ME. *lach(che)*.]

calde. See calle.

calle *v.* call (summon, name) 610; *pr. pl.* 1882; calde, callyd *pt. sg.* 228, 490, 1184, etc.; *pp.* (*pass.*) 319. [ON. *kalla;* OE. (late) *ceallien*.]

callyd. See calle.

cam(e). See come.

can *v.* know, know how to, can *1 pr. sg.* 249, 350, 375; *3 pr. sg.* 169, 215, 598, etc.; *pr. pl.* 399, 417, 654; conne *pr. pl.* 1952; cowde, cowthe *pt. sg.* 59, 62, 524, etc.; *pt. pl.* 782. [OE. *can, con, cūþe*.]

can *v. auxil.* used with *infin.* as *equivalent of simple pt.* (*can dye* = died, 69) 21, 69, 138, etc. [Confused with ME. *gan*, did.]

candyll *n.* candle 1645. [OE. *cándel, cóndel*.]

cardynale *n.* cardinal 1395; cardynals *n. pl.* 2146. [OFr. *cardinal*.]

care *n.* woe, misery 687, 1450, 1596, etc.; anxiety 919, 2015. [OE. *caru*.]

care *v.* be concerned for 273. [OE. *carian*.]

carefull *adj.* full of grief, anxious 1577. [OE, *carful, cearful*, f. *caru*, care.]

caryage *n.* carriage 164. [ONFr. *cariage*.]

caste *n.* stroke, trick 1404, 2049. [ON. *kast*.]

caste *v.* cast, put 823. *3 pr. sg.* 1427, 1432, 1447, etc.; *pr. pl.*

1157, 1367; *pr. pl.* scheme 1782. [ON. *kasta.*]

castell *n.* castle 1230, 1548. [ONFr. *castel.*]

cawser *n.* originator, author 1580. [f. ME. *causen.*]

cawsyd *pt. sg.* 130, 1581, 1589; *pt. pl.* 2109. [ML. *causare.*]

certen *adj.* certain, sure, definite 306, 621, 1359, etc. [OFr. *certain.*]

certenly *adv.* certainly 1822. [OFr. *certain.*]

certys *adv.* certainly, truly 1123, 1357. [OFr. *certes.*]

chalenge *1 pr. sg.* defy, dare 685. [OFr. *ca-*, *chalonger*, *-langer*, *-lenger.*]

charbokull *n.* red-coloured precious stone 392. [OFr. *charbuncle.*]

chare *n.* chariot, car 592. [OFr. *char.*]

charge *imper.* burden 1008. [OFr. *charger.*]

chargyd *pt. pl.* burdened 125, 202. [OFr. *charger.*]

charyte *n.* charity, Christian love 1702; *for charyte* (formula used in prayers or requests) 1909. [OFr. *charité.*]

chasyng *pr. p.* chasing 1115, 1163. [OFr. *chac(i)er.*]

chaste *adj.* chaste, pure 2163. [ad. L. *costus*, *casta.*]

chastlayne *n.* governor of a castle 1984. [AF. *castelain.*]

chaumber, -ur, chawbur *n.* room (usually a small private room or bedroom) 229, 239, 833, etc. [OFr. *chambre.*]

chaumburlayne *n.* chamberlain, groom of the chamber 691. [OFr. *chamberlain.*]

chawnce *n.* chance, fortune 271; *per chawnce* perhaps 942. [OFr. *ch(e)ance.*]

chawngyd *pt. sg.* changed 819. [OFr. *cha(u)ng(i)er.*]

chefe *n.* leader, head 596. [OFr. *chef*, *chief.*]

chefe *adj.* chief, principal 17. [OFr. *ch(i)ef.*]

chekys *n. pl.* cheeks 578. [OE. *cē(a)c.*)

chere *n.* (expression of) face 812, 819. [OFr. *ch(i)ere.*]

cherye *n.* cherry 1761. [AF. *cherise*, taken as *pl.* form, but with the vowel of OE. *cirse*, *ciris-beam.*]

chese *pt. sg.* made his way 470. [OE. *céosan.*]

chesten *v.* to put in a chest 1474. [f. ME. *chest(e).*]

cheualry *n.* knighthood, knightly conduct 570. [OFr. *chevalerie.*]

chylde *n.* child 31, 36, 56, etc.; **chyldur** *n. pl.* 415. [OE. *cīld*, pl. *cildru.*]

chyualrous *adj.* chivalrous 2. [OFr. *chevalerie.*]

chorle *n.* man (of low birth) 1474. [OE. *ceorl.*]

church(e) *n.* church 1894, 1996. [OE. *cirice*, *circe.*]

cyte *n.* city 17, 116, 150, etc. [OFr. *cité.*]

claymed *pt. sg.* claimed 1192. [OFr. *clamer.*]

clave *pt. sg.* cleaned 1870. [OE. *clifan.*]

cled(d) *pt. sg.* clad 1691; *pp.* (*pass.*) 211. [OE. *clǣþan; pt. clædde.*]

clene *adv.* entirely 9, 277, 533, etc. [OE. *clǣne.*]

clere *n.* fair lady 78, 1797, 2007. [OFr. *cler.*]

clere *adj.* fair 574, 894, etc.; bright 326, 1225. [OFr. *cler.*]

clerkys, *n. pl.* priests 1363. [OFr. *clerc.*]

clyne *v.* incline or tend 1128. [OFr. *cliner*.]

cloystur *n.* monastery 1899, 2012. [OFr. *cloistre*.]

close *imper.* close, fasten 532. [OFr. *clos*, n.]

clothe *n.* cloth 823, 1157; *n. pl.* **cloþys, clothys** clothes 134, 182, 385; cloths 203. [OE. *claþ*.]

cloþyng, clothyng *n.* clothing 211, 1666. [f. ME. *clothe* v. + *yng*.]

cofurs *n. pl.* strong boxes 1182. [OFr. *cofre, coffre*.]

coghyth *3 pr. sg.* coughs 248. [Akin to MDu. *cuchen* and LG. *kuchen*, of echoic origins.]

colde *n.* cold 209. [OE. *cáld*.]

colde *adj.* cold 95. [OE. *cáld*.]

comawndyd *pt. sg.* commanded 283, 1180, 1555. [OFr. *commander*.]

come *v.* come 314, 1373, 1403, etc.; *1 pr. sg.* 434, 952, 1738; *3 pr. sg.* 1928; *pr. pl.* 147, 341, 504, etc.; *pr. subj. sg.* 253, 272; *pt. subj. sg.* 1110; *jussive subj.* 695; **cometh, comyth** *3 pr. sg.* 334, 488, 1068; **cam** *pt. sg.* 1368; **came** *pt. sg.* 7, 15, 165, etc.; *pt. pl.* 4, 192, 469, etc.; **comyn** *pp.* (*pass.*) 122, 236, 444, etc. [OE. *cuman, cóm, comon, cumen*.]

come *n.* arrival, coming 1577. [OE. *cyme*.]

comely *adj.* fair, beautiful. [OE. *cymlic*, infl. by assoc. with ME. *becomen*.]

cometh. See **come.**

comyn. See **come.**

comyng *vbl. n.* coming, advent 1528. See **come.**

comyth. See **come.**

condyte *n.* conduit 334. [OFr. *conduit*.]

confownde *v.* throw into con-

fusion or disorder 51, 938. [OFr. *confondre, confundre*.]

conne. See **can.**

conqueste *pp.* conquered 1199. [OFr. *conquerre*.]

cornell *n.* circlet worn on head 808. [AF. *coronal* (in sense of head of spear) and L. *coronál, -is* adj.]

corse *n.* body 1088. [OFr. *cors*.]

covenawnt *n.* agreement 1786. [OFr. *covenant*.]

couenawnt *adj.* agreed, agreeable, trustworthy 945. [OFr. *covenant, convenant*.]

couer *v.* shield, protect (*fig.*) 328; **couyrde** *pp.* (*pass.*) covered 163. [OFr. *cuvrir, courir*, later *couvrir*.]

cowde. See **can** *v.*

cowncelde *pt. sg.* advised, counselled 886, 943; *pt. pl.* 880. [OFr. *co(u)nseill(i)er*.]

cowncell, counsell *n.* counsel, advise 240, 260, 899, etc. [OFr. *co(u)nseil*.]

cowncell *n.* council 233, 251, 1097. [OFr. *cuncile*. In English confused with ME. *conseil*, later *counsel* until the sixteenth century.]

cowre *v.* cower 785. [Perhaps f. Norse; cf. Sw. *kura*, to squat.]

cowthe. See **can** *v.*

crachyd. See **crake.**

crake *v.* crack 92, 1476; **crakyd** *pt. pl.* 1850; **crachyd** *pp.* 2025. [OE. *cracian*, to crack (sound).]

creature *n.* creature 1537. [OFr. *creature*.]

crye *n.* shouting, clamour, proclamation 174, 544, 1518, etc. [OFr. *cri*.]

crye *v.* proclaim; *made to crye*, had proclaimed 551; **cryed** *pt. sg.* shouted 761. [OFr. *crier*.]

cryed. See **crye.**

crystalle *n.* crystal 326. [OFr. *cristal.*]

crysten *adj.* Christian 620. [OE. *crı̆sten.*]

crysten *v.* to administer baptism 36. [OE. *crı̆stnian.*]

crystendome *n.* Christian lands 17, 998. [OE. *crı̆sten, -dōm,* Christianity.]

crystyante *n.* Christianity 830, 903. [OFr. *crestienté.*]

crokyd *adj.* crooked 1977, 2025. [ON. *krókr, n.*]

crompylde *pp.* crimpled 1977. [Echoic, dim. of ME. *crump.*]

cronykyle *n.* chronicle 2174. [a. AF. *chronicle* = OFr. *cronique.*]

crosse *n.* cross 1903. [ON. *kross,* from OIr. *cros.*]

crowlande *pr. p.* trembling, quivering 844. [OFr. *croler, croller, crouler.*]

crowne *n.* crown of the head 92. [OFr. *coroune*; cf. ON. *krúna.*]

crowne *v.* crown 995, 1256; **crowned, -yd**; *pt. pl.* 1232; *pp.* (*pass.*) 1025, 1200, 1262. [AFr. *coruner, corouner.*]

crowned, -yd. See **crowne**.

cuntre *n.* land 115, 1196, 1491, etc.; **cuntreys** *n. pl.* 1221. [OFr. *cuntrié, contrée.*]

cursyd *pp.* cursed 1279. [OE. (late) *cŭrsian,* from OIr. *cúrsagim.*]

curten *n.* curtain 1628. [a. OFr.; L. *cortina.*]

curtes *adj.* gracious 129, 526, 810, etc. [OFr. *corteis, curteis.*]

curtesye *n.* courtesy, grace 300, 524. [OFr. *corteisie, curteisie.*]

curteslye *adv.* courteously 508, 1714. See **curtes**.

D

day(e) *n.* day 159, 311, 316, etc.;

on a day, one day 29, 1925; *mony a day,* many days, a long time 350; *oones on a day,* once upon a time 418; **dayes** *n. pl.* 43. [OE. *dæg.*]

dayes. See **day**.

dale *n.* (bottom of) valley 1398. [OE. *dæl.*]

dame *n.* dame, lady 1980, 2082, 2122. [OFr. *dame.*]

damysell *n.* damsel 58, 1464, 1843. [OFr. *damisele.*]

dar *1 pr. sg.* dare 737. [OE. *dearr, dorste.*] See **durste**.

dare *v.* cower 93. [OE. *darian.*]

date *n.* date 2174. [OFr. *date.*]

dawyd *pt. sg.* dawned 1029. [OE. *daȝian.*]

dedd *n.* death 976, 1582, 1821, etc. [A variant, usually northern, of ME. *deþ.*]

dedd *adj.* dead 34, 48, 406, etc. [OE. *dēad.*]

dede *n.* deed 882, 1621, etc.; *as obj. of do* 669. [OE. *dēd.*]

dedly *adj.* deadly 330. [OE. *dēadlic.*]

defendyd *pt. sg.* defended 2052. [OFr. *defendre.*]

deyse *n.* high table 1759. [AF. *deis* and CF. *dois.*]

delay *n.* delay 1362. [ad. Fr. *délai,* f. OFr. *delaier, delayer.*]

dele *n.* part, detail 251; *euery dele,* in every detail 251, 1733. [OE. *dæl.*] See **somedele**.

dele *v.* deal; *wyth them dele,* have to do with them 2115. [OE. *dælan.*]

delyte *n.* delight 868, 1943. [OFr. *delit.*]

delyuyr *imper.* set free, liberate 944. [OFr. *de(s)livrer.*]

delyurd *pt. sg.* delivered, set free 1737. [OFr. *de(s)livrer.*]

dentyd *pp.* inlaid 326. [OFr. *denté* and L. *dentātus.*]

depe *adj.* deep (sea) 132, 1298, 1417. [OE. *dēop.*]

dere *n.* harm 369. [OE. *daru,* infl. by *derian.*]

dere *adj.* dear, prized 72, 801, 1298, etc.; derrest *sup.* 1065. [OE. *deore.*]

dere *adv.* dearly, at great cost 244, 561, 1477, etc. [OE. *dēore.*]

deryd *pt. pl.* afflicted, hurt 657. [OE. *derian.*]

derne *adv.* stealthily 1956. [OE. *derne.*]

derrest. See dere *adj.*

derworthe *adj.* sumptuous 1956. [OE. *dēorwurþe.*]

desyre *n.* desire 763. [OFr. *desir.*]

dethe *n.* death 1043, 1688; dethys *n. gen.* 915. [OE. *deaþ.*]

dethys. See dethe.

deuyll *n.* devil 731, 1991. [OE. *dēofol.*]

dewkys *n. pl.* dukes 188, 319, 838, etc. [OFr. *duc.*]

dyd. See do.

dye *v.* die 69, 257, 356, etc.; dyed *pt. sg.* 31, 1430, 1511, etc.; *pt. pl.* 644, 1041. [ON. *deyja.*]

dyed. See dye.

dyght, dyȝt *pt. pl.* arranged, prepared 795; dressed 1672; *pp.* 1301, 1394, 1446; *to dedd ys dyght,* put to death 930. [OE. *dihtan.*]

dyntys *n. pl.* strokes, blows 653, 661. [OE. *dynt.*]

dyscownfortyd *pp.* distressed, grieved 1718. [OFr. *desconforter.*]

dyscrye *v.* write 60. [OFr. *descrire,* var. of *descrivre.*]

dysheryted *pp.* disinherited 940. [OFr. *desheriter.*]

dyssees *n.* death 618. [L. *decessus,* f. *decedere.*]

dystawnce *n.* quarrelling; *wythowt distawnce,* indisputably 2138. [OFr. *destance.*]

dystroye *v.* destroy 116, 220, 278, etc. [OFr. *destruire.*]

do(o) *v.* 235, 283, 641, etc.; *3 pr. sg.* 272; *pr. pl.* 845, 905, 1769, etc.; dyd, dud *pt. sg.* 251, 726, 854, etc.; *pt. pl.* 369, 802, 803, etc.; done, doone *pp.* 656, 689, 772, etc.; *haue done . . .,* get it done, be quick 210, 223. [OE. *dōn.*]

doghtely *adv.* mightily, valiantly 1169. [f. *doghty(e).*]

doghty(e) *adj.* doughty, brave 256, 665, 680, etc.; as *n.* hero 644, 713; doghtyar *sup.* 23. [OE. *dohtig.*]

doghtyar. See doghtye.

doghtur, -yr *n.* daughter 23, 72, 90, etc. [OE. *dohtor.*]

dolefull *adj.* doleful 582, 1859. [OFr. *dol, doel, deol, diol + -ful.*]

dome *n.* judgement, doom 153. [OE. *dōm.*]

done. See do(o).

doone. See do.

dore *n.* door 1480, 1610, 1636, etc. [OE. *duru, dor.*]

down(e) *adv.* down 467, 474, 488, etc. [OE. *of dūne, adūne.*]

dowte *n.* fear 457, 863. [OFr. *doute.*]

dowve *n.* dove 422, 424, 487, etc. [OE. **dūfe; ON. dúfa.*]

dragon *n.* dragon 599. [OFr. *dragon.*]

drawe *v. intr.* approach 225; drewe *pt. sg.* drew to, became 1456; droghe *pt. sg.* drew, approached 2016. [OE. *dragan.*]

drawe *v. tr.* pull 532; drewe *pt. sg.* 722; drowe *pt. pl.* 142; drawyn *pp.* 1224. [OE. *dragan.*]

drawyn. See drawe.

dredd, drede *n.* fear 885; *for drede for fear* 837, 1601, 1611. [From OE. *drǣdan.*]

drede *adj.* fearful 966. [f. prec.]

drede *pr. subj. sg.* (might) dread 1622. [OE. *drǣdan*.]

dredyd *pt. pl.* feared 153. [OE. *drǣdan*.]

drery *adj.* sad, melancholy 798, 1029, 2105; **dreryar** *comp.* 1838. [OE. *dreoriʒ*.]

dreryar. See **drery.**

drewe. See **drawe.**

drye *adj.* dry 1305, 1886. [OE. *drȳge*.]

drynke *n.* drink 1760; *esp. in mete and drink.* [f. OE. *drincan*.] See **mete.**

droghe. See **drawe.**

drowe. See **drawe.**

drowned *pt. sg.* drowned 378; *3 pt. pl.* 1872; *pp. (pass.)* 1736, 1865, 1878. [See *MED.*]

drowpe *v.* drop 93. [OE. *dropian*.]

dud. See **do(o).**

durste *pt. sg.* dared 429, 1047, 1233, etc.; *3 pt. pl.* 457. [OE. *dearr, durron; dorste*.] See **dar.**

dwelle *v.* live, dwell 303, 428, 452, etc.; **dwellyth** *3 pr. sg.* 1951; **dwellyd** *pt. sg.* 1591, 1613, 1913, etc. [OE. *dwellan*.]

dwellyd. See **dwelle.**

dwellyth. See **dwelle.**

E

eere, ere *n.* ear 1753, 2116. [OE. *ēare, ēaran* (pl.).]

effect *n.* essential content, sum and substance 346. [L. *effectus*, OFr. *effect*.]

efte *adv.* a second time, once more 520; afterwards, then 1200. [OE. *eft*.]

egyll *n.* eagle 392. [OFr. *egle, aigle*, f. L. *aquila*.]

eyder. See **eyther.**

eye *n.* eye 1588, 1748; **eyen, yen** *n. pl.* eyes 353, 2027. [OE. *ēage*, pl. *egan*.]

eyen. See **eye.**

eyen *n. pl.* young hawks 845. [Var. of *nyesse* (ODan. *nyas*) and *eyes* (ODan. *eyas*), a nestling hawk; OFr. *niais* nestling.]

eylyth *3 pr. sg.* troubles, afflicts 1300. [OE. *eglian*.]

eyther *pron.* either 1791; each one 675; *eyther odur, eyder odur* each the other, one another 47, 1450. [OE. *ǣghwæþer, ǣgþer*.]

eke *adv.* also 1919. [OE. *ēc*.]

elde *n.* age 94, 555, 973. [OE. *éldo*.]

elder *comp. adj.* older 671. [f. *elde*.]

eldyst *sup. adj.* oldest 896. [f. *elde*.]

ellys *adj.* following a limiting noun, *noght ellys* 932 nothing else. [f. adv.]

ellys *adv.* otherwise 1358, 1735. [f. OE. *elles*.]

ellys *conj.* unless 217. [f. adv.]

emperes, -ys *n.* consort of the emperor 34, 2150. [OFr. *emper-(e)ris, emperesse*.]

emperowre *n.* emperor 19, 25, 35, etc.; **emperowrs** *gen. n.* 173, 322. [OFr. *empereor*.]

emperowrs. See **emperowre.**

empyre *n.* realm 74, 764, 1208, etc. [OFr. *empire, empere*.]

encheson *n.* reason or grounds (for a given opinion, decision, or act); *encheson why* 102. [OFr. *enchaison*.]

encresyth *3 pr. sg.* grows, prospers 1950. [AF. *encreisser, encresser*.]

ende *n.* end, concluding part 600, 1745, 1794; conclusion 2178. [OE. *ende*.]

endyd *pp.* ended, ceased 697. [OE. *ge-endian, endian*.]

endyth *3 pr. sg.* ends 2185. [OE. *ge-endian, endian*.]

enhabyted *pt. sg.* inhabited, dwelled 9. [OFr. *enhabiter*.]

enmye *n.* enemy 1064; **enmyes** *n. pl.* 428, 799. [OFr. *enemi, anemi*.]

enqueryd *pp.* asked 1315. [OFr. *enquerre*.]

entent *n.* mind, heart, spirit 1997. [OFr. *entente*.]

enteryd *pt. sg.* buried 869. [OFr. *enter(r)er*.]

entyrd(e) *pt. pl.* entered 151, 191. [OFr. *entrer*.]

erbys *n. pl.* herbs 1549. [OFr. *erbe*.]

erles, -ys *n. pl.* nobles 188, 838. [OE. *eorl*.]

errande *n.* errand 1775; petition, prayer 1855. [OE. *ærende;* ON. *erendi*.]

erthely *adj.* wordly 1667. [OE. *eorþlic;* ME. *ĕrthe*.]

este *n.* east 1414. [OE. *ēast*.]

estyrs *n. pl.* dwellings, buildings 293. [OFr. *estre;* ? also OFr. *estree*, road.]

ete 1 *pr. sg.* eat 1463; *pt. sg.* ate 525, 1468, 1471. [OE. *etan*.]

etyn *pp.* eaten 263. [OE. *etan*.]

euenynge *n.* evening 1456. [OE. *ēfnung*.] See **euyn**.

euery *pron. euery oon*, everyone 155. [OE. *æfre*.]

euery *adj.* every 161, 316, 362, etc. [OE. *æfre*.]

euerychon *pron.* one and all 359, 1555. [*euery* + ME. *on*.]

euerydele *adv.* completely, thoroughly 251, 1733. [*euery* + *dele*.]

euyll *n.* misfortune 1616, 1950; disease 1933, 1990, 1994; sin 1983; *n. pl.* diseases 1919. [OE. *yfel*.]

euyll *adj.* bad 254, 815, 876, etc.; defective 1824. [OE. *yfel*.]

euyll *adv.* badly 715. [OE. *yfele*.]

euyn *n.* evening 114. [OE. *ēfen*.]

euyn *adj.* smooth 327. [OE. *efen, efn*.]

euyn *adv.* straight, directly 445, 470, 747, etc. [OE. *efen, efne*.]

euyr *adv. with particularising force:* at any time at all 139, 308, 717, etc.; always, at all times 149, 167, 172, etc.; forever 1386; *comb. and phr.* **euyr:** *euyrmore*, for ever afterward 1220, 1808; *foreuyr*, for all time 1341; *euyrsyth*, ever since 2105; in a comparison: at any time, in any way or manner *as . . . as euyr* 2142; at any time at all 2181. [OE. *æfre*.]

euyrmore. See **euyr**.

F

face *n.* face 566, 1540, 1809. [OFr. *face*.]

fadur *n.* father 115, 180, 250, etc.; applied to God 1124, 1676; applied to the Pope 1421; **fadurs** *n. pl.* 649; *gen. n.* 246, 762, 818, etc. [OE. *fæder*.]

fadurles *adj.* without a father 1220. [OE. *fæderlēas*.]

faght. See **fyght**.

fayle *n.* failure 137, 1310. [OFr. *faille*.]

fayleste, faylyst *pr. pl.* lack, want 555; disappoint 1854. [OFr. *faillir, falir*.]

faylyd *pt. pl.* failed 1831. [OFr. *faillir, falir*.]

fayne *adj.* joyful, happy 294, 967, 1074, etc.; *for fayne*, for joy 967. [OE. *fægen*.]

fayre *adj.* beautiful, attractive 33. [OE. *fæger*.]

falle *v.* fall 1067, 1081; **felle** *pt. sg.* 474, 632, 699, etc.; happened 418; *pt. pl.* 48, 677. [OE. *fallan* (*fēol, fēollon, feallen*).]

fals, false *adj.* disloyal, treacherous

737, 751, 1089, etc.; **falsyst** *sup.* 716. [OFr. *fals.*]

falsehed(d) *n.* deceitfulness 1076, 1128. [From *fals.*]

fame *n.* good reputation 252. [OFr. *fame.*]

famysched *pp.* (*pass.*) starved 875. [Prob. from AF; cp. OFr. *afamer.*]

fande. See **fynde.**

farde. See **fare.**

fare *n.* behaviour, conduct 270, 1957; fortune 1580, 1877. [OE. *faru.*]

fare *v.* advance 593; go 833, 1599, 1707, etc.; journey, travel 432, 1014; **farde** *pt. sg.* 563, 2080; *pt. pl.* 1683; **fared** *pt. sg.* behaved 660. [OE. (i) *faran* (*fōr, faren*); (ii) *fēran* (*ferde*).]

fared. See **fare.**

farre *adj.* distant 891. [OE. *feor(r).*]

faste *adv.* quick 705, 1053, 1319, etc.; tight, firm 858, 1638, 2052. [OE. *fæste.*]

faste *pp.* (*pass.*) bestowed 404. [OE. (*ge-*)*fæstan.*]

fasten *imper.* set 851. [OE. (*ge-*) *fæstan.*]

faxe *n.* hair of the head 1543. [OE. *feax.*]

febull *adj.* unhappy, sorry 2108. [OFr. *feble.*]

feche *v.* go after, get 219; *imper.* 1016. [OE. *fetian, feccan.*]

fed *pt. pl.* supplied with food 1552. [OE. *fēdan.*]

fedyll *n.* a bowed stringed instrument, viol, violin 1012. [OE. *fipele.*]

feele *adj.* bold, audacious 593; treacherous 2112. [OFr. *fel.*]

feyre *n.* good fortune 317. [Partly f. OE. *fæger* n., partly f. *fæger* adj.]

feyre *adj.* beautiful, fair 28, 37,

79, etc.; **feyrest(e)** *sup.* 195, 307, 1250, etc. [OE. *fæger.*]

feyre *adv.* splendidly 141, 175, 295. [OE. *fægre.*]

feyrenes *n.* beauty 349. [OE. *fægernes.*]

feyrest. See **feyre.**

feythe *n.* in oaths: *in feythe*, truly 1769. [OFr. *feid* (early), later *fei.*]

fekyll *adj.* of human beings: inconstant, changeable. [OE. *ficol.*]

felde, fylde *n.* plain 380, 531, 632, etc.; **feldys** *n. pl.* 568. [OE. *feld.*]

felle *n.* the skin as one of the parts of the body, *fleshe and felle* 309 [OE. *fel(l).*]

felle *adj.* fierce in combat 427; grievous, virulent 1971. [OFr. *fel.*]

felle. See **falle.**

felowe *n.* man, chap 928; **felows** *n. pl.* comrades 503. [ON.; cp. OI. *felagi* share-holder.]

fende *n.* mortal foe 1669. [OE. *fēond.*]

fende *jussive subj.* defend 1441. [Aphet. **defend.**]

fere *n.* of persons: in a group, in company, together *in fere* 443, 461, 503, etc.; **ferys** *n. pl.* forces 461. [OE. *gefēr*, company.]

fere *n.* spouse, mate 81. [OE. *gefēra.*]

fere *n.* fear 822, 923, 1906. [OE. *fēr.*]

fe(e)re *v.* fear 462, 2004, 2084. [OE. (*ge-*)*færen.*]

ferly *n.* astonishment, *have ferly* be astonished 431. [From ME. adj. *fērlī*, OE. **feorlic*, strange.]

ferre *adj.* much 671. [OE. *feor(r).*]

ferre *adv.* far, afar 1, 104, 1482. [O.E (i) *feorh;* (ii) *feorran.*]

ferse *adj.* ferocious, wild 427. [OFr. *fers.*]

feste *n.* feast, banquet 2128. [OFr. *feste.*]

festurd *pp.* ulcered 1943. [From ME. *festre* n.; OFr. *festrir.*]

fete *n. pl.* feet 640. [OE. *fōt*; pl. *fēt.*]

fett *pt. sg.* fed 1760. [OE. *fēdan.*]

feturs *n. pl.* shackles, fetters 1148. [OE. *feotor.*]

fyftene *card. num.* fifteen 391. [OE. *fiftēnē.*]

fyfty *card. num.* fifty 458; a set of fifty persons 466. [OE. *fiftig.*]

fyght *n.* fight 485, 498, 591, etc. [OE. *fe(o)hte.*]

fyght *v.* fight 531, 548, 705, etc.; **faght** *pt. sg.* 44; *pt. pl.* 475, 679, 1039, etc.; **fyghtande, fyghtyng** *pr. p.* 708, 744, 925; *used as n.* 681, 697. [OE. *fe(o)htan (fæht, fuhton, fohten).*]

fylde. See **felde.**

fylle *n.* one's heart's desire 1405. [OE. *fyll.*]

fylle *pt. subj. pl.* (might) fill 1182. [OE. *fyllan.*]

fyllyd *pp.* (*pass.*) filled 328. [OE. *fyllan.*]

fynde *v.* find, encounter; *1 pr. sg.* 2117; **fande** *pt. sg.* 714, 1697; *pt. pl.* 1230; *used as infin., That was so feyre to fande* 1656. [OE. *findan (fand, fundon, funden).*]

fyne *adj.* consummate in virtue 2123. [OFr. *fin.*]

fyne *adv.* in the end, at last 1137. [Aphet. form of ME. *afin.*]

fyre *n.* fire 73, 97, 500, etc. [OE. *fȳr.*]

fyred *pp.* kindled (a fire) 709. [From **fyre** n.]

fyrmament *n.* sky 46. [OFr. *firmament.*]

fysches *n. pl.* fishes 390. [OE. *fisc*; pl. *fiscas, fixas.*]

fyve *card. num.* five 991; *before*

'thousand' 454; *with a common noun* 913, 1848. [OE. *fīf(e).*]

flankys *n. pl.* sides of the abdomen 109. [CF. *flanc.*]

fledd(e). See **flee.**

flee *v.* run away, flee 783, 1041, 1381; **fledd(e)** *pt. sg.* 723, 1352; *pt. pl.* 497. [OE. *flēon.*]

flemed *pp.* (*pass.*) banished, exiled 2087. [OE. *(ge-)flēman.*]

flesche *n.* flesh 94, 309, 1517. [OE. *flǣsc.*]

flete *v.* float, drift 1989; **flett** *pt. pl.* drifted, sailed 137; **fletyd** *pp.* floated 1874, 2102. [OE. *flēotan (flēat).*]

fletyd. see **flete.**

flett. See **flete.**

flyre *v.* mock, sneer, 1767. [Cp. Norw. *flire,* giggle, grin.]

flode *n.* river 131, 390. [OE. *flōd.*]

flowre *n.* flower 194, 616, 901, etc.; the most excellent 570. [OFr. *flour, flor, flur.*]

fode *n.* food 1552. [OE. *fōda.*]

folde *n.* earth, world 342, 758, 873. [OE. *fólde.*]

folde *v.* fold 1323; embrace 1849. [OE. *fáldan.*]

folke *n.* (*coll. or pl.*) people, persons 141, 318, 575, etc. [OE. *folc.*]

folowe *v.* follow 547; *jussive subj.* 1703. [OE. *folgian.*]

fomen *n. pl.* enemies 719. [OE. *fāhmon.*]

fomes *n. pl.* seas 137. [OE. *fām.*]

fonde *pt. sg.* found 631, 748, 1138, etc. [OE. *findan.*]

fonge *pp.* seized 1829. [OE. *fōn.*]

for *prep.* as regards 6; *with infin.* 24, 64, 101, etc.; for the space of 43; for the sake of 52, 183, 558, etc.; on account of 94, 96, 252, etc.; as 125, 302; suitable for 134; in spite of 270, 282. [OE. *for.*]

for *conj.* because 716, 1059, 1128, etc. [From prep.]

for. See **fowre**.

forbede *imper.* prohibit, stop; in exclamations; *Jhesu forbede* 243; *God forbede hyt* 267, *God forbede* 904. [OE. *forbēodan*.]

forbode *3 pt. pl.* prohibited 955. [OE. *forbēodan*.]

foreste *n.* wilderness 1448, 1521, 1708. [OFr. *forest*.]

forgeue *v.* forgive 1837; *pp.* 1286. [OE. *forgefan*.] See **geue**.

forjusted *pt. pl.* defeated in battle 466. [Cp. *juste*.]

formast(e) *adj.* first 172, 375. [From **forme**; L. *forma*, OFr. *fourme*.]

forme *n.* shape 1004, 1101. [L. *forma*, OFr. *fourme*.]

forne *prep.* on behalf of, on account of 67. [From adv. *fŏrn*; OE. *foran, forne*.]

forows *n. pl.* ditches, trenches 746. [OE. *furh*.]

forronne *pp.* overcome with walking 1902. [OE. *for* + *runnen*.]

forty *num.* forty; *cardinal as adj.* 121, 124, 443, etc. [OE. *fēowertig*.]

forþy, forthy *adv.* on that account 96, 302, 1022, etc. [OE. *forþȳ, forþī*.]

fote *n.* foot 388, 1139, 1366, etc. [OE. *fōt*; pl. *fēt*.]

forthe *adv.* forward, ahead, onward 138, 373, 375, etc. [OE. *forþ*.]

fowle *a;j.* ugly 920, 2178; **fowlest** *sup.* 2021. [OE. *fūl*.]

fowlys *n. pl.* birds 46. [OE. *fugol, fuglas*.]

fownde *v.* proceed, set out 281, 371. [OE. *fundian*.]

fownde *pt. sg.* found 1459; *pt. pl.* 451, 705; *pp.* 2126. [OE. *findan*.]

fownder *n.* the founder (of a country) 11, 1888. [From L. *fundator*.]

fowre *num.* four 991. [OE. *fēower*.]

fowrtenyght *n.* two weeks 1735, 2158. [From the early ME. phrase.]

fra. See **from**.

frawde *n.* dishonest act 1820. [OFr. *fraude*.]

fre. See **free**.

fre(e) *adj. of a people:* politically independent 318; noble in character, gracious 480, 900, 1096, etc.; *as n.;* person of noble character 1910. [OE. *frēo*.]

frende *n.* friend 126, 1065, 1803. [OE. *frēond*.]

fresche *adj. of water:* not salt 342; **frescher** *comp. of colours:* brighter 158. [OFr. *freis*; fem. *fresche*; cp. OE. *fersc*.]

freschly *adv.* boldly 548, 1042. [From **fresche**.]

fro(o). See **from**.

from *prep.* from 2043; **fra** 1110, 1737; **fro(o)** 15, 200, 209, etc. [OE. *fram* and ON. *frá*.]

fulfylle *v.* comply with, execute 237. [OE. *fulfyllan*.]

full *intensive with adv.* very 152, 273, 505, etc.; *intensive with adj.* very, most 156, 162, 174, etc.; *adv. with num.* fully 189; *adj.* filled 425. [OE. *ful(l)*.]

furste *ord. num. as adj.* first 8, 139, 623, etc.; *ord. num.* 1102; *altherfurste* first of all 292, 1804. [OE. *fyrst*.] See **alther**.

further *adv.* to a greater degree 411. [OE. *furþor, forþor*.]

G

ga. See **go**.

gabuls *n. pl.* heavy ropes used

on ships 1862. [Var. of ML *cabulus*.]

gaf(e). See geue.

gayne *n.* advantage, help 147, 149. [ON. (cp. OI. *gegn* adj.) and OFr. *gäin*.]

gayne *adj.* of persons: ready, well-disposed 491. [ON. *gegn*.]

gayne *adv.* close by, near 1985. [From *adj.*]

galow(e)tree *n.* gallows, place of execution 1724, 2090. [OE. *galga*.]

galows(e) *n.* gallows, place of execution 1711, 1737, 2092. [OE. *galga*.]

game *n.* revelry, amusement, 266. [OE. *gamen, gomen*.]

gare *v. auxil. with infin.:* to cause (something to be done) 92; gart *pp.* 36, 56, 74; prepared (one-self) 1132, 1363. [ON.; cp. OI. *göra, görva, gera, gerva*. Cp. also OE. *gearwian*, ME. *yaren*.]

garson *n.* retainer, follower 118, 626, 779; garsons *n. pl.* 256, 371, 397, etc. [OFr. *garçon*.]

gate. See gete.

gates *gen. n.* journey's, expedition's. 149 [ON.; cp. OI. *gata*.]

gatys *n. pl.* roads 1419. [ON.; cp. OI. *gata*.]

gaue. See geue.

geest *n.* an invited guest 1012. [ON.; cp. OI. *gestr*.]

gente *adj.* graceful, attractive 395, 479, 971; *adv.* courteously 2133. [OFr. *gente*.]

gentyl(l) *adj.* of noble rank or birth 444, 1266, 1654, etc. [OFr. *gentil*.]

gere *n.* fighting equipment, armour 456; the equipment of a riding horse 678; wearing apparel 1559, 1754. [ON.; cp. OI. *görvi, gervi*. Also cp. OE. *gearive*.]

gete *v.* bring 1473; *3 pr. sg.* obtain 269; gate *pt. sg.* went 16; *pt. pl.* obtained, got 2164; getyn *pp.* got 968, 1165, 1978, etc. [ON.; cp. OI. *geta*; pt. *gat*, pl. *gatum*; pp. *getenn*.]

getyn. See gete.

gethe *n. only in phr.: yn a gethe*, spiritedly, hastily [ON.; cp. OI. *geð*, mind, spirit; OE. *ge(h)þu*.]

geue, geve *v.* give, bestow gratuitously 224, 616, 691, etc.; *3 pr. sg.* 440; geuyth *3 pr. sg.* 305; gaf(e), gaue *pt. sg.* 693, 961, 1234, etc.; *pt. pl.* 1729, 2130; yf *pr. subj.* 1474; geuyn *pp.* 917. [ON. *gefa*; OSw. *gifa*. See *OED*.]

geuyn. See geue.

geuyth. See geue.

gyf *conj.* if 1271. [Northern var. of ME *ȝif*.]

gyftys *n. pl.* gifts 305, 1729, 2156. [ON. *gift*.]

gyle *n.* crafty trick 1791. [OFr. *guile*.]

gylle *n.* gully 1417. [ON. *gil*.]

gylte *n.* transgression, misdeed 556. [OE. *gylt*.]

gyltles *adv.* guiltless 1678, 2088. [From gylte(OE. *gylt*).]

gladd *adj.* joyful 1317. [OE. *glæd*, Merc. **gled*.]

glemed *pt. sg.* radiated, shone 381, 1709. [From ME. *glem* n., a beam.]

glyde *v.* pass through (the sea, etc.) 1053; glode *pt. sg.* 1709. [OE. *glidan (glād, glidon, gliden)*.]

glyste *pt. sg.* glared, stared 1657. [OE. *glisnian*.]

glyteryng *pr. p.* glittering 157. [Blend of ON. (cp. OI. *glitra* to glitter) and OE. (cp. *gliddrian* to slip, be unstable.).]

glode. See glyde.

go(o) *v.* go 848, 944, 949, etc.; *pr. pl.* 233, 259; goys *3 pr. sg.*

547, 747; **gon(e), goon** v. walk 1386, 1920 *ryde or gone*, ride on horseback or walk 1; *pp.* 862; (*pass.*) 358, 1009. [OE. *gān.*] See **ȝede, ȝode.**

god(d) n. God, 244 267, 405; **god(d)ys** n. pl. 955; *gen. n.* 1422, 1892. [OE. *god.*]

gode adj. good 97, 102, 393, etc. [OE. *gŏd*, adj.]

godhede n. divinity 1680. [From *God*; also cp. OE. *godhād.*]

goys. See **go.**

golde n. the metal gold 86, 125, 134, etc. [OE. *góld.*]

gome n. man 26, 968. [OE. *guma.*]

gon(e). See **go.**

goon. See **go.**

goost n. soul of a dead person 778; *holy goost*, the Holy Ghost 1676. [OE. *gāst.*]

gowte n. gout 1919. [OFr. *gote, goute*, and ML. *gutta.*]

grace n. God's favour 1458, 1511, 1806, etc. [OFr. *grace.*]

graceles adj. worthless, contemptible 1963. [From *grace.*]

graye adj. grey 1776. [OE. *grēg* and ON. (cp. OI. *grār*).]

graspyd *pt. pl.* reached for 678. [? OE. *grǣpsan*; cp. Norw. *krafse.*]

graunt, grawnt adj. *used as noun*, great one, king 26, 127, 298, etc. [OE. *grēat.*] See **grete.**

graunt v. concede (something to someone) 1074, 1721; *pr. pl.* permit 1194; **grauntyd** *pt. sg.* permitted 624. [OFr. *granter*, var. of *crēanter.*]

grauntyd. See **graunt.**

grefe n. hardship, distress 1243, 1280, 1994. [CF. *gref* and CF. *grief, grieve.*]

grekys n. pl. Greeks 709; *gen. n.* 1884. [OE. *Grēc.* pl. *Grēcas.*]

grene adj. green 1449. [OE. *grēne.*]

grete adj. great, large 50, 69, 94, etc.; **grettyst** *sup.* 903, 998. [OE. *grēat.*] See **graunt, grawnt.**

grete 1 *pr. sg.* greet 127. [OE. *grētan*, weak.]

grettyst. See **grete.**

greue v. injure 954, 1460. [OFr. *grever.*]

grome n. a youth, young man. [Prob. OE. **grŏm, *grōma*) Akin to OE. *grōwan*. Infl. by OE. *guma.*]

grones *3 pr. sg.* groans 248. [OE. *grānian.*]

grope v. feel 1631. [OE. *grāpian.*]

grownde, grounde n. ground 48, 381, 699, etc. [OE. *grúnd.*]

gruchyng *vbl. n.* grumbling 91. [OFr. *gr(o)ucher.*]

ȝ

ȝaa adv. yea, yes 1734. [OE. *gǣ, gē(a).*]

ȝatys n. pl. gates 151, 532, 857, etc. [OE. *gæt* (pl. *gatu*).]

ȝede *pt. sg.* went 240; *pt. pl.* 1674. [OE. *ēode.*]

ȝelde v. take vengeance on 542. [OE. *geldan.*]

ȝelle v. utter a loud cry 1486. [OE. *ȝellan.*]

ȝelowe adj. yellow 1544. [OE. *ȝeolu.*]

ȝeme v. govern, control. [OE. *ȝieman.*]

ȝerde n. branch of a tree 1516. [OE. **ȝiérd, ȝyrd, ȝird.*]

ȝerne adv. quickly 1950, 1959. [OE. *ȝéorne.*]

ȝylde v. yield 528; 1 *pr. pl.* 1208; **ȝyldyd** *pt. sg.* handed over 1226; *pr. subj. sg.* 1411; *pr. subj. pl.* 515; *ȝyldyd þe goost*, died 778. [OE. *geldan.*]

ȝynge adj. young 1391, 1568, 1731, etc. [OE. *ȝiong.*]

ȝyt *adv.* yet, still 5, 354, 697, etc. [OE. *gēt, gȳt.*]

ȝode *pt. sg.* went 606, 1610, 1627, etc. [Prob. altered form of OE.] See ȝede.

ȝonder *adj.* over there, away there 229. [ME *ȝonder, ȝender,* corresp. to OS. *gendra,* adj., on this side.]

ȝondur *adv.* there 815. [OS *gendra,* adj., on this side.]

ȝowle *n.* December or January 1895. [OE. *ȝeól.*]

H

habyte *n.* monastic habit 1910. [OFr. *(h)abit.*]

had. See haue, have.

hadyst. See haue, have.

hafte *n.* hilt of a knife 1634. [Merc. **heft* and ON. (cp. OI. *hepti*).]

hale. See hole.

halfe *n.* a half part of an object 358. [OE. *half.*]

halle *n.* royal residence 187, 337; large public room in a palace 192, 262, 325, etc.; halles *n. pl.* 295. [OE. *hal(l).* Also cp. OFr. *hale.*]

hals *n.* neck 1472, 2091. [OE. *hals.*]

hame, home *n.* a plot of enclosed ground, home 225, 265, 364, etc. [OE. *hām.*]

hamperde *pt. pl.* enclosed 1173. [? From ME. *hamper* n., a receptacle.]

hande, honde *n.* human hand 109, 161, 238, etc.; handys, hondys *n. pl.* 817, 836, 838, etc. [OE. *hónd, hánd* and ON. (cp. OI. *hönd*).]

handylde *pt. sg.* touched 2110. [OE. *handlian.*]

hange, hynge *v.* hang 1628, 1712, 1970; hangyd *pt. sg.* 1514, 1532, 2058; *pp.* 1747. [OE. *hangian* and ON. (cp. OI, *hengja*).]

happe *n.* luck, fortune 2106. [ON. (cp. OI. *happ*); also cp. OE. *gehæp* adj.]

happe *v.* embrace 112. [? Blend of ME. *lappen* and OFr. *happer,* to seize.]

harbarde, harberde *pt. sg.* sheltered 1969, 1985. [From ME. *herberwe* n. temporary dwelling. Also cp. OE. *herebeorgian,* to lodge.]

harburgens *n. pl.* coats or jackets of mail 637. [OFr. *hauberjon.*]

harburgerye *n.* temporary lodging-place 1758. [OFr. *herbergerie, herberge.* Cf. ME. *herberwe.*]

harde *adj.* difficult to bear, full of hardship 435; near, close by 562, 636, 676. [OE. *hearde.*]

harde. See here.

hardy *adj.* strong in battle, stout-hearted 6, 75, 545, etc. [OFr. *hardi.*]

hare *n.* hair of the head 87, 2058. [OE. *hēr* and ON. (cp. OI. *hār*).]

harme *n.* injury, damage 284, 1325. [OE. *hearm.*]

harnes *n.* body armour 104, 1046. [OFr. *harneis.*]

harpe *n.* harp 63, 1012. [OE. *hearpe* and OFr. *harpe.*]

harte *n.* heart of a human being or an animal 528, 754, 770, etc. [OE. *heorte.*]

harteblode *n.* lifeblood 633. [From *harte* and ME. *blod.*]

haste *n.* speed in phr., *in haste* 779, speedily 779. [Cp. OFr. *en haste.*]

haste. See haue, have .

hastely *adv.* quickly, in a hurry 210, 215, 223, etc. [From *haste.*]

hasty *adj.* swift, quick 73. [From *haste.*]

hastyd *pt pl.* hurried 1959. [OFr. *haster.*]

hate *adj.* high in temperature, hot 768. [OE. *hāt.*]

hath. See haue, have.

haue, have *v.* possess, own 81, 227, 266, etc.; *1 pr. sg.* have (an abstraction) 212, 400, 431; *pr. pl.* 932; *haue need*, to be under compulsion 230; *haue done*, to finish 210, 223; *finite v. as auxil. before pp.* 78, 106, 199, etc.; haste *2 pr. sg.* 1212, 1383, 1507, etc.; hath *3 pr. sg.* 355, 510, 556, etc.; had(d) *pt. sg.* 28, 71, 97, etc.; *pt. pl.* 263, 466, 680, etc.; hadyst *2 pt. sg.* 1747. [OE. *habban, haf-.*]

hauyn *n.* refuge 139. [OE. *hæfen,* port and ON. (cp. OI. *höfn*).]

hawkys *n. pl.* hawks 842, 1523. [Merc. *heafuc.*]

haylestones *n. pl.* hailstones 641. [OE. *hagol-stān.*]

haylsyd, haylese(y)d *pt. sg.* greeted (with respect) 193, 1714, 2000. [ON.; cp. OI. *heilsa.*]

he *pron.* he 22, 28, 36, etc.; *used indefinitely*: he that, he who, the one who 279, 1340; hym *acc. and dat.* him: *as object of a v. or prep.* 116, 120, 126, etc.; *dative of interest* 228; hymselfe himself: *emphatic pron. having same referent as subject* 374, 993; hys *adj.* his: *modifying a n. which denotes something owned or in one's charge* 74, 116, 117, etc.; *modifying a n. denoting a relation* 38, 72, 90; *modifying a n. denoting a part* 94, 95, 96. [OE. *hē; him,* dat.; *his,* gen.]

hed(d), hede *n.* human head 134, 181, 744, etc.; leader, chief 999,

1668; hedys *n. pl.* 640. [OE. *hēafod.*]

hede. See hed(d), hede.

hedeows *adj.* horrible 1657. [OFr. *hidous, hideus.*]

hedur *adv.* hither, here 254, 511. [OE. *hider.*]

hedurcome *n.* coming to this place 515. [From *hedur* adv. and *come* n.]

hedurward *adv.* in this direction 255. [OE. *hiderw(e)ard.*]

heere. See heyre.

heyle *v.* salute, hail 989. [From ME. *heil* adj., interj.]

heyre, heere *n.* heir 38, 651, 911, etc. [AF. *heir, aire.*]

helde *v.* move, go, 1713. [OE. *hēldan.*]

helde *pt. pl.* contained 1380. [OE.; cp. A. *haldan (heold, halden).*]

hele *n.* health 1967. [OE. *hǣlu, hǣl.*]

hele *v.* cure, heal 1982, 2106; helyd *pt. sg.* 1922, 1942. [OE. *hǣlan*; ? also cp. OI. *heila,* to make whole.]

helyd. See hele.

helle *n.* hell 1487, 1669. [OE. *hel, helle.*]

helme *n.* helmet 1939. [OE. *helm* and ON. (cp. OI. *hjalmr*).]

helpe *n.* assistance 482, 489, 1847, etc. [OE. *help.*]

helpe *v.* to rescue, preserve 976; *God helpe . . .* 405. [OE. *helpan* and ON. (cp. OI. *hjālpa*).]

hende *adj.* courtly, refined 129, 226; near, close by 1800, 1998. [OE. *gehende.*]

hens *adv.* from this place, away 259. [From *henne* adv.]

hent(e) *pt. sg.* took hold of 238; *pt. pl.* arrived at (a place) 139, 587. [OE. *hentan.*]

herawde *n.* king's messenger 611. [AF. *heraud, herald.*]

here *adv.* in this place, here 1212, 1340, 1494, etc. [OE. *hēr*.]

here *v.* hear 411, 994, 1163, etc.; *imper.* 1855; **herde, harde** *pt. sg.* 70, 766, 1527, etc.; *pt. pl.* 856, 1457. [OE. *hēran*.]

hereynne *adv.* herein 1865. [OE. *hēr* + OE. *inn*.]

herytage *n.* inheritable property 1067. [OFr. *iretage, iritage, (h)eritage*.]

herkenyth *imper.* pay attention 20. [OE. *hercnian*.]

herte *n.* heart 1055, 1685. [OE. *heorte*.]

hete *n.* high body temperature 771. [OE. *hētu, hētē*.]

heuydd *n.* head 475, 1306. [OE. *hēafod*.]

heuyn *n.* heaven 65, 324, 482; **heuyn-trone** *n.* heaven's throne 1839, 2018. [OE. *heofon, heofen*.]

heuynkynge *n.* king of heaven 1371, 1725. [OE. *heofon-cyning*.]

hewe *n.* colour 990, 1261. [OE.; cp. Merc. *hēow, hīow, hīo*; Nth. *hīw*.]

hye *adj.* high, lofty 1144, 1299, 1747, etc.; *in hye* in haste 199, 1715; **hyest** *sup.* 1229. [OE. *hēh*.]

hye *v.* go quickly, travel rapidly 130, 199; **hyed** *pt. sg.* 1295, 1612, 1861; *pt. pl.* 1825, 1863. [OE. *hīgian*.]

hyely *adv.* high up 807. [From ME. *heigh* adj. and OE. *hēalīce*.]

hyght *pt. sg.* named 7, 626, 1519, etc.; promised 1118, 1346; *refl.* be named 13, 26, 118, etc.; **hyghtyst** *2 pt. sg.* called 1187. [OE. *hātan*.]

hyʒt, hyght *n.* height; *on hyʒt, vpon hyght adv. phr.* up high, aloft 472, 767. [OE. *hēhþo*.]

hylle *n.* hill 723, 807, 1746. [OE. *hyll*.]

hym. See **he**.

hymselfe. See **he**.

hynge. See **hange**.

hyppyng *pr. p.* limping, hobbling 1991. [OE. **hyppan*.]

hyred *pp. (pass.)* rented 1798. [OE. *hȳrian*.]

hys. See **he**.

hyt *pron.* it: *as sybject of v.* 295, 315, 335, etc.; *as object of v.* 333; *as a grammatical subject emphasising a clause which precedes hyt* 49; *pleonistic uses accompanying a subject emphasising a clause which precedes hyt* 4, 18, 20, etc.; *indefinite subject in impersonal constructions having to do with weather* 43, *with time* 377, 418, *with the actions of an indefinite agency* 404. [OE. *hit*.]

hodur *v.* cuddle, hug 112. [Cp. MnE. dial. *howder*, to huddle and LC. *hudern*, to shelter, cover.]

holde *n.* restraint 540, 864, 1173, etc.; *hath ... in holde*, possesses 1329. [OE. *geháld*.]

holde *v.* have in one's possession 975; keep 1205; *1 pr. sg.* consider 1692; *holde the stylle*, keep still, be silent 1749; **holdyst** *2 pr. sg.* 1187. [OE. *háldan*.]

ho(o)le, hale, holy *adj.* healthy 57, 1130, 2032; cured 2033, 2111. [OE. *hāl*.]

holy *adj.* holy, divine 1034, 1124, 1459, etc. [OE. *hālig*.]

holy goost *n.* the third person of the Trinity 1676. [OE. *hālig gāst, sē hālga gāst*.]

home. See **hame**.

homecome *n.* homecoming, return 1742. [OE. *hōm-cŏme*.]

honde. See **hande**.

honowre *n.* honourable use 56; splendour 1228. [OFr. *hono(u)r*.]

hoole. See **hale.**

hoost *n.* army 959. [OFr.]

hope *n.* trust, confidence 212. [OE. *hopa.*]

hope *1 pr. sg.* hope 1725, 1835. [OE. *hopian.*]

hopyd *pt. sg.* hoped 1296. [OE. *hopian.*]

hopped *pt. pl.* bounced 640. [OE. *hoppian.*]

hors *n.* horse 584, 640, 926, etc.; **horsys** *n. pl.* 202, 1446. [OE. *hors.*]

horsyd *pt. sg.* helped (somebody) to mount a horse 703. [OE. *horsian.*]

hoscht *adj.* silent, quiet; *hoscht and stylle* 813. [Prob. imitative; cp. ME. *hissen* v.]

hoselde *pt. sg.* administered Holy Communion 776. [OE. *hūslian.*]

how *adv.* in which manner or way 795, 796, 1114, etc. [OE. *hū.*]

howndys *n. pl.* dogs used in hunting 842, 1523, 2059. [OE. *hund.*]

hows *n.* house, dwelling 446, 1484, 1755, etc. [OE. *hūs.*]

hundred, hu(o)ndurd *adj. card. num. as adj.* 83, 296, 338, etc.; *as noun* 189, 1046, 1066, etc.; **hundurdys** *n. pl.* 1133. [OE. *hundred* and ON. (cp. OI. *hundrað*).]

hungurd *pt sg.* suffered from hunger 1451. [OE. *hyngrian.*]

hur. See **sche, she.**

hurselfe. See **sche, she.**

I

i *n.* The Roman numeral for one, used alone and to form other numerals 2014, 2108, 1995, etc.

I *pron.* I 66, 212, 359, etc.; *me acc. and dat.* me: *direct obj.* 62, 76, 89, etc.; *governed by prep.*

111, 115, 401, etc.; *for the nom.* 113, 979; **my** *adj.* my 81, 108, 109, etc.; *as obj. of prep.* 2075; **myn(e)** *pron.* mine: *qualifying a following n.* 959, 1064, 1338, etc.; *qualifying a preceding n.* 2091 [OE. *ic, mē, mīn.*] See **Y.**

Y *pron.* I 40, 77, 78, etc. [OE. *ic.*] See **I.**

yen. See **eye.**

yf. See **geue, geve.**

yf *conj.* (*usually with subj.*) if 91, 214, 241, etc. [OE. *gef, gi(e)f.*]

ylle *adv.* cruelly 726; ill 739, 804, 834, etc.; badly 1418. [ON. *illr*; *illa* adv.]

in *adv.* within 3, 334, 337, etc.; surrounded by 1443; *fig. context:* in state of 499, 513, 885, etc.; clad in 104, 155, 178, etc.; during the period 254, 275, 459, etc. [OE. *inn.*]

yn *adv.* in 151, 314, 727, etc. [OE. *innan,* prep., adv.; *inne* adv.]

in *prep.* within 42, 46, 54, etc.; enclosed in 161, 187, 323, etc.; clothed in 398, 866, 1046. [OE. *in* and L. *in* and ON. (cp. OI. ī).]

yn *prep.* in 91, 1344. [OE. *in.*]

yngynes *n. pl.* engines of war 859. [a. OFr. *engin.*]

ynne *n.* lodging, *they toke ther ynne* they took up their quarters 447. [OE. *inn.* n.]

ynogh *adj.* enough 400, 2010. [OE. *ȝenōh.*] See **ynowe.**

ynowe *adj. pl.* of 'enough' 143. [OE. *ȝenōh.*]

insondur *adv.* separately 47, 1327, 1632, etc. [From ME. phr. *in sonder.*]

into *prep.* into (a liquid) 131; into (an enclosed space) 191, 192, 199, etc. [OE. *inn to.*]

yre *n.* anger 499, 658. [OFr. *ire.*]

yron *n.* iron 1335. [OE. *īren*.]

js *3 pr. sg.* as copula or auxiliary with *pp.* 437. [OE. *is*.]

ys *3 pr. sg.* is 79, 80, 107, etc. [OE. *is*.]

yssewed *pt. pl.* came out (of persons), *yssewed out* 458. [From OFr. *issu*, pp. of *issir*.]

yvore *n.* ivory 598. [OFr. *ivoire*.]

ywroght *pp.* formed 1625. [OE. *ʒe-worht*, pp. of *ʒewyrcan*.]

J

juste *v.* fight with spear or lance on horseback with another knight 459, 672. [OFr. *jo(u)ster*, *juster*.]

K

keye *n.* key 1225. [OE. *cæg*.]

kene *adj.* bold 6, 788, 1089; sharp-pointed 1321. [OE. *cēne*.]

kenne *v.* give instruction to (n.) 1564; **kende** *pt. pl.* knew 2184. [OE. *cennan*; senses influenced by ON. (cp. OI. *kenna*).]

kepe *v.* contain (persons), hold 141, 540, 597, etc.; *fig.* preserve 209, 1031, 1061, etc.; *imper.* 533, 535; **kepyd, kept** *pt. sg.* kept (n. in a certain state) 57; *pt. pl.* 2163; *pt. sg.* preserved 1325. [OE. *cēpan*.]

kydde, kythe *n.* offspring 1234; homeland 2043. [OE. *cȳþ, cȳþþu*.]

kynde *n.* natural disposition, temperament 2169. [OE. *(ge)cȳnd*.]

kyndely *adv.* courteously, pleasantly 1313. [Cp. OE. *(ge)cȳnd elīce*.]

kyndylde *pp. fig.* caused, produced 2015. [From ME. *kindel* v.]

kyndyst *sup. adj.* (heir) having most rights by birth, most lawful (heir) 1257. [Cp. OE. *(ge)cȳnde*.]

kynge *n.* king 406, 415, 553, etc.; **kynges, kyngys** *n. pl.* 187, 509, 916. [OE. *cyning*.]

kynne *n.* race, clan, family 122, 444, 1266, etc. [OE. *cyn*.]

kyns *suff. combining with no (no-kyns*, 2017) *to form adj. denoting* no certain . . ., no specific . . . [OE. *nanes cynnes*.]

kyrke *n.* entire community of Christians; also, church of Rome 1804; *holy kyrke* 1034. [OE. *cir(i)ce* and ON. *kirkja*.]

kyrtell *n.* cloak or coat for men 1644. [OE. *cyrtel*.]

kyste *pt. sg.* kissed 1803. [OE. *cyssan*.]

kythe. See **kydde**.

knagg *n.* peg, fastener 1793. [Cp. E.Fris. *knagge*, Sw. *knagg*, Dan. *knage*.]

knaue, knave *n.* servant 1721, 1751, 1774, etc. [OE. *cnafa* (? Merc. **cneafa*), infl. *cnafan*.]

knee *n.* knee 951. [OE. *cnēo(w)*.]

knelyd *pt. sg.* knelt 951, 1903. [OE. *cneowlian*.]

knewe *pt. sg.* knew 2010; *pt. pl.* 2017. [OE. *cnāwan*.]

knyfe *n.* knife 1624, 1650, 2077. [Late OE. (from ON.) *cnif* and ON. (cp. OI. *knīfr*).]

knyght *n.* a noble warrior 23, 473, 484, etc.; **knyghtys, knyʒtys** *p. pl.* 4, 166, 229, etc. [OE. *cniht*; pl. *cnihtas*.]

knighthedd *n.* skill in fighting 425. [From ME. *knight* and *-hēd(e)* suff.; cp. OE. *cnihthād*.]

knyghtly *adv.* in a warlike manner 712. [From *knyght* n.]

knok *v.* attack or injure (n.), fight 281. [OE. *cnucian* and *cnocian* and ON. (cp. OI. *knoka*).]

knowyn *pp.* known about 891. [OE. *cnāwan.*]

L

lace *n.* noose, snare 1815. [OFr. *laz, las.*]

lad(d). See lede.

lady *n.* consort of a ruler 28, female head of a household 213, 824, 971, etc.; ladyes *n. pl.* 566, 832. [OE. *hlǽfdige.*]

lagh, lawe *v.* laugh 290, 1767; loghe *pt. sg.* 2019. [OE. *hlæhhan.*]

lande, londe *n.* earth 3, 717, 1258; *fig.* domain 362, 1199, 1211; property 1227, 1236; landys, londys *n. pl.* properties 220, 359, 829, etc. [OE. *land, lond.*]

lappe *1 pr. sg.*, *refl.* me lappe, I wrap myself 113. [From ME. *lappe* n., loose sleeve.]

large *adj.* spacious 1175. [L. *larga.*]

lasse. See lesse.

laste *adj. sup.* latest; *in phr.* at the (*þe*) laste finally at last 855, 917, 2180; to the laste every bit, to the last detail 2046. [Prob. from adv. Also cp. OE. *læt adj.* and *lætest.*]

laste *v.* endure 1410. [OE. *lǽstan.*]

lawe *n.* law 261. [OE. *lagu*; cp. OI. *lög* pl., from **lagu.*]

lawe *v.* See lagh, lawe.

lawmpe *n.* lamp 1645. [L. *lampas.*]

lay *v.* set watch, *wach . . . lay* 1358; *1 pr. sg.* wager, bet 737, 808; *3 pr. sg.* exposes (himself) to view 394, 478; leyde *pt. sg.* set watch 740, placed 1547; *pt. pl.* 1600; *pp.* laid out (corpse) 1088; layned *pt. pl.* put (something) upon the ground 799; layeng *pr. p.* overthrowing 729. [OE. *lecgan.*]

layne *v.* grant the loan of, forgive 1283, 1587, 1617. [f. ME. *loan* n.]

leche *n.* physician 1942. [OE. *lǽce.*]

led(d). See lede.

lede *n.* man 716. [OE. *lēod.*]

lede *n.* direction, guidance 249. [From lede v.]

lede *v.* conduct, guide 802, 1559, 1665, etc.; pass (one's life) 876; le(e)de *3 pr. sg.* 817; *pr. pl.* 229; lad(d), led(d) *pt. sg.* 161, 764, 1415, etc.; *pt. pl.* 133, 1228, 2171. [OE. *lǽdan.*]

le(e)de. See lede.

leen *v.* grant temporary possession of a thing 791. [OE. *lǽnan.*]

lees *n.* property, protection 940. [a. AF. *les.*]

lees *n.* leash 1318. [OE. *leas.*]

leest *n.* lowest in power or position 1013. [OE. *lǽst.*]

leeve *n.* permission 2134. [OE. *lēaf.*]

lefe *adv.* willing 1244; *adj. absol.*, *esp. in* for lief or loath 1490; *quasi-n.* friend 1720. [OE. *lēof, līof.*]

lefte. See le(e)ue.

ley3tenyng *n.* lightning 1642. [Special use of ME. *lightening.*]

lele *adj.* loyal 988, 1966. [OFr. *leal,* AF. *leël.*]

leman, lemman *n.* sweetheart 1829, 1988, 1594. [Early ME. *leofmon.*]

lende *v.* go, depart 1056. [OE. *lendan.*]

lene *v.* grant the temporary possession of (a thing) 1458; lente *pp.* 2136. [OE. *lǽnan.*]

lenger *adv.* longer 1018, 1047, 1530. [OE. *lengra, lengre.*]

lenkyth *n.* length 1175. [OE. *lengþu.*]

lente. See **lene.**

lepe *pr. pl.* rise up; *pt. sg.* 586, 963; sprang upon (a horse's saddle) 1529; *pt. pl.* rose up 1019. [OE. *hléapan (hléop, hlupon).*]

lere *v.* teach 417, 1215; **lerydd** *pp.* 1316. [OE. *lǽran.*]

lerne *v.* teach 420, 464, 1565, etc. [OE. *leornian.*]

lesynge *n.* lie 1292. 1374, 1567, etc. [OE. *léasing.*]

lesse, lasse *adj.* comp. of little, not so much 449, 2125, 2149; **leste** *sup.* slightest 962. [OE. *lǽs* adv., *lǽssa* adj.]

leste *adj.* slightest 962. [OE. *lǽssa, lǽs(es)t.*]

let *n.* stoppage 722. [From **let** v.]

let *v.* allow 949, 1402; *pt. sg.* 2067, 207; *let awt,* allowed to go 1369; *pt. pl. let . . . be,* left undisturbed 1188; *imper.* 557, 695, 889, etc. *let be,* leave undisturbed 789. [OE. *lǽtan, létan.*]

leve *n.* permission asked for or granted 960; *toke ther leue,* departed (with expression of farewell) 285, 2139, 2159. [OE. *léaf.*]

le(e)ue *v.* subsist 932, live 1838; **leuyd** *pt. sg.* 717; *pt. pl.* 941; **leu(e)yng** *pr. p. adj.* living 1720, 1897, 1908. [OE. *libban.*]

le(e)ve *v.* depart 439, 1633; leave alone, depart from 1730; *pr. pl.* 234, 793; **leuyth** *3 pr. sg.* 885; **lefte** *2 pt. sg.* 1219; *pt. pl.* 1334; *pt. sg.* abandoned 1484, 1531, 1098; *pt. pl.* 521; *pp.* abandoned 1003; remained 1030; (*pass.*) 496; **leuyd** *pt. sg.* left, caused to remain 1049. [OE. *lǽfan.*]

leuyr *adv. in construction with 'have': had leuyr,* would rather have 245, 941, 1453, etc. [OE. *léof, líof.*]

lewde *adj.* unlettered 1316. [OE. *lǽwede.*]

lye, lygg *v.* lean 171, to lie (in bed) 247, 108, 207, etc.; **lygge** *pr. pl.* dwell?; **lay(e)** *pt. sg.* was situated 1414, 1603, 1932; lay (dead) 1092; slept 1637, 1773; *pt. pl.* 1566; **layne, leyn** *pp.* slept (with) 688; slept (by) 1071, 1438, 1496, etc.; **lygyng** *pr. p.* 1303. [OE. *licgan.*]

lyfe *n.* life 29, 222, 510, etc. **lyuys** *n. pl.* 476, 656. [OE. *líf.*]

lyfte *pt. sg.* raised 767. [ON. *lypta.*]

lyght *v.* descend (from a horse) 399; *1 pr. pl.* 1420; *pt. sg.* set burning 1645; **lyghtyd** *pt. sg.* 1504. [OE. *líhtan.*]

lyghtly *adv.* cheerfully 2019, foolishly 912. [OE. *lĕ(o)htlice,* f. *lĕoht.*]

lyghtnes *n.* brightness 184, 393. [OE. *líhtnes.*]

lyke *adj.* having the same characteristics, like 18, 1808, 1991. [Early ME. *lích, lík* (? late OE. **líc*).]

lykeande *pr. p. adj.* agreeable 1890. [f. ME. *lyke* v.] See **lykyng.**

lykyd *pt. sg.* was pleased 739, 834, 2041, etc.; *pt. pl.* 804, 1179. [OE. *lícian.*]

lykyng *n.* pleasure (sensual) 1309, 1444, 1499. [OE. *lícung.*]

lykyng *pr. p. adj.* agreeable 519. [f. ME. *lyke* v. + *ing.*] See **lykeande.**

lylly *n.* lily 901, 1024, 1538. [OE. *lilie.*]

lyme *n.* cement used in building; usually coupled with stone; *lyme and stane* 1146. [OE. *lím.*]

lymmes *n. pl.* limbs 2028. [OE. *lim.*]

lyon *n.* lion 335, 423, 427, etc. [L. *leo, leōnem.*]

lyppes *n. pl.* lips 96. [OE. *lippa*.]

lyste *pt. sg.* paid attention 290. [OE. *hlystan*.]

lyter *n.* a framework supporting a bed 1547. [AF. *litere*, OFr. *litiere*.]

lytyll *adv.* little 608, 706, 1520, etc. [OE. *lȳtel*.]

lythe *adj.* supple 841. [OE. *liðe*.]

lythe *v.* listen 40, 1189. [ON. *hlȳða*.]

lyþys *n. pl.* warm shelters 1118. [? var. of ME. *lewth*.]

lyve *n.* life; *used in phrase*: *sworne . . . be lyve*, sworn . . . with one's life 992. [OE. *līf*.]

lyue *adj.* alive, living 1049; *attrib. use in on lyue*, alive 662. [OE. *on līfe*.]

lofe *n.* loaf 1453, 1465. [OE. *hlāf*.]

logge *n.* temporary dwelling 1436. [OFr. *loge*, *loige*, arbour, hut.]

logyd *pt. sg.* dwelt 874; *pp.* (*pass.*) has his abode 437. [OFr. *logier*.]

loke *v. fig.* to turn or fix one's regard 235, 237; *imper.* see, find out 726; behold 852; **loky(e)d** *pt. sg.* looked 706, 742; *pt. pl.* 1818, 1897. [OE. *lōcian*.]

longe *adj.* long, with reference to duration 311, 874, 1309, etc. [OE. *lang*, *long*.]

longe *v.* depart 1828. [OE. *langian*.]

longyth *pr. pl.* belong 321. (Aphet. f. OE. *ʒelang*, at hand.]

loone *n.* gift 1914. [a. ON. *lán*.]

loouyd. See **loue.**

lorde *n.* lord, one who has dominion 161, 276, 298, etc.; **lordys** *n. pl.* 74, 121, 169, etc. [OE. *hlāford*.]

lore *n.* learning, scholarship 176, 1215. [OE. *lār*.]

lorne *pp.* lost 510, 827, 1358. [ME. *leese* v.]

lose *n.* fame, reputation 753. [OFr. *los*.]

lose *v. intr.* perish 453. [OE. *losian*.]

lose *v. tr.* destroy, be the ruin of 222; be deprived of 1857; **loste** *pt. sg.* 29, 753; *pp.* 1119, 1868, 2006, etc. [OE. *losian*.]

lothe *n.* harm, injury 1490. [OE. *lāð*, orig. neut. of adj. *lāð*, loath.]

lothe *adj.* reluctant, unwilling 1126, 1244, 1460, etc. [OE. *lāð*.]

loudyng *pr. p.* praising 1881. [L. *laudare*.]

loue *n.* a beloved person 643; *in religious sense, applied to paternal affection of God: For godys love* 1287, 1570. [OE. *lufu*.]

loue *v.* hold dear 1104. *3 p. sg.* 302; **loou(e)yd** *pt. sg.* praised 704, 1904; *pt. pl.* 2149, 2161; **loueyng** *pr. p.* 1914. [OE. *lufian*.]

louely *n.* beautiful person 1815. [See **louely** adj.]

louely *adj.* beautiful 113. [OE. *luflic*, f. *lufu*, love n. + *lic*, *-ly*.]

lowde *adj.* loud 2036. [OE. *hlūd*.]

lowsyd *pt. pl.* set free 1543. [f. *loose* adj.]

M

M¹ *abbrev.* Roman numeral symbol for a thousand 571.

ma. See **moo.**

madde *adj.* mad, insane 554. [Aphet. OE. *gemœd(e)d*.]

made. See **make.**

madyste. See **make.**

mageste *n.* greatness and glory of God 483, 1443. [a. OFr. *majestét*.]

may(e) *n.* maiden 71, 349, 525, etc. [OE. *mæʒden*.]

may *1 pr. sg.* can, may: *auxil. of predication with a following simple infin.* 66, 828, 912, etc.; *2 pr. sg.* 1405, 1855; *3 pr. sg.*

209, 828; *pr. pl.* 486, 1189,
1896; *pr. subj. sg.* 942; *with
ellipsis of 'do'*, 680; *God ... all
may* 736. [OE. *mæȝ (maȝon,
meahte)*.]

maydyn *n.* maiden 520, 565, 574,
etc.; **maydyns** *n. pl.* 757, 809,
1391. [OE. *mæȝden.*]

maydynhedd, -hede *n.* virginity
1857, 1868, 2051. [f. **maydyn** +
ME. *hedd.*]

maye *n.* May. [OFr. *Mai* and L.
Maium.]

mayne *n.* power; *wyth myȝt and
mayne* 2161. [OE. *mæȝen.*]

mayntene *v.* defend, protect 883.
[ME. *maintene, -teine*, f. OFr.
maintenir.]

maystr *n.* master 2180. [OE.
mæȝester, maȝister.]

maystres *n.* mistress, as a title
of courtesy prefixed to the
Christian name 820. [OFr.
maistresse.]

make *n.* mate 881. [OE. ȝ*emaca.*]

make *v.* cause to become 847;
bring into existence 1495, 1664,
2119; *pr. subj. sg.* 91; **makyste** 2
pr. sg. cause to become 1413;
makyth 3 *pr. sg.* causes to
become 2004; *the boke makyth
mynde*, the book records 2166;
madyste 2 *pt. sg. const. infin.
with 'to'* 1217; **made** *pt. sg.* made
416; caused (something to
happen) 416; brought into
existence 647, 1292, 1416, etc.;
const. inf. with 'to' 988, 1084,
1108, etc.; caused to become
1122, 1317, 1479, etc.; pro-
duced (a sound) 1350; com-
posed of 1146; *pt. pl.* made
144; caused to become 692;
*const. inf. with 'to': made to
crye* had announced 551, *made
... to dye* caused to die 713
(also 785, 864); produced (a
sound) 554; *pp. (pass.)* made
159, 309; caused to become
1824, 1911; *pp.* brought into
existence 1824; **makeyng** *pr. p.*
bringing into existence 168.
[OE. *macian.*]

makeynge. See **make.**

makyste. See **make.**

makyth. See **make.**

man, mon *n.* human being (irres-
pective of sex or age) 51, 65,
68, etc.; adult male person 14,
353, 554, etc.; *n. pl.* 816; **men**
n. pl. human beings (irrespec-
tive of sex or age) 1, 62, 135,
etc.; adult males 365, 371, 398,
etc. [OE. *man(n), mon(n).*]

maner(e) *n.* species, kind, sort.
Often with ellipsis of *of* 1002;
customary mode of acting 2001.
[a. AF. *manere.*]

manhode *n.* qualities becoming a
man; manliness, courage, valour
417. [OE. *man(n), mon(n) +
hood.*]

many, mony *adj.* many, *used
distributively with a sg.: many
a oon*, many a person 21, 51,
68, etc.; *with 'an' or 'a' prefixed
to the n.:* 92, 222, 332, etc.;
many, a great number of 872,
1049, 1278, etc.; *placed after
the n.: odur many* 170; *any
many* 1569; *n.* 303. [OE. *maniȝ,
moniȝ.*]

manly *adv.* courageously 541. [f.
man n. + *ly*; OE. *mannlice.*]

mantell *n.* sleeveless cloak 1323.
[OE. *mentel* and OFr. *mantel.*]

mare, more *adj.* more, greater in
number or amount 84, 438, 674;
*absol. and quasi-n. in the sense
'greater': more and lesse* 449,
the more and the mynne 549,
2037 = persons of all ranks; all
without exception; something
that is more 1008. [OE. *māra.*]

G

mare, more *adv.* again 1571; more 1579; chiefly with prefixed word *no more* (*mare*) 690, 1717, *euyrmore* 956, *neuyrmare* 1423. [OE. *māra*.]

marynere *n.* sailor 1784, 1814, 1835, etc. [a AF. *mariner*.]

marred *pt. sg.* hindered, interfered with 863. [OE. *merran*.]

masse *n.* Eucharistic service 1805, 1997, 1999. [OE. *mæsse*.]

maste *n.* mast 1826, 1861. [OE. *mæst*.]

mate *adj.* overcome 771. [OE. a. OFr. *mat* (at chess).]

matrymony *n.* action of marrying 1137. [a. OFr. *matremoine*.]

me. See **I.**

mede *n.* duty; *Euyll quytt he . . . hys mede,* He did his duty poorly 715; reward 1671. [OE. *mēd.*]

medowe *n.* any tract of grass land 382, 399, 419. [OE. *mædive.*]

meene *1 pr. sg.* intend 2182. [OE. *mænan.*]

meete *v.* meet, encounter 1995; **mete** *pr. pl.* come upon 850; **mett** *pt. sg.* met 628, 728; *pt. pl.* 652. [OE. *mētan.*]

meyne *n.* body of retainers 1396, 1402, 1526. [a. OFr. *meyné, mesne.*]

meke *adj.* gentle, courteous 32. [Early ME. *meoc,* a. ON. *miuk-r.*]

mekenes *n.* gentleness of spirit 426. [From *meke* + *nes.*]

mekyll *adj.* great, *in various applications* 67, 273, 299, etc. [OE. *micel.*]

men. See **man.**

mercy *n.* compassion 1193, 1853. [a. OFr. *merci.*]

merye *adj.* joyous 1764. [OE. *myr(i)ȝe.*]

mesell(e) *n. fig.* foul person 2021, 1965. [a. OF. *mesel,* leprous, leper.]

message *n.* the carrying of a communication; a mission 123. [a. OFr. *message.*]

messengere *n.* messenger 1258; **messengerys** *n. pl.* 154, 190, 232, etc. [ME. *messager, -ier* (OFr. also *messagier*).]

mete *n.* dinner 522; food 879, 1009, 1462, etc. [OE. *mete.*]

mete *v.* See **meete.**

mett. See **meete.**

mewse *v.* ponder 332. [a. *Fr. muser.*]

my. See **I.**

myddyl *n.* the middle point 604. [OE. *middel, midl* adj., also n. masc. by ellipsis of *dæl,* part.]

myddys *prep.* midst 337, 343, 612. [Evolved from ME. *in-middes, on-middas.*]

myght *n.* bodily strength 45, 1287; power 1500; **mytghys** *n. pl.* (Of God): with reference to commanding influence 1675, 1832. [OE. *miht.*]

myght *pt. sg.* could: expressing ability or power 65, 368, 501, etc.; *pt. pl.* 135, 332, 339, etc.; *pt. subj. sg. expressing subjective possibility* (*with infin.*) 539, 623, 735; *pt. subj. pl.* 196, 1053; *pt. subj. sg. statement of future contingency deemed improbable: myȝt Y come,* If I might 1738; *used with infin. to convey a suggestion* 312. [OE. *mæȝ* (*maȝon meahte*).] See **may.**

myghtfull *adj.* mighty 1443. [From *myght* n. + *-full.*]

mykyll. See **mekyll.**

mylde *adj.* Of a person's disposition: kind 32, 565, 1500: low 481; quiet, kind (general application) 1510, 1763, 1904. [OE. *milde*.]

myle *n.* miles (*sg. form used with a pl. number: Syxty myle* 376). [OE. *mīl*.]

myn(e). See **I**.

mynne *adj.* less. Always coupled with *more, mare* 549, 2037. [a. ON. *minne*.] See **more, mare**.

mynstralcy *n.* practice of playing and singing 1010; *Makeyng sweete mynstraley*, making sweet music 168. [ad. OFr. *menestralsie-trancie*.]

mynstrals *gen. n. pl.* minstrells', singerss' 2155. [a. OFr. *menestral*.]

myrakyls *n. pl.* miracles 872. [a. OFr. *miracle*.]

myrthe *n.* musical entertainment 2155. [OE. *myrgþ*.]

mystyr *n.* need 97, 512. [a. OFr. *mestier, mester*.]

mode *n.* fierce courage 603; humour, disposition 1510. [OE. *mōd*.]

modur *n.* feeling, *in phr.*: *mode and mayne* 291. [OE. *mōd*.]

modur *n.* mother 409, 936, 1915. [OE. *mōdor*.]

molde *n.* earth, ground 1946; *vpon molde*, in the world 158. [OE. *molde*.]

mo(o)ne *n.* complaint, lamentation 467, 1350. [OE. **mān, rel.* to *mǣnan* v.]

monythys *n. pl.* months 358. [OE. *mōnað*.]

moo *adj.* more 572, 1212; *n.* the greater 1079; **ma** *adv.* more, to a greater extent 1104. [OE. *mā*.] Cp. **mare, more**.

moone *n.* moon 1833. [OE. *mōna*.]

moost, moste *absol.* (*quasi-n.*) greatest persons. *Usually in association with leest: moost and leest* 1013; *adj.* greatest, with

reference to power 1287, 1675. [OE. *mǣst*.]

more. See **mare**.

morne *n.* morning 454, 501, 805, etc. [OE. *morȝen* (inflected also *morȝn-, morn-*).]

morne *v.* grieve 543; **mornyd** *pt. sg.* grieved 291. [OE. *murnan*.]

mornetyde *n.* the morning. [OE. *morȝen* (inflected also *morȝn-, morn-*) + *tyde*.]

mornyng *pr. p. adj.* sorrowing, lamenting 812. [f. ME *morne* v. + *yng*.]

mornynge *n.* morning 1390. [ME. *morivening, morning*, f. *morwen, morne* + *yng*.]

moste. See **moost**.

mote *pr. subj. sg. In wishes forming a periphrastic subj.*: **may**: *mote Y the* ... 668, 724, 1186, etc.; *pr. subj. pl.* *mote yow befalle* ... 198. [OE. *mōt*.]

mownt *n.* mountain. *Used in proper names of mountains: Mownt Devyse* 986. [OE. *munt*.]

mowthe *n.* mouth 1606, 1609, 1618. [OE. *mūþ*.]

muste *1 pr. sg.* must: *used to express a certain futurity* 979; *3 pr. sg.* 2039, 2071; *pr. pl.* 224, 669, 672; *imper.* 1193, 1238. [OE. *mōste*, pl. *mōston*, pt. of *mōt*.]

N

nay *adv.* nay, no: *introductory word, without direct negation* 559, 1198, 1705; *used to express negation* 1422, 2100; *to seye hur nay* to make denial to her 1727, *sche seyde nay* she made denial 1846, 1907. [a. ON. *nei*.]

nakyd *adj.* unsheathed (sword) 1426; unclothed 1517. [OE. *nacod*.]

name *n.* name 1184; *n. pl.* 2146. [OE. *nama, noma.*]

nane. See **none.**

narowe *adj.* narrow 2030. [OE. *nearu, nearo.*]

nave *n.* fleet 1246. [a. OFr. *navie.*]

ne *conj.* nor: *following a negative clause* 351; *adv.* not: simple negative 1952. [OE. *ne, ni.*]

nede *n.* need; *in phr.* haue nede, require 230; necessity 1854. [OE. *nēd.*]

nede *adv.* (*with* 'must') necessarily, of necessity 2071. [OE. *nēde, nēdes.*]

nede *pt. sg.* stood in need of, required 1553, 879. [OE. *nēdian,* f. *nēd* n.]

neeve *n.* fist 1634. [ad. ON. *hnefi, nefi.*]

nere *adv.* close 217, 377, 457, etc.; almost 658, 875, 921, etc.; *in phr.* far and neer 891. [a. ON. *nǣr.*]

nerre *adj. comp.* nearest 1036. [OE. *nērra,* comp. of *nēh.*]

neuer. See **neuyr.**

neuyn *v.* mention 64. [a. ON. *nefna.*]

neuyr, neuer *adv.* never, at no time 3, 5, 54, etc. [OE. *nǣfre,* f. *ne* + *ǣfre.*]

newe *adj.* new 984, 1200, 1235, etc. [OE. *nēowe.*]

newe *adv.* newly, recently 936. [OE. *nēowe.*]

nygh *adv.* near: *in predicative use with the v.* 'to be' 217. [OE. *nēh.*]

nyght *n.* night 159, 402, 535, etc.; **nyghtys** *n. pl.* 1109, 1355. [OE. *niht, nǣht.*]

nyghtyd *pp.* (*pass.*) overtaken by night 1435. [From the n.]

no *adj.* not any 65, 153, 266, etc. [OE. *nān.*]

no *adv.* no: *used to express a negative reply to a question* 1430.

[Southern and midland form of OE. *nā.*]

nobull, nubull *adj.* illustrious 55, 122, 197, etc.; splendid, impressive 1694. [a. OFr. *noble.*]

nodur *conj.* neither 746, 1012, 1442; *pron.* neither (of two persons) 1877. [OE. *nowðer.*]

noght *adv.* not at all 269; not 351, 556, 1049, etc.; *n.* nothing 907, 932, 1769. [OE. *nōwiht,* f. *ne* + *awiht.*]

nome *v. intr.* go, pass 254. [Var. of ME. *nyme* v. by assimilation to the pt. forms.]

nomore *n.* nothing more 66. [From OE. *nā* + *more* n.]

none *n.* midday 1377. [OE. *nōn* neut.]

none, nane, noon *pron.* not any 18, 260, 1010, etc.; no one 1923, 1469, 1705, etc. [OE. *nān,* f. *ne* + *ān.*]

nonne *n.* nun 1911, 1913, 1951, etc.; **nonnes** *n. pl.* 1889, 1924, 2130. [OE. *nunne.*]

nonnery *n.* a place of residence for nuns 1961. [Prob. ad. AF. **nonnerie,* f. *nonne,* nun n.]

nonnes. See **nonne.**

noon. See **none.**

noonre *n.* nunnery 1882. [prob. ad. AF. **nonnerie.*]

nor *conj.* nor 4, 159, 390. etc. [Prob. a cont. of ME. *nother.*]

norysch *v.* nurture 56. [ad. OFr. *noris(s), nuris(s).*]

northweste *adv.* north-west 2102. [f. OE. *norð, norþ* + OE. *west.*]

nose *n.* nose 1609. [OE. *nosu.*]

not *adv.* not: *following the v.* 39, 80, 249, etc.; *following an auxil.* 77, 273, 432, etc.; *preceding infin.* 23, 1314; *with adverbs* 214; *after* 'or' 272; *with terms of number: not oon* 1140. [Abbrev. of ME. *nought* adv.]

nothynge *adv.* not at all 1407. [From *no* adj. + *thynge*.]

now(e) *adv.* now, at the present time, 210, 403, 841, etc. [OE. *nū*.]

nowmberde *pt. pl.* amounted to 571. [ad. OFr. *nombrer*.]

nubull. See **nobull.**

O

odur, odyr, oþer *adj.* other 260, 341, 371, etc.; *pron. eyther odur, eyder odur* one another 47, 1450; *odur many,* many other 170, other persons 1147; *odur day* another day 1231; *feyreste of odur* fairest of any 1250; *oon aftur odur* one after another 1830. [OE. *oþer, oðer.*]

of *prep.* of: *indicating origin or source* 4, 8, 10, etc.; *indicating the cause of an action, feeling, etc.* 31; *introducing the agent after a pass. v.* 104; *indicating the material or substance of which anything consists* 14, 86, 98, etc.; *after intr. verbs especially those of learning, knowing, hearing* 41, 59, 63, etc.; *indicating a distinguishing mark by which a person or thing is characterised* 184, 185, 349, etc.; *in partitive expression* 195, 347; *in the sense of 'belonging to' or 'pertaining to'* 169, 176, 257, etc. [OE. *of.*]

offyce *n.* public service 1235. [a. AF. and OFr. *office.*]

ofte *adv.* many times 76, 1324, 1428, etc. [OE. *oft.*]

oght *pt. sg.* owed 1983; *pt. pl.* owned 650. [OE. *āhte.*]

olde *adj.* old 208, 580, 1064, etc.; of any specified age 61, 83; great, grand (after *gode*) 681; *n.* 870, 981, 1731, etc. [OE. *ald.*]

oldely *adv.* in the manner of one who is old 248. [*olde* + *ly.*]

on *adv. used idiomatically: ... mewse on* 332; movement into a position above 472. [OE. *on*].

on *prep.* upon 181, 310, 381, etc.; *expressing contact with any surface* 249, 478; *expressing position with reference to a place* 362, 477, 551, etc.; *indicating the day of an occurrence* 29, 377, 418, etc.; *of state or condition on blode* 609, *on lyue* 662, 1049. [OE. *on.*]

ones, oones, -ys *adv.* at one time 2072; *preceded by a prep.: at ones* 190, 340; under any circumstances 1557; *oones on a day* one day 418. [OE. *ānes.*]

ony *adj.* any 1033, 1906. [OE. *ǣnig.*] See **any.**

onslayne *pp.* made assault 496. [*on slay.*]

oon *num. adj.* one 2, 881, 887, etc.; *pron.* a person 7, 343, 378, etc.; *after pronominal adj. without a contextual reference: many a oon* 21, 873, 1674; *many oon* 476, 701, 785; *oon aftur odur,* one after another 1830; *eueryoon* 155; a single person 1140; a single thing 1246, 2128, 2152. [OE. *ān.*]

oones, -ys. See **ones.**

oost, oste *n.* host 448, 606, 625, etc. [OFr. *host.*] See **host.**

openyd *pt. pl.* opened 1222. [OE. *openian.*]

openlye *adv.* without concealment, so that all may hear 1925, 2035. [*open* adj. + *lye.*]

or *prep.* before 272, 357, 358, etc. [OE. *ār* adv. The sense is that of the comparative, OE. *ǣr.*]

or *conj.* or 1, 116, 227, etc. [Phonetically reduced form of ME. *odur* conj.]

ordeygn *v.* furnish 1013; **ordeygned**

pt. sg. ordered 365, 1396; *pt. pl.* prepared 877; *pp.* prepared 1087. [a. OFr. *ordener*.]

ore *n.* oar 1989, 2104. [OE. *ār*.]

os *conj.* as 464. [contr. OE. *ealswā*.] See **as.**

oste. See **oost.**

ostes *n.* hostess 448. [OFr. *hôtesse*.] See **hostess.**

othe *n.* promise 1127, 1489, 1495; **othys** *n. pl.* acts of swearing 355. [OE. *āþ*.]

oþer. See **odur.**

ouer, -yr *adv.* on the other side 329, over 1040; across 1114; surpassing 1942. [OE. *ofer* adv. and prep.]

ouyr *prep.* across 88, 132, 137, etc.; over 475, 1746. [OE. *ofer*.]

ouyrend *n.* top 600. [**ouyr** + ME. *end* n.]

ouyrmore *adv.* moreover, furthermore 956. [*ouyr* adv. + *more* adv.]

ouyrnyght *adv.* night before 1393. [*ouyr* prep. + *nyght* n.]

own *adj.* own: *used after possessive case or adj. to emphasise possessive meaning* 647, 801, 1691, etc. [OE. *āȝen*.]

owre. See **we.**

owt(e) *adv.* out 53, 171, 314, etc.; through 463; from 625; *with ellipsis of intr. v., functioning as a v. without inflexion: Mylys owte wyth a swyrde,* Mylys drew out a sword 1321; *from a contained condition into one of accessibility hys nose braste owt on blood* 1609, *The tethe be smetyn owt of my mowþe* 1618, *broght owt of . . . bale* 2033, etc. [OE. *ūte*.]

owt *v. intr.* to go out 710, 1172. [OE. *ūtan*.]

owttakyn *pp.* excepted 1034. [*owte* adv. + *take* v.]

P

paye *n.* satisfaction 615, 941, 2094. [a. OFr. *paie*.]

paye *v.* pacify, content 1388. [a. Fr. *payer*.]

payne *n.* suffering 1422, 1944. [a. OFr. *peine*.]

pales, paleys *n.* palace 322, 173, 1109, etc. [a. OFr. *palais, paleis*.]

palfray(e), palfrey *n.* a saddle-horse for ordinary riding 310, 1288, 1425, etc. [a. OFr. *palfrei*.]

palmer *n.* pilgrim 430, 451. [a. AF. *palmer, paumer*.]

palsye *n.* palsy, disease of the nervous system 1976. [OFr. *paralisie, -lysie*.]

parell *n.* preparation, equipment 85. [Aphet. form of ME. *apareil*, apparel.]

parte *n.* faction 1079, 1791. [OE. ad. L. *pars*; thirteenth-century a. Fr. *part*.]

passed, -yd, paste *pt. sg.* went through 463, 966; *pt. pl.* 463; *pt. sg.* travelled 1398; *pt. pl.* 148; *pt. sg.* surpassed 1790; *pt. sg.* escaped 2055. [a. OFr.*passer*.]

pavylon *n.* stately tent 384; **pavylons** *n. pl.* 379, 964. [a. Fr. *pavillon*.]

pees *n.* peace 941. [Early ME. *pais*, a. OFr. *pais*.]

peyntyd *pp.* (*pass.*) painted 329, 331. [ad. OFr. *peindre*.]

perchawnce *adv.* as is possible 942. [a. AF. *par chance*.]

perde *adv.* By God!, assuredly 1878. [a. OFr. *par dé*.]

pere *n.* pear; a type of something small: *deryd not a pere*, risked not a thing 657. [OE. *pere, peru*.]

perys *n. pl.* peers 233, 319. [a. OFr. *per, peer*.]

perre *n.* jewellery 184. [a. OFr. *pierrie, pierie.*]

pyllere *n.* pillar 1141; *n. pl.* 325. [a. OFr. *piler.*]

pyne *n.* suffering 2085. [OE. **pin*, a. L. *poena.*]

pyte *n.* tenderness 1682. [a. OFr. *pit(i)é.*]

pytt *n.* hole of captivity 1147. [OE. *pytt.*]

place *n. short for* 'place of battle' 607; quarters 1355; general designation for city 1812; convent 1891. [a. Fr. *place.*]

play(e), plawe *v.* practise sport 419, 1523; *pr. pl.* move energetically 258. [OE. *pleȝ(i)an.*]

playnere *n.* assembly 317. [a. AF. *plener.*]

plawe. See **playe.**

plente *adj.* abounding 400. [a. OFr. *plentet.*]

plyte *n.* guilt 2108. [OE. *pliht.*]

pokkys *n. pl.* pustules 2022. [OE. *poc, pocc.*]

pole *n.* small body of still water 1736. [OE. *pōl.*]

pomels *n. pl.* balls 391. [a. OFr. *pomel.*]

pope *n.* Pope, head of Roman Catholic Church 775, 868, 994, etc. [OE. *pápa.*]

pore *n.* needy. [a. OFr. *povre.*]

portreyed *pp.* (*pass.*) represented 389. [a. OFr. *portrai-, pourtray-.*]

poscescon *n.* control 1178. [a. OFr. *possession, -un.*]

posterne *n.* side way 463. [a. OFr. *posterne.*]

powere *n.* body of armed men 218. [a. AF. *pouair.*]

pownde *n. pl.* English money of account 1195, 1373. [OE. *pund* (pl. *pund*).]

praye *n.* troop 1020; victim 1831. [OFr. *proie* and ML. *praeda.*]

praye *v.* beseech 1981; *pt. sg.*

1837; **preyed** *pt. sg.* 1282, 1497, 1573, etc. [a. OFr. *preier.*]

precyus *adj.* of great price 1106, 1535. [a. OFr. *precios.*]

prees *n.* multitude 469, 612, 1319. [a. OFr. *presse.*]

preest *n.* priest 1005; **preestys** *n. pl.* 1101. [OE. *prēost.*]

preyed. See **praye.**

preyer *n.* prayer 1439; **preyers** *n. pl.* 2008. [a. OFr. *preiere.*]

preke *v.* ride fast 1020. [Late OE. *prician.*]

prekyng *vbl. n.* galloping 469; 1319. [ME. *preke* v. + *yng.*]

present(e) *n.* gift 199, 125. [a. OFr. *present.*]

presyd *pt. pl. Of an attacking force:* bore heavily on 1082; crowded 1660. [a. OFr. *presser.*]

preson, pryson *n.* prison 1304, 1367. [a. OFr. *prisun, prison.*]

prest *adj.* ready for action 162. [a. OFr. *prest.*]

preuely *adv.* stealthily 1956. [ME. *prive, privy* adj. + *ly.*]

preuely *adv.* bravely 979. [ME. *preue* + *ly.*]

preuyd *pp.* proved, shown to be 751. [a. OFr. *prover.*]

pryce *n.* value; in adj. phr. *of pryce,* of great worth 305. [a. OFr. *pris.*]

pryde *n.* splendid ornamentation 183; arrogance 282, 550, 646; inordinate self-esteem, 471, 1218. [OE. *prȳdo.*]

pryson. See **preson.**

procescyon *n.* festive marching 797. [Early ME. a. Fr. *procesion.*]

prowde *adj.* lordly 118, 626, 779. [Late OE. *prūt, prūd.*]

put *v.* push 1327; *pt. sg.* placed 1304, 1634, 1974; *pt. pl.* 2029; *pp.* 1144; *imper.* send by force 580, thrust 1796. [Late OE. *putian.*]

Q

quarell *n.* a short, square-headed arrow 773, 1940; **quarels** *n.* *pl.* 861. [a. OFr. *quarel, quarrel,* etc.]

quene *n.* king's wife 2160. [OE. *cwēn.*]

quyte *v.* hand over 1671; reward 1733; **quytt** *pt.* *sg.* acquitted himself (of a task) 715. [a. OFr. *quiter.*]

quod *3 pt. sg.* said 731. [pt. of ME. *quethe.*]

qwelle *v.* kill 1670. [OE. *cwellan.*]

qwyte *adv.* completely 944, 1192. [ME. *quyt* adj.]

R

rayne *n.* rain 845. [OE. *reʒn.*]

rampande *adj.* rearing 845. [a. Fr. *rampant, pr. p.* of *ramper.*]

range *pt. pl.* rang 167, 1892. [OE. *hringan.*]

ranne *pt. sg.* of liquids: flowed 1040; went on foot 1259; *pt. pl.* flowed 578, 609. [OE. rinnan (*ran, *runnon, ʒerunnen*).]

rase *pt. sg.* got up 565. [OE. *rīsan.*]

rave *v.* show signs of madness 1835. [? a. OFr. *raver.*]

rawnsome *n.* ransom 663. [a. OFr. *rancon.*]

rechyd, rekyd *pt. sg.* aimed 1646; *pt. pl.* launched 132. [OE. *reacan.*]

recke *v.* heed 1154. [OE. *reccan* (? *rēcan*).]

recomforde *pt. pl.* consoled 1313. [ad. F. *renconforter.*]

redd *n.* reason, faculty of deliberation 35, 407; counsel 259; advise 1098. [OE. *rǣd, rēd.*]

redd *adj.* red 163, 179, 380, etc. [OE. *rēad.*]

rede *1 pr. sg.* advise 1207, 1420. [OE. *rǣdan, rēdan.*]

rede *pr. pl.* read 645, 1539. [OE. *rǣdan, rēdan.*]

redy *adv.* already 590. [Early ME. *readi.*]

redylye *adv.* with willingness 105. [f. *redy* + *lye.*]

refte *pt. pl.* deprived (by force) 926; pp. 2051. [OE. *rēafian.*]

reygned *3 pt. sg.* ruled 25. [a. OFr. *regner.*]

rekyd. See **rechyd, reykyd.**

reyned *pt. sg.* descended like rain 43. [OE. *reʒnian.*]

reyset *n.* refuge 1744. [a. OFr. *recet.*]

reysyd *3 pt. sg.* lifted 472. [a. ON. *reisa* = OE. *rēran.*]

rekenyth *3 pr. sg.* amount to, number 188. [OE. *(ge)recenian.*]

remes *n. pl.* kingdoms 117. [a. OFr. *reaume.*]

remouyd, remeuyd *pt. sg.* moved 606; taken away 1827. [a. OFr. *remouvoir.*]

rennyng *pr. p.* flowing 343, 383. [OE. *rinnan.*] See **rennande.**

rennyth *3 pr. sg.* flows 335, 1884. [OE. *rinnan.*]

renowne *n.* fame 1031. [a. AF. *renoun, renun.*]

rente *n.* source of income 1118, 1346, 2130. [a. OFr. *rente, rende.*]

rente *pt. sg.* tore 47. [OE. *rendan.*]

rerde *n.* cry 1427. [OE. *rēord.*]

rerewarde *n.* third division in the line of battle 605. [a. AF. *rerewarde.*]

rescowde, -ed *pt. sg.* saved 712; *pt. pl.* 702; *pp.* 718, 725; *pp.* (*pass.*) 489. [a. OFr. *rescoure.*]

resseyuyd *pp.* (*pass.*) welcomed 175. [ad. ONFr. *receivre, receyvre;* OFr. *recoivre.*]

revedd, revydd *pp.* robbed 1934, 1307. [OE. *rēafian.*]

reuerence *n.* power 1145, 1277. [a. OFr. *rēverence.*]

rewe *v.* regret 368, 942, 993, etc.; **rewyd** *pt. sg.* 2064. [OE. *hrēowan.*]

rewfull *adj.* pitiable 1427, 1518. [f. ME. *rew* + *ful.*]

ryall *adj.* noble 174; grand 178, 918, 1160, etc. [a. OFr. *roial.*]

ryally *adv.* with pomp 152, 505. [f. *ryall.*]

rybbes *n. pl.* ribs 1850. [OE. *rib, ribb.*]

ryche *adj.* valuable 85, 184, 386, etc.; mighty 218, 890, 1931, etc. [OE. *rīce.*]

ryde *v.* ride (a horse, a ship) 1, 117, 152, etc.; *pr. pl.* 1418; *pt. sg.* 588, 1259, 1384, etc.; *pt. pl.* 155, 373, 445, etc. [OE. *rīdan.*]

rydynge *vbl. n.* a mounted combat 623. [f. *ryde* + *ynge.*]

ryfe *adj.* abundant 1122. [Late OE. *ryfe.*]

rygge *n.* back (animal's) 746. [Northern form of ME. *rydge.*]

ryght *n.* that which is consonant with equity 261; duty 405; justifiable claim 933. [OE. *riht.*]

ryght *adj.* just 42, 1498; legitimate 651, 2066; correct 1414. [OE. *riht.*]

ryght, ryȝt *adv.* in due order 165; straight 202, 568, 597, etc.; with intensive force: *before adj.* 178, 386, 573; to the full 492; exactly 977; without delay 1290, 1612, 1646. [OE. *rihte.*]

ryke *n.* kingdom 1807. [OE. *rīce.*]

rynge *n.* circlet of precious metal (token of marriage) 889, 996. [OE. *hring.*]

rynge *v.* ring 1457. [OE. *hringan.*]

ryse *v.* rise 1858; **ryseth** *3 pr. sg.* mounts up 216; **rose** *pt. sg.* got up 750, 1860. [OE. *rīsan.*]

ryseth. See ryse.

ryve *v.* arrive 225; **ryved** *pt. pl.* 376. [ad. OFr. *river*, aphet. form of *arriver.*]

robe *n.* long outer garment 178; **robys** *n. pl.* 2157. [a. OFr. *robe.*]

roche *n.* rock 1875, 1917. [a. OFr. *roche, rocche.*]

rode *n.* cross 1105, 1511, 2186. [OE. *rōd.*]

romans, romance *n.* romance, tale in verse 82, 1539, 1546, etc.; used without article (with plural sense) 645. [a. OFr. *romanz, romans.*]

roo *n.* rest 840. [a. ON. and Icel. *ró* = OE. *rōw.*]

rope *n.* rope 2091; **ropys** *n. pl.* 386. [OE. *rāp.*]

rose. See ryse.

roton *pp.* rotted 2028. [OE. *rotian.*]

rowe *v.* row 1217. [OE. *rōwan.*]

rownde *adj.* spherical 54. [a. OFr. *ro(u)nd-.*]

rowned *pt. sg.* cried out 1753. [ad. OFr. *roungier.*]

S

sa. See so.

sadylde *pt. sg.* saddled 1294. [OE. *sadolian.*]

sadull, sadyll *n.* saddle 1534, 1802; **sadyls** *n. pl.* saddles 156, 677. [OE. *sadol.*]

safe *adj.* free from hurt 1916. [OFr. *sa(u)f.*]

say *imper.* try 126. [Aphet. form of ME. *assay.*]

say(e), sey(e) *v.* speak, say, tell 70, 274, 516, etc.; *1 pr. sg.* 154, 322, 614, etc.; *3 pr. sg.* 1026, 1387; *imper.* 1063; **sayne** *v.* 814, 1112, 1590, etc.; *pr. subj. sg.* 297; **seyth** *3 pr. sg.* 84, 439, 494, etc.; **says** *3 pr. sg.* 1205; **seyde** *pt. sg.* 76, 88, 223, etc.; *pt. pl.* 253, 452, 805, etc. [OE. *secgan.*]

sayle *n.* sail 136, 1051, 1826,

etc.; **seylys** *n. pl.* 373. [OE.
seȝ(e)l.]

sayled *pt. sg.* sailed 1842. [OE.
siȝlan.]

sayne. See say(e), sey(e).

says. See say(e), sey(e).

sake *n.*; for my sake, on my
account 576. [OE. *sacu.*]

salutyd *pt. pl.* addressed with
respect 505. [ad. L. *salūtāre.*]

same *n.* the same, the aforesaid
person or thing 365, 551, 1077,
etc. [a. ON. *same.*]

sange. See synge.

sare *adj.* in pain 1927. [OE. *sār.*]

sare *adv.* Of suffering: severely
684, 1424, 1451, etc. [OE. *sāre.*]

sate. See set, sytt.

sate. See sytt.

saue *pr. subj. sg.* protect 297, 696.
[a. OFr. *sauver.*]

sawe *n.* story 1281. [OE. *saȝu.*]

sawe. See see.

sawtrye *n.* stringed musical instru-
ment 63. [OE. *(p)saltere.*]

schall, shall *auxil. forming* (*with
pr. infin.*) *the future: 1 pr. sg.*
92, 116, 359, etc.; *3 pr. sg.* 108,
112, 279, etc.; *pr. pl.* 227, 257,
266, etc.; **schalt** *2 pr. sg.* 725,
763, 1423; **sch(o)ulde,** *auxil.
forming* (*with pr. infin.*) *the
conditional pt. sg.* 40, 51, 283,
etc.; *pt. pl.* 464, 531, 576, etc.;
schulyst *2 pt. sg.* 1191. [OE.
sceal, scūlon, scōlde.]

schake *v.* tremble 1976. [OE.
scacan.]

schakyng *pr. p.* (*adv.*) trembling
2024. [OE. *scacun.*]

schalt. See schall, shall.

schame *n.* infliction of disgrace
689; disgrace 1183, 1856; *god
gyf þe schames dedd*, God give
thee a shameful death 1474,
1821. [OE. *schamu, scamu.*]

schame *v.* shame 1442; **schamyth**
3 pr. sg. 2180. [OE. *scamian.*]

schare *pt. sg.* cut through 1632.
[OE. *sceran* (**scer, scēron,
scoren*).]

scharpe *adj.* keen-edged 679, 1624.
[OE. *scearp.*]

schawe *n.* thicket 1502. [OE.
sceȝa.]

sche, she *pron.* she 59, 67, 108,
etc.; **scho(o)** 1466, 1980; **hur**
acc. and *dat.* her 37, 57, 81,
etc.; *adj.* her 29, 64, 109, etc.;
subjective gen. 68; **hurselfe** *refl.
as indir. obj.* herself 1532. [OE.
prob. fem. demons. pron. *sēo*
and *hēo*; *hire.*]

scheldys. See schylde.

schende *v.* disgrace 1442; **schent**
pp. (*pass.*) 1615, 2045. [OE.
scéndan.]

schene *adj.* beautiful 559, 1452,
1823, etc. [OE. *scēne.*]

schepe. See schyp.

schewe *pr. pl.* exhibit to view
1101. [OE. *scēawian, sceāivian.*]

schylde *n.* shield 27, 366, 421, etc.;
protection 1497; **scheldys** *n. pl.*
shields 569. [OE. *scild.*]

schyp(p)e, schepe *n.* ship 16, 1050,
1056, etc.; **schyppes, -ys** *n. pl.*
131, 144, 146; *n. gen.* 1874.
[OE. *scīp.*]

schyre *adj.* bright 98. [OE. *scīr.*]

scho. See sche.

schone *n. pl.* shoes 655. [OE.
scoh.]

schone, schoon *pt. sg.* radiated
186; gleamed 655, 1540, 1545;
pt. pl. gleamed 156, 391, 1534.
[OE. *scīnan* (*scán, scinon*).]

schope *pt. sg.* created 1833. [OE.
sceppan (*scōp, scapen*).]

schoulde, sculde. See schall, shall.

schryue *v.* hear confession of 2035;
schrofe *pt. sg.* 776. [OE. *scrīfan*
(*scrāf, scrifon,* (*ȝe*)*scrifen*).]

schyppborde *n.* side of a ship 1794. [*schypp* + ME. *borde* n.]

scole *n.* school 58. [OE. *scōl.*]

scryed *pt. sg.* described 333. [Aphet. form of ME. *descry.*]

se. See **see.**

seconde *adj.* second 2097. [a. Fr. *second.*]

seculors *n. pl.* non-ecclesiastical men 1133. [a. OFr. *seculer.*]

see *n.* sea 88, 1063, 1114, etc. [OE. *sǣ.*]

see *v.* perceive 353, 486, 741, etc.; *2 pr. sg.* 1382; **sawe** *pt. sg.* 289, 1004, 2103; *pt. pl.* 1897; **sye** *pt. sg.* 667, 1157, 1885, etc.; *pt. pl.* 397, 1787; **seen** *pp.* 790, 1455; *pp.* (*pass.*) 3, 1080, 1247. [OE. *seon,* (*seah, sāwon, sēgon, ӡesewen.*)]

sege *n.* a beleaguering 874, 1168. [a. OFr. *sege.*]

segyd *pt. sg.* laid siege to 1174. [f. *sege.*]

seyde. See **say(e), sey(e).**

seylys. See **sayle.**

seynt *adj.* saint (prefixed to name of canonised persons) 434, 514, 694, etc. [a. OFr. *sainte, seint.*]

seyth. See **say(e), sey(e).**

seke. See **se(e)ke, syke.**

se(e)ke, syke *v.* find 1967; go in search of 21, 434, 2004; **sekyth** *3 pr. sg.* 2175. [OE. *sēcan.*]

se(y)ke *adj.* sick 1918, 1927. [OE. *sēoc.*]

sekenes *n.* disease 1971. [*seke* adj. + *nes.*]

sekyr *adj.* certain, sure 1129, 1331. [OE. *sicor.*]

selde *adv.* seldom 33. [OE. *seldan.*]

selde *pp.* paid for, avenged 561. [OE. *sellan.*]

sembyll *v.* assemble 74, 634; **sembelde** *pt. pl.* 370. [Aphet. variation of ME. *assemble.*]

sembelde. See **sembyll.**

semely *adj.* of a pleasing appearance 527, 1485, 1541, etc.; of great proportions 498. [a. ON. *sœmiligr.*]

semely *adv.* handsome 1158. [a. ON. *sœmiliga.*]

semyth *3 pr. sg.* appears to be 945. [ME. *seme,* a. ON. *sœma.*]

sende *v.* commission to go to a place or person 89, 115, 128, etc.; *2 pr. sg.* 214; *pr. pl.* 860; *pt. sg.* 120; *pt. pl.* 775; *pp.* 1975; **sent(e)** *pt. sg.* 124, 454; dispatched (a message) 1393; *pt. pl.* 2007; *pp.* 206. [OE. *sendan.*]

sendell *n.* thin silken material 163. [a. OFr. *cendal.*]

sent(e). See **sende.**

sent *v.* assent 241. [a. OFr. *a(s)sēnter.*]

sere *adj.* various 331, 1221. [ON. *sēr.*]

serue *v.* render service (to) 1732, 1752, 2094; *imper.* 231; **seruyd** *pt. pl.* 1554; *pp.* 1461. [a. OFr. *servir.*]

set(t) *v.* place; *1 pr. sg. set my soule,* bet my soul for 1131; *3 pr. sg.* 1840; *pr. pl.* 1693; *pt. sg.* 523, 629, 653, etc.; put in the way of following a course 58; caused to be in a certain condition 684; *pt. pl.* 373, 592, 721; set up, raised to an elevated position 1051; *pp.* 1535; **sete** *3 pr. sg.* 1481; **sate** *pt. sg.* caused to be in a certain condition 684. [OE. *settan.*]

set. See **sytt.**

sete. See **set.**

sethyn *adv.* next in order 1090, 1481. [OE. *siþþan.*]

seuyn *adj.* seven 330, 674. [OE. *seofon.*]

syclatowne *n.* cloth of gold or other rich material 179. [a. OFr. *ciclaton, -un.*]

syde *n.* side 108, 180, 362, etc.; sydes *n. pl.* 1550. [OE. *sīde.*]

syghed *pt. sg.* sighed 1094, 1424, 1701. [ME. *sihen, sizen,* etc.]

syghyng *vbl. n.* sorrow 919. [f. ME. *sihen v.*]

sygned *pt. pl.* assigned 865. [Aphet. f. ME. *assygned.*]

syght *n.* sight 798, 1541. [OE. *sihð.*]

sygnyfyed *pt. sg.* foreshadowed 49; betokened 424, 601, 1227. [ad. F. *signifier.*]

syke *v.* See se(e)ke, syke.

syke *adj.* See se(e)ke.

sylke *n.* silk 86, 385. [OE. *seoloc.*]

syluyr *n.* silver 328. [OE. *siolfor, seolfor.*]

sympull *adj.* simple 539, 577, 1672. [a. OFr. *simple.*]

syn *adv.* subsequently 1192. [Contracted from ME. *sithyn.*]

synge *v.* say mass 1005; sange *pt. pl.* sang 166; syngyng *pr. p.* singing 2147. [OE. *singan.*]

syngyng. See synge.

synke *v.* fall, degenerate 921. [OE. *sincan (sanc, suncon, suncen).*]

synne *n.* a sin (without article) 1692; synnes *n. pl.*; *dedly synnes seuyn,* seven deadly sins 330. [OE. *syn(n).*]

syr *n.* title of honour of a knight, placed before the Christian name 19, 26, 55, etc.; *n. pl.* 88; syrrys *n. pl.* 265, 198, 431, etc. [Reduced form of ME. *syre.*]

systur *n.* nun 1918. [OE. *sweoster.*]

syte *n.* care, *in phr.: sorowe and syte* 1629, 2107. [a. ON. **sýt.*]

sytt *v.* sit 1148; sate *pt. sg.* 177, 310, 1876; set *pt. sg. of things:* was situated 181. [OE. *sittan (sæt, sæton, zeseten).*]

sythe *adv.* afterwards 1190, 2050. [Reduced form of OE. *siððan.*]

sythyn, sethyn *conj.* then 1753, 2056; since 673. [OE. *siþþon.*]

sythys *n. pl.* times 1324. [OE. *sīþ, sīð.*]

syxe *adj.* card. num. six, *used with a noun* 595, 987. [OE. *sex, six,* etc.]

syxty *adj.* card. num. sixty, *used with a noun* 319, 370, 376, 438, etc. [OE. *syx-, sextiz.*]

skapyd *pp.* escaped 1191. [Aphet. var. of ME. *eskape.*]

skorne *n.* derision 513. [OFr. *escorne.*]

slayn(e). See slee.

slee *v.* kill, 221 1140; slewe *pt. sg.* 786, 1065, 1213, etc.; *pt. pl.* 467, 1037, 1083; slayn(e) *pp.* 68, 788, 893; *(pass.)* 704, 1102, 1337; slone *pp. (pass.)* 1347; slo *imper.* 850. [OE. *slēan (sloz, slōh, slōzon, slæzen).*]

slepe *v.* sleep 135, 1655; slepyd *pt. sg.* 1070, 1638. [OE. *slēpan (slēp, slēpon, -slāpen).*]

slewe. See slee.

slyly(lye) *adv.* stealthily 1947; cleverly? [f. ME. *slyh* adj. + *ly.*]

slo. See slee.

slone. See slee.

slope *n.* sleep 1630. [OE. *slāp.*]

small(e) *adj.* small 52, 338, 395, etc. [OE. *smæl.*]

smartely *adv.* promptly 1143. [f. ME. *smart* adj.]

smetyn *pp.* infected 2005; *pp. (pass.)* struck 1618. [OE. *smītan (smāt, smiton, smiten).*]

smyle *v.* smile 1788. [OE. **smīlan.*]

smote *pt. sg.* struck 1940, 2075; lowered (down) 1306. [OE. *smītan (smāt, smiton, smiten).*]

so(o), sa *adv.* in the manner described 267, 381, 517 etc.; *with the v. 'do', passing into the sense of* 'that' 272; *at the be-*

ginning of a clause with continuative force 251, 874; *to that extent* 33, 107, 1110, etc.; *in oaths* 297; *so* (that), *in limiting sense* 422; *thus* 494, 539, 772, etc.; *conj.* so that 1182. [OE. *swā.*]

soche *demons. adj.* of the character described 39, 71, 80, etc.; *pron.* persons or things before mentioned 323, 1463. [OE. *swelc, swilc.*]

socowre *n.* protection 631, 1602. [a. OFr. *sucurs, soc(c)ours.*]

softe *adj.* producing agreeable sensations 100; smooth 1550; pleasing 1763. [OE. *sǒfte.*]

solde *pt. sg.* sold 2096; *pt. pl.* 1784. [OE. *sellan.*]

solempnyte *n.* observance of ceremony 1161. [a. OFr. *solempneté.*]

some *adj.* certain (*with pl. nouns*) 100; a certain (*with sg. nouns*) 1669; *some tyme*, at one time or another 1241, 1259. [OE. *sum.*]

somedele *adj.* a little 674. [f. OE. *sum* adj. + *dēl*, n.]

somedele *adv.* somewhat 674. [OE. *sume dēle.*]

somer *n.* pack-horse 277. [a. OFr. *somer.*]

somersday *n.* a day in summer 311, 1434. [Cf. OFris. *sumersdey* Midsummer day.]

somned *pp.* (*pass.*) summoned 2146. [a. OFr. *somondre.*]

sone. See **soon.**

son(n)e *n.* son; God the Son 1676, 1779; **sonnes** *n. pl.* sons 407, 509. [OE. *sunu.*]

sonne *n.* sun 518, 1833, 1908. [OE. *sunne.*]

soon(e), sone *adv.* within a short time 142, 131, 214, etc.; *Also soon as*, as soon as 1054. [OE. *sōna.*]

sore *adj.* painful 1550. [OE. *sār.*]

sore *adv.* with great exertion, laboriously 21; with verbs of lamenting and denoting fear 1601, 1622, 1653, etc. [OE. *sāre.*]

sory *adj.* distressed 1022; unfortunate 1820. [OE. *sāriȝ.*]

sorowe *n.* grief 839, 921, 1055, etc. [OE. *sorȝ.*]

sorowfull *adj.* unhappy 1658. [OE. *sorȝful.*]

sorte *n.* fate 1089. [a. OFr. *sort.*]

sothe *n.* truth 306, 741, 1112, etc. [OE. *soð.*]

sotheyr *n.* soldier 1281; **sowdears** *n. pl.* 401, 512, 931. [a. OFr. *soud(i)er.*]

souereygn *n.* king 789, 863. [a. OFr. *soverain.*]

sowdears. See **sotheyr.**

sowle *n.* soul 1131. [OE. *sāwol, sāwel.*]

sownde *adv.* in safety 57, 696, 1574, etc. [f. ME. *sownde* adj.]

sowne *n.* sound (produced by the voice) 761. [a. AF. *soun*; OFr. *son.*]

sowþe *adv.* towards the south 2012. [OE. *suð.*]

sowtheweste *adv.* towards the south-west 1415. [OE. *suðwest.*]

space *n.* without article: lapse of time 608, 1011. [ad. OFr. *espace.*]

spaynysch *adj.* Spanish 133. [f. ME. *Spayne* + *ysh.*]

spake. See **speke.**

spare, spere *v.* save 293; refrain from using 403, 1556; leave unused 1011; **spared** *pt. sg.* refrained from using 746; *pp.* left unused 662; **speryd** *pt. pl.* refrained from using 448. [OE. *sparian.*]

sparryd *pt. sg.* bolted 1772. [var. of ME. *sparre* v.]

speche *n.* words 907, 1409. [OE. *sp(r)ēc.*]

specyally *adv.* expressly 1439. [OFr. *(e)speciaument.*]

spede *n.* pace 1295, 1863. [OE. *spēd.*]

speke *v.* talk 1546, 1920; *speke wyth*, talk to 1405; *pr. pl.* utter 513; discourse 794; **spake** *pt. sg.* 2098; **spekynge** *pr. p.* 2013. [OE. *sp(r)ecan, (sp(r)eac, sp(r)econ, ӡesp(r)ecen).*]

spere. See **spare.**

spere *n.* spear 366, 465, 472, etc.; **sperys** *n. pl.* 721. [OE. *spere.*]

speryd *pt. sg.* shut up 172. [a. MLG. *speren.*]

spering *pr. p.* closing 149. [a. MLG. *speren.*]

spyed *pt. sg.* watched 1595. [ad. OFr. *espier.*]

spylle *v.* destroy 837; run out 633; **spylte** *pp.* (*pass.*) wasted 557. [OE. *spillan.*]

spyr *v.* publish 2013. [Special sense of ME. *spir, speir* v.]

spyrytualte *n.* body of ecclesiastical persons 1132. [ad. OFr. *spiritualté.*]

spytt *3 pr. sg.* spit out 1607. [Northern OE. *spittan.*]

sprang *pt. sg.* spread (of fame, rumour) 1930. [OE. *springan.*]

sprede *v.* unfurl 803. [OE. *sprēdan.*]

spurrys *n. pl.* spurs 745. [OE. *spura, spora.*]

squyers *n. pl.* squires 835. [ad. OFr. *esquier.*]

stabull *n.* stable 1558. [a. OFr. *estable.*]

stabull *v.* make stable 1236. [a. OFr. *establer.*]

stadde *pp.* (*pass.*) burdened 1311. [Early ME. *stude, stede.*]

stake *n.* post 1663. [OE. *staca.*]

stalle *n.* stable 201. [OE. *steall.*]

standard(e) *n.* flag 547, 592, 598, etc. [Aphet. a. OFr. *estandard.*]

stande, stonde *v.* stand 711, 1899; wait for 271; *agenste hym stande*, oppose 1233; *pr. pl.* 325; **standys** *3 pr. sg.* 221; **standyth, stondyth, standyþ** *3 pr. sg.* 337, 1340, 1883; **stode** *pt. sg.* 384, 506, 562, etc.; *in stede stode me* was of service to me 948; *... nede stode*, required 1553; *pt. pl.* stood in position (*with infin. expressing accompanying action*) 264; *stode owte* 2027; **stondyng** *pr. p.* 324. [OE. *standan (stōd, stōdon, ӡestanden).*]

standys. See **stande, stonde.**

standyth, stondyth, standyþ. See **stande, stonde.**

stane *n.* rock 1146. [OE. *stān.*]

starte *pt. sg.* jumped 1643. [OE. **stertan;* cp. *styrtan.*]

stavys *n. pl.* walking sticks 1991. [OE. *stæf.*]

stedd, stede *n.* another 409; place 1095, 1160, 1554, etc.; an enclosure 379. [OE. *stede.*]

stede *n.* stallion 160, 586, 642, etc.; **stedys** *n. pl.* 124, 133, 143, etc. [OE. *steda.*]

stekyth *pr. sg.* sticks 1472. [OE. *stician.*]

stele *n.* steel 638, 1335, 1625; *trewe as any stele*, thoroughly trustworthy 398. [OE. *stēle.*]

stelyng *pr. p.* coming stealthily 720. [OE. *stelan.*]

steppyd *pt. sg.* stepped 1879. [OE. *steppan (stōp, (be)stapen).*]

stepull *n.* tall tower 1885. [OE. *stēpel.*]

stere *v.* govern, rule 414; guide 825, 1236. [OE. *stȳran.*]

sterne *adj.* resolute in battle 398; *adv.* harshly 414. [OE. *styrne.*]

steuyn *n.* voice 333, 481, 2155. [OE. *stefn.*]

steward *n.* a major-domo 228. [OE. *stiweard.*]

styckyd *pp.* (*pass.*) pierced 642. [OE. *stician.*]

styffe *adj.* resolute, steadfast 573. [OE. *stif.*]

styf(fe)ly *adv.* firmly 711; hard 485. [f. *styffe* + *ly.*]

stylle *adj.* calm, quiet 630, 813. [OE. *stille.*]

stylle *adv.* silently 234; motionless 908, 1185, 1749. [OE. *stille.*]

stylle *v.* quiet 831. [OE. *stillan.*]

styrryth *3 pr. sg. refl.* acts energetically 485. [OE. *styrian.*]

stythe *adj.* strong 842. [OE. *stīð.*]

stode. See **stande, stonde.**

stokkes *n. pl.* stocks (instrument of punishment) 1148. [OE. *stoc(c).*]

stolyn *pp.* (*with 'away'*) gone unobserved 1353. [*stelan* (*stæl, stælon, stolen*).]

stondyng. See **stande, stonde.**

ston(e) *n.* stone 340, 392, 1879, etc.; **stones** *n. pl.* 641, 860. [OE. *stān.*]

store *n.* accumulated goods, supply 878, 1166; *fig.* 1657. [aphet. f. *astore* n., a. OFr. *estor.*]

store *v.* furnish 654. [Aphet. var. of *astore* v., a. OFr. *estorer.*]

story *n.* tale 2173. [a. AF. *estorie.*]

storme *n.* storm 1858, 1864. [OE. *storm.*]

stownde *n.* moment 372, 702, 1421. [OE. *stund.*]

stowre *n.* armed conflict 708, 727, 743, etc.; *in phr. styffe in stowre*, brave in battle 573. [a. AF. *estur*; OFr. *estour.*]

straunge *adj.* unusual 435. [a. OFr. *estrange.*]

strekyn *pp.* (*pass.*) *in phr.: strekyn in age,* driven inwards with age 670. [OE. *strīcan* (*strāc, stricon, stricen*).]

strekk *adv.* straightway 1153. [f. ME. *streke adj.*]

streme *n.* stream 1777; *n. pl.* 1217. [OE. *strēam.*]

strenkyþ, -th *n.* fortress 497, 1174. [OE. *strengðu.*]

strenkyþfull *adj.* full of strength 1583. [f. *strenkyþ* + *full.*]

strete *n.* road 641, 851; **stretys** *n. pl.* 2030. [OE. *strēt.*]

stryfe *n.* discord 216, 1125. [a. OFr. *estrif.*]

stryke *v.* to deal a blow 24; **strykeþ** *3 pr. sg.* 488; **stryked** *pt. sg.* made (his) way into 127; **stroke** *pt. sg.* 745 *pt. pl.* 1862; *stroke in,* made his way into 784. [OE. *strīcan.*]

strynde *n.* lineage 2172. [OE. *strỹnd.*]

stryve *pr. pl.* wrangle 1851. [ME. *striven,* a. OFr. *estriver.*]

stroye *v.* destroy 848, 855. [Aphet. f. ME. *destroye.*]

stroke. See **stryke.**

strong(e) *adj.* physically powerful 14, 143, 495, etc.; *of suffering:* hard to bear 839. [OE. *stráng, stróng.*]

strote *n.* projection 2027. [OE. **strūt.*]

struglynge *vbl. n.* the action of struggle 185. [ME. *strugle* v. + *ynge.*]

suffur *v.* endure 707, 915; **suffurde** *pt. sg.* 913, 1848. [a. AF. *suffrir, soeffrir.*]

swayne *n.* servant 1872. [a. ON. *sveinn.*]

swalme *v.* faint 770. [f. ME. *swalm* n.]

sware *n.* speech. [Partly OE. **swaru,* partly ON. *svar.*]

sware *adj.* loth 90. [OE. *swer, swēre.*]

sweme *n.* swoon, dizziness 770. [OE. *swīma.*]

swepe *v.* drive along 138. [ME. *swepe.*]

swere *v.* swear, take an oath 988, 1084, 1489; *pt. sg.* 499; **sworne** *pp.* 355, 806, 992; *pp. (pass.)* 980, 1123, 1357. [OE. *swerian (swōr, sworen).*]

swete *adj.* dearly loved 1106, 1467, 1469; lovely 90; pleasing to the ear 168, 441. [OE. *swēte.*]

swylke *adj.* such 386. [Northern form corresponding to OE. *swilc.*]

swymmyng *pr. p.* swimming 390. [OE. *swimman (swamm, swummon, swummen).*]

swyrde *n.* sword 585, 722, 1224, etc.; **swyrdys** *n. pl.* 679. [OE. *sweord.*]

swythe *adv.* without delay 1111. [OE. *swiðe.*]

sworne. See **swere.**

swowned *pt. sg.* swooned 824; *pp.* 1093. [ME. *swoȝene, swoȝeny, swowene.*]

T

ta. See **take, ta, too.**

take, ta, too *v.* seize 277, 585, 887, etc.; accept 880; *1 pr. sg.* bring 1856; *imper.* seize 268, 1792, 1796; accept 896; *weakened sense of* seize 1060; **toke** *pt. sg.* seized 2122; accepted 415; brought 493, 675, 1079; *toke ... leue*, departed 960; *pt. pl.* captured 950; brought 443; ate and drank 447; *toke ... leue* departed 285, 2139, 2159 (see **leue**); *toke downe*, cut down 1279; *toke hym tome*, took the opportunity 292; **takyn** *pp.* captured *pp. (pass.)* 53; seized 1034; *weakened sense of* seized 607; **tane** *pp.* captured 787, 892, 924 *(pass.)* 1103, 1143; con-

veyed 700; *(pass.)* accepted (advice) 259. [Late OE. *tacan (toc, tacen).*]

tale *n.* story 1129, 1331, 1392. [OE. *talu.*]

talme *v.* become exhausted, faint 769 [Akin to ON. *talma.*]

tame *adj.* domesticated 45. [OE. *tam.*]

tane. See **take, ta, too.**

taste *n.* trial, attempt 852. [a. OFr. *tast.*]

taste *v.* explore by touch 109. [a. OFr. *taster.*]

telle *v.* recount 40, 306, 350, etc.; make known 294; *þe boke telle*, read the book 59; *1 pr. sg.* recount 164, 1970; **tolde** *pt. sg.* made known 346, 564, 757, etc.; recounted 105, 451, 734, etc.; reckoned 1320; *pt. pl.* discerned 296; recounted 62, 82, 345, etc.; made known 1091. [OE. *tellan.*]

tempeste *n.* storm 2101. [a. OFr. *tempeste.*]

temporalte *n.* laity [app. a. AF. **temporelté.*]

te(e)ne *n.* rage, wrath, 560, 1083. [OE. *tēona.*]

tene *v.* injure 1322. [a. OE. *tēonian.*]

terys *n. pl.* tears 578. [OE. *tēar.*]

tethe *n. pl.* teeth 1618, *fortethe* front teeth 1607, 2075. [OE. *tōþ, tōð.*]

th-. See **þ, th.**

tyde *n.* any definite time in the course of the day, *mornetyde* morning 114; time 189, 285, 426, etc. [OE. *tīd.*]

tyght *pt. pl.* set firmly 379. [Obscure.]

tyl(l), tyll(e) *prep.* of time: until 59, 418; *adv.* unto 228, 833, 624, etc.; until 741, 965, 980, etc. [ONth. *til.*] See **þertylle.**

tylleth *3 pr. sg.* persuades, wins over 991. [OE. **tyllan.*]

tyme *n.* a particular period 19, 1214; general state of affairs at a particular period 254; *þat tyme,* a particular period characterised in some way 406; *some tyme* occasionally 1241, 1259; **tymes** *n. pl.* used to express the multiplication of a number: *ix tymes* 1705. [OE. *tīma.*]

tymely *adv.* soon, quickly 591, 1394, 1501. [Late OE. *tīmlice.*]

tymberde *pp. fig.* caused, brought about 560. [OE. *timbran.*]

tyre *n.* apparel 2120. [Aphet. f. ME. *atyre.*]

tyte *adv.* smart, alert 289, 656, 693, etc. [ad. ME. *thyght.*]

tyþyngys, tythandys, tythadys *n. pl.* events 236; news 435, 449, 846, etc. [Late OE. *tidung.*]

to(o) *prep.* to expressing motion towards 15, 16, 48, etc.; expressing purpose, condition, or status 28, 72, 81, etc.; before an infin. in adverbial relation 111, 130, 235, etc.; before infin. 551, 617, 635, etc.; indication obj. 529, 754, 846, etc.; *adv.* according to, in order to 881, 938. [OE. *tō.*]

tobrokyn *pp.* broken down 103. [OE. *tobrecan.*]

today, todey *adv.* today 613, 1856. [OE. *to dæg.*]

todusched *pt. pl.* dashed to pieces 638. [ME. *todaschen.*]

togedur, togodur *adv.* together 258, 636, 676, etc. [OE. *to gædere.*]

togodur. See **togedur, togodur.**

toyle *n.* strife 1936. [a. AF. *toil, toyl.*]

toke. See **take.**

tolde. See **telle.**

tome *n.* opportunity 292. [a. ON. *tóm.*]

tome *adj.* empty 144. [OE. *tōm.*]

tomorne *n.* tomorrow 1376. [f. *to* + OE. *morȝenne.*]

too. See **to.**

too. See **take, ta, too.**

toppe *n.* highest part 1861. [OE. *top(p).*]

torusched *pt. sg.* dashed in pieces 637. [ME. *to-ruschen,* f. *to* + *ruschen.*]

town(e) *n.* city 2, 341, 535, etc.; village 140, 166; **townes** *n. pl.* 650; *gen. n.* 1745. [OE. *tūn.*]

towre *n.* tower 567, 1144, 1229, etc.; **towres, -ys** *n. pl.* 296, 650. [OE. *torr.*]

trayne *n.* deceit 1416, 1623. [a. OFr. *traine.*]

traytur *n.* betrayer 1027, 1381, 1431, etc. [a. OFr. *traitre.*]

trauayle *n.* labour 1309. [a. OFr. *travail.*]

trauelde *pp. (pass.)* tormented 104. [a. OFr. *travaillier.*]

tre(e) *n.* tree 1437, 1505, 1514; the cross on which Christ was crucified 1430; pieces of wood 1348. [OE. *trēo.*] See **galow(e).**

tredd *n.* path 1880. [Early ME. *trede.*]

tree. See **tre.**

trembyll *v.* quiver 635; **trembylde** *pt. sg.* 94. [a. Fr. *trembler.*]

treson *n.* treachery 1272, 1284. [a. AF. *treysoun, tresun, treson.*]

tresory *n.* a place for valuables 204. [a. OFr. *tresorie.*]

tresowr(e), tresur *n.* a store of anything valuable 142, 165, 268, etc. [a. OFr. *tresor.*]

tresse *n.* braid of the hair 1513. [a. OFr. *tresse.*]

trewage *n.* tribute 947. [a. OFr. *treuage.*]

trewe *adj.* of persons: steadfast 301, 987, 1206; honest 620, 906,

945; **trewest** *sup.* most honest 2184. [OE. *trēowe*.]

trewly *adv.* honestly 82; used to emphasise statement: indeed 738, 1038, 2079. [OE. *trēowlice*.]

trybulacyons *n. pl.* miseries 50. [a. OFr. *tribulacion*.]

trynyte *n.* in phr.: *Hym in trynyte* 'Him in threeness' 1847; trinity 1881. [a. OFr. *trinite*.]

troyan *n.* inhabitant of Troy 13. [ad. L. *Trōiānus*.]

trone *n.* seat of God 1839. [a. OFr. *trone*.] See **heuyn**.

trowe *pr. sg.* believe, trust 670, 732, 791, etc.; *imper.* 738, 1038. [OE. *trēowan, trēowian*.]

trowed *pt. sg.* believed 1392. [OE. *trēawan, trēowian*.]

trumpes *n. pl.* trumpets 635. [a. F. *trompe*.]

tuggelde *pt. sg.* dragged about 1936. [app. rel. to ME. *tugge*.]

turne *v.* change 1243; *turne again* return 1037; **turned** *pt. sg.* changed 1685; *pp.* (*pass.*) returned 1125. [OE. *turnian*.]

turnement *n.* a meeting for knightly sports 1616. [OFr. *turnement*.]

twenty *adj.*: *as multiplier before a num.* 320; *in conjunction with a n.* 1147; *used for the ordinal* twentieth 1895. [OE. *twentiʒ*.]

twyes *adv.* two times 1093. [Late OE. *twiʒes*.]

twynkylde *pt. sg.* blinked 1748. [OE. *twinclian*.]

two *adj. card. num.* two, *with n.* 415, 1078, 1401, etc. [OE. *twā*.]

Þ, Th

thay. See **þey, they.**

than. See **then.**

þankyd, -ed, thankyd *pt sg.* gave thanks 520, 1731, 1806; *pt. pl.* 2133, 2160. [OE. *þancian*.]

þar(e), thare, þer(e), ther(e), thore *adv.* in (or at) that place 216, 317, 339, etc.; *with v.* 'to be' 18, 158, etc.; *used unemphatically to introduce a clause: with intr. verbs* 41, 334. [OE. *þēr, þēr*.]

þar *3 pr. sg.* need 23. [OE. *þearf*.]

þat, that *dem. adj.* that: *indicates a thing or person pointed out* 10, 26, 52, etc. [OE. *þæt*.]

þat, that *rel. pron.* introducing a clause defining or restricting the antecedent 12, 15, 19, etc. [Unstressed form of the dem. pron.]

þat, that *conj.* introducing a dependent clause 21, 49, 61, etc. [OE. *þæt*.]

þe, the. See **þou, thou.**

þe, the(e) *def. art* the 8, 13, 17, etc.; *generally or universally* 19, 22, 26, etc. [OE. *se* (late *þe*).]

thede *n.* nation 246, 1536. [OE. *þēod*.]

þedur, thedur *adv.* to that place 287, 962, 1048, etc. [OE. *þider*.]

thee. See **þe, the(e).**

thefe *n.* thief 1279, 1633, 1712, etc.; **thefys** *n. pl.* 1744. [OE. *þēof*.]

thefte *n.* larceny 1730. [OE. *þēofð*.]

þey, they, thay *pron. pl.* they 44, 130, 132, etc.; **þem, them** them: *as dir. obj.* 105, 130, 138, etc.; *indir. obj.* 305, 653; *obj. of prep.* 124, 133, 257, etc.; *refl.* 462, 571; **þer, ther** *poss. adj.* their: 142, 143, 144, etc.; **þemselfe** themselves: *as emphatic nom.* 1203. [OE. *þā*; ? ON. *þeim*, ?OE. *þæm*; OE. *þēra*; See *OED*.]

þemselfe. See **þey, they, thay.**

þen, then, than *dem. adv.* at that time 7, 18, 216, etc. [OE. *þanne, þænne, þon*.]

þen, then *conj.* than: *used after comp. adv.* 2, 4, 101, etc.; *with ellipsis of preceding comp.* 247; *conj. adv. of time:* then 499, 502, 520, etc. [OE. *þanne, þænne, þon.*]

thens *adv.* from there 434. [ME. *þannes.*]

þer, ther. See þey, they, thay.

þer(e), ther(e). See þar(e), thare, þer(e), ther(e), thore.

thereaftur *adv.* after that time 787, 1094, 1586. [OE. *þǣr æfter.*]

þereby, thereby *adv.* near that, adjacent to 412, 1520, 1960. [OE. *þǣrbi.*]

þerfore, ther- *adv.* for that reason 368, 557, 599, etc. [Early ME. *þerfore.*]

therforne *adv.* therefore 356. [Alteration of ME. *therfore,* from OE. *-foran.*]

therfro *adv.* from that place 1969. [ME. *ther + fro.*]

þeryn, theryn(ne) *adv.* in that place 447, 1368, 1944; in that particular 2088. [OE. *þǣrin.*]

therof, therof *adv.* of it 1468, 1471, 1629. [OE. *þærof.*]

thertylle *adv.* thereto 241. [ME. *þar till.*]

þerto, therto(o) *adv.* besides 301, 327, 760, etc. [OE. *þēr tō, þærtō.*]

þes, thes *dem. adj. sg.* this 191; *pl.* these 190, 466, 581, etc. [See *OED.*]

thetodur *n. pron.* the other 731, 1079, 1275, etc. [ME. *þe toþer.*]

þy, thy. See þou, thou.

þyck, thyck *adj.* dense 1435, 1642, 1660. [OE. *þicce.*]

thyckfolde *adv.* in quick succession 873. [OE. *þicce + fōld* suff.]

thyn(e). See þou, thou.

thynge, þonge *n.* thing 962;

applied to a person 307, 1667, 1728, etc.; *all thynge,* everything, all things 60, 230; *no maner of thynge* 1003; þyngys *n. pl.* 331. [OE. *þing.*]

thynke *pr. sg.* consider 913; *pr. pl.* intend 1722; *pr. subj. sg.* intend 906. [OE. *þyncan (þǔhte, ʒepǔht).*]

thynke *n.* possession 918. [OE. *þing.*]

þynkyth, thynkyth *pr. sg.* imagines 1738, 2108. [OE. *þyncan (þǔhte, ʒepǔhte).*]

þys, thys *dem. adj.* this: *used in accord with n.* 5, 36, 37, etc. [See *OED.*]

tho *dem. pron.* those 416, 692, 987, etc. [OE. *þā.*]

thogh, thowe, tho *conj.* howbeit: *introducing a subordinate clause* 310, 663, 1155, etc.; *introducing a restricting statement:* however 1479. [OE. *þēh.*]

þoght *n.* idea 1768. [OE. *þoht.*]

þoght, thoght *pt. sg.* considered 526, 1469, 1577, etc.; *pt. pl.* 2038; *pt. sg. with on:* remembered 1249; *pt. sg.* contemplated 1639; *pt. pl.* planned 462. [OE. *þync(e)an, (þǔhte, ʒepǔht).*]

thonderblaste *n.* clap of thunder 1641. [OE. *þunor + blæst.*]

þonge. See thynge, þonge.

thore. See þar(e), thare, þer(e), ther(e), thore.

þorow, thorow *adv.* through 117, 148, 152, etc. [OE. *ðurh, þurh.*]

thorowly *adv.* fully, completely 1647. [OE. *þurh + ly.*]

þou, thou *pron.* thou 214, 554, 670, etc.; þe, the *acc.* thee 668, 724, 929, etc.; *refl.* thyself 910; þy, thy(n)(e) *adj.* 201, 204, 206, etc. [OE. *þu, þē, þin.*]

þousand(e), thousand(e) *n.* card. num., thousand: *after another*

num. sg. used as coll. pl. 356,
370, 438, etc.; adj. followed by
pl. n. 320, 1373. [OE. þusend.]

thowe. See thogh.

thra adj. persistent 1113. [ME. a.
ON. þra-r.]

thraste pt. sg. pressed 1647. [OE.
þræstan.]

þre, three adj. card. num. three
in accord with n. 43, 358, 1133,
etc.; in phr.: be two and three,
by twos and threes 786. [OE.
þrī.]

thretty adj. card. num. thirty 119.
[OE. þritiჳ.]

thryd(d) adj. third, ord. num.:
with n. expressed 13, 377. [OE.
þridda.]

thryes adv. three times 1094. [ME.
þriჳes.]

thrynge v. press hard, use op-
pression 1368. [OE. þringan,
(þrang, þrungon, þrungen).]

throo adj. angry, violent 2118.
[ME. a ON. þrár; þráliga.]

throte n. throat 1631. [OE. þrote.]

þus, thus adv. in this way 367, 957,
991, etc. [OS. thus.]

V (vowel)

vndo imper. undress 1509. [OE.
on-, undon.]

vndur prep. below 65, 324, 518,
etc.; with reference to something
which covers; clothes, etc. 27, 135.
[OE. under.]

vndurne n. third hour of the day;
about 9 a.m. 1504. [OE. undern.]

vndurnethe prep. beneath 1437.
[OE. underneoðan..]

vndurstande, vndurstonde v. to
have knowledge 1896; 1 pr. sg.
110, 160, 344, etc. [OE. under-
stonden, -standen.]

vndurtake 2 pr. sg. take in hand
905. [OE. underniman with sub-
stitution of take.]

vnfayne adj. displeased 692. [OE.
unfæჳen.]

vnfrendely adv. in an unfriendly
manner 2087. [vn + ME.
frendely.]

vngayne adj. of ways: not plain or
direct 1421; difficult of access
1875. [vn + ME. gayne; cp.
ON. úgegn, unreasonable.]

vnhele n. misfortune 1338. [OE.
unhēlu.]

vnnethe adv. scarcely 1339. [OE.
uneaðe, f. un + eaðe.]

vnnethys adv. scarcely 2132. [f.
prec. + s.]

vnpees n. strife 615. [vn ME. +
pees, prob. after unfrith.]

vnto prep. until 19, 2063; directed
towards 50, 147, towards 150,
173, 497, etc.; with a view to
271; indicating the persons to-
wards whom action is directed
284, 538, 790, etc.; to 1333; as
high ME. 1826. [f. on the analogy
of ME. vntill. Cp. OS. untō.]

vnwelde adj. weak, feeble 95. [vn
ME. + welde adj.]

vp adv. up 142, 373, 494, etc.;
with verbs denoting consuming
or destroying, stroye up 848.
[OE. up(p).]

vpholde v. support, stay 883. [Cf.
OFris. op-, uphalaa.]

vpon prep. on 158, 342, 683, etc.;
indicating the cause espoused by
the agent 404; against 548;
on top of 1120, 1876, 2104;
up towards 767; indicating day
of an occurrence 1597. [OE. upp-
on.]

vs. See we(e).

V (consonant)

v The Roman numeral symbol for
five: vij, 296; vx 1195.

vanysched, -t pt. sg. disappeared

1444, 1499. [Aphet. ad. OFr. *evanissir*.]

vawewarde *n.* vanguard 604. [Reduced form of *vamward*.]

venge *v.* avenge 976; **vengyd** *pt. sg.* 1582; *pp.* 1621. [ad. OFr. *vengier, venger*.]

venome *n.* poisonous fluid 2114, 2116. [a. AF. and OFr. *venim (venym)*.]

verament *adv.* really, truly 455, 1805, 1940, etc. [ad. AF. *veirement*.]

verraye *adv.* in truth 1926. [From OFr. *verai*.]

vetaylyd *pt. sg.* supplied with victuals 1166. [ad. AF. and OFr. *vitailler*.]

vylenye *n.* wrongdoing of a shameful nature 689. [a. AF. *vile(i)nie, vilanie*.]

vysage *n.* face 1563. [a. AF. and OFr. *visage*.]

vysyon *n.* dream 1639. [a. AF. *visiun, visioun;* OFr. *vision*.]

vysyted *pt. sg.* went (in order to assist the sick) 1921. [ad. OFr. *visiter*.]

voyce *n.* without article: singing 1904. [a. AF. *voiz, voice;* OFr. *vois*.]

W

waa *n.* distress 1743. [OE. *wā*.]

wach *v.* attend diligently 1356. [OE. *wæcc-*, a doublet of *wacian*.]

way, wey *n.* course of travel 1289, 1414, 1700, etc.; **wayes, weyes** *n. pl.* 1952; roads 172; *be Godys wayes*, by God's providence 1204. [OE. *weȝ*.]

wakenyd *pt. sg.* stirred up 2076. [OE. *wæcnan*.]

wakenyng *vbl. n.* rousing 1658. [OE. *wæcnan*.]

wakenyth *3 pr. sg.* awakens 1743. [OE. *wæcnan*.]

wall(e) *n.* wall, rampart of stone 394, 478, 965; **walles** *n. pl.* 860. [OE. *wall*.]

wan(ne). See **wynne.**

wanne *adj.* deadly 1992. [OE. *wann*.]

wante *v. tr.* to be destitute of 2109. [Prob. a ON. *vanta*.]

ware *adj.* watchful, vigilant 304. [OR. *ȝewær*.]

wared *pp.* guarded 661. [OE. *warian*.]

waryson *n.* reward 546. [a. OFr. *warison*.]

warme *adj.* warm 100; rich 878, 1166. [OE. *wearm*.]

warnyd *pt. sg.* denied 559. [OE. *wiernan; wearnian*.]

warre *n.* war, 104, 404, 941. [Late OE. *wyrre, werre*, a. northeastern OFr. *werre*.]

warre *adj., predicative use:* aware, conscious 1528, 2014. [OE. *wær*.]

warse *adj.* worse 2086. [OE. *wyrsa, wiersa*.]

warste *adj. used as the sup. of the adjs.* bad, evil *or* ill 956; most inferior 649. [OE. *wyrresta, wyrsta*.]

warste. See **was.**

was *pt. sg.* was 2, 3, 5, etc.; **were** *pt. sg.* came from 1557; *pt. pl.* were 44, 75, 122, etc.; *pt. subj. sg.* might (would) be 315, 404, 453, etc.; **ware** *pr. subj. sg.* 267, 601, 673, etc.; **warste** *pt. subj. sg.* 245. [OE. *wæs (wes); wǣron*, etc.; ON. pl. *várum*, etc.]

wasche *v.* wash 339. [OE. *wascan*.]

waste *adj.* uninhabited 1503. [a. OFr. *wast(e)*.]

wate. See **wytt.**

water, watur *n.* water 383, 334, 1466, etc.; *n. pl.* rivers 341. [OE. *wæter*.]

waxe *n.* wax 1544. [OE. *weax.*]

waxe *pt. sg.* became 32, 73, 380, etc. [OE. *weaxan.*]

we(e) *pron.* we 197, 224, etc.; **owre** *adj.* our 200, 233, 259, etc.; **vs** *acc.* us 236, 345, 533, etc.; *obj. of a prep.* 482, 980; *refl.* ourselves 1207. [OE. *wē, ūre, ūs.*]

wed(d)(e) *v.* marry 101, 212, 619, etc.; *1 pr. sg.* 1097; *pt. sg.* 2048; *pp.* 77, 409, 1351; *pp.* (*pass.*) 936, 1023, 1099. [OE. *weddian.*]

weddyng *n.* marriage 1136. [f. *wedd(e)* + *yng.*]

wede *n.* garment 1533, 1691; **wedys** *n. pl.* 398. [OE. *wǣd; wǣde.*]

wede *v.* become mad 1683, 2080. [OE. *wēdan.*]

wedows *n. pl.* widows 1221. [OE. *widwe, widuwe.*]

wedur *n.* weather 768. [OE. *weder.*]

wey. See **way.**

weyght *n.* weight 1706, 1790. [OE. *wiht.*]

wel(l), wele *adv.* skillfully 62, 1181, 1732; *with v. of greeting:* with friendly words 127; satisfactorily 250, 456, 661, etc.; *used as intensive to strengthen v., with verbs of pleasing* 302, 170, 290, etc. [OE. *wel(l).*]

welcomed *3 pt. sg.* greeted 1762. [OE. *wilcumian.*]

welde *v.* possess 30, 354, 558, etc.; handle with skill 534; *1 pr. sg.* 830. [OE. *(ge)weldan.*]

wele. See **wel(l).**

weleawaye *interj.* wellaway 1428. [OE. *weȝ lá weȝ.*]

welle *n.* source 300. [OE. *well(a).*]

welnere *adv.* wellnigh 1055. [Early ME. f. *wel* + *nere.*]

wemon, woman *n.* woman 369, 577; **wemen, women** *n. pl.* 1654, 2176. [OE. *wīfmon, wīfman.*]

wende *v.* return 123, 1059, 1196; travel 1238, 1700, 1797; depart 1289; go forward 1370; *pr. pl.* go forward 1777; go 227; depart 536; **went(e)** *pt. sg.* travelled 1276, 1360, 1397, etc.; returned 314, 898; departed 1772, 1922; *impers.* with *hyt happened* 377; *pt. pl.* travelled 985, 1112, 1245, etc.; returned 288; departed 239, 419, 821; thought 1816; turned 970; *went crowlande* (see **crowlande**), [OE. *wendan.*]

wene *n.* misery 12, 1086, 1822, etc. [OE. *wēa.*]

wenyst *pr. pl.* expect, think 958. [OE. *wenian.*]

went(e). See **wende.**

wepe *v.* shed tears 1654, 1686; **wepyd** *pt. sg.* 1095; **wepte** *pt. pl.* 870. [OE. *wēpan.*]

wepon *n.* weapon; **wepons** *n. pl.* 534. [OE. *wǣpen.*]

were. See **was.**

wery *adj.* weary 430, 536. [OE. *wēriȝ.*]

werkys *n. pl.* moral actions 1364. [OE. *we(o)rc.*]

werre *n.* war 459, 672. [Late OE. *wyrre, werre,* a. ONFr. *werre.*]

werryd *pt. sg.* made war upon 20, 1937. [f. *werre.*]

wete *v.* know 1717; **wetyn** *pp.* 1623. [ME. *wēte(n)* var. f. *wite(n).*]

wete *adj.* bloody 1992. [OE. *wēt.*]

wetyn. See **wytt.**

wethur *n.* violent wind 138. [OE. *weder.*]

whan, when, whon *adv.* at what time; on what occasion 34, 70, 106, etc. [OE. *hwanne, hwonne, hwenne.*]

what *pron. elliptical for what the thing* 235, 1190, 1492, etc.; *interrogative pron. of neut. gender*

928, 958, 1124, etc.; *adj.* whatever 2181. [OE. *hwæt.*]

whedur *conj.* whether 237, 272, 453, etc. [OE. *hiνæþer, hweþer.*]

whelebarowe *n.* wheelbarrow 2029. [ME. *whele + barowe.*]

whelme *v.* swell 683. [f. *whalme* n., possibly represents unrecorded OE. derivative **wælman.*]

wheme *adj.* pleasing 145. [ME. *cweme, queme.*]

when *rel.* when *in reference to an occurrence in the past* 628, 652, 667, etc.; *in reference to future time* 688, 952, 1188. [OE. *hwanne, hwænne.*]

whens *n.* from which place 196, 1492, 1557, etc. [thirteenth-century ME. *whannes, whennes,* f. *whanne.*]

where *adv.* at what place 507, 730, 1578; *rel.* 850. [OE. *hwær.*]

whereuyr *conj.* wherever, at any place which 314; *adv.* wherever 547. [f. *where + euyr.*]

whether *conj. introducing an alternative statement* 1244. [OE. *hwæþer.*]

why *rel. pron.* an account of which 20, 102, 734. [OE. *hwī.*]

whych *pron. rel.* which 1329; who 1662, 1933. [OE. *hwilc.*]

whyle *n.* time 922, 1162, 1785, etc. [OE. *hwīl.*]

whylys *adv. preceded by a demonstrative adj.: þys whylys,* this time 1378. [orig. OE. *sumehwiles, oðerhwiles,* etc.]

whyll *conj.* during the time that 799. [abbrev. of OE. *þā hwīle þe.*]

whyte *adj.* white 87, 194, 422, etc. [OE. *hwīt.*]

who *pron. rel.* who (of person or persons) 188, 279, 613, etc.; (of an animal) 422; *in dependent clause without correlative,* whoever 2175. [OE. *hwā.*]

whon. See **whan, when, whon.**

wychyd *pp.* affected (a person) with witchcraft 1507. [OE. *wiccian.*]

wyck *adj.* wicked 1436, 1661. [adj. use of OE. *wicca.*]

wyde *adj.* having a great extent 151, 393, 1524. [OE. *wīd.*]

wyde *adv.* over a large region 186, 361, 1222. [OE. *wīd.*]

wyfe, wyve *n.* wife 28, 219, 914, etc. [OE. *wīf.*]

wyght, wyȝt *n.* a living being in general 12, 39, 80, etc. [OE. *wiht.*]

wyght *adj.* courageous 27, 495, 527, etc. [a. ON. *vigt.*]

wyght *adj.* white 162, 310. [OE. *hwīt.*]

wyghtly *adv.* bravely 534. [f. *wyght* adj. + *ly.*]

wykkyd *adj.* bad in moral character 627, 1406, 1479. [app. f. ME. *wick* adj.]

wykkydly *adv.* immorally [f. as prec. + *ly.*]

wylde *adj.* untamed 45, 1503; unruly, uncontrolled 35, 407. [OE. *wilde.*]

wylys *n. pl.* ruses 1167. [Obscure.]

wyll *auxil.* of the future (*with infin.*) will: *1 pr. sg.* 32, 81, 351, etc.; *3 pr. sg.* 212, 217, 220, etc.; *pr. pl.* 237, 401, 432, etc.; **wolde** *auxil. of cond.* would: *pt. sg.* 77, 241, 500, etc.; *pt. pl.* 40, 450, 452, etc.; *pt. subj. sg.* 546, 899; *pt. subj. pl.* 339. [OE. *willan, wyllan; wōlde, walde.*]

wylle *n.* pleasure 231, 242, 828, etc.; disposition 627, 810, 1406; intention 729, 740, 956. [OE. *willa.*]

wynde *n.* wind 136. [OE. *wind.*]

wyndowe *n.* window 1185; **wyndow.** *n. pl.* 171. [a. ON. *vindauga.*]

wyne *n.* wine 1761. [OE. *wīn.*]

wynne *v.* obtain 546, 1241, 1263, etc.; obtain as a wife 354, 360; be victorious 453; go 857; tempt 2054; **wan(ne)** *pt. sg.* gained (land) 2104; *pt. sg.* arrived at 1258; *pt. pl.* acquired 1181. [OE. *winnan* (*wann, wunnen*).]

wynnyng *vbl. n.* taking, conquest 655. [f. ME. *wynne* + *yng.*]

wyrke *v.* cause, bring to pass 853, 1197; wield (a weapon) 1033; **wyrkyth** *3 pr. sg.* 615. [OE. *wyrcan.*]

wys. See **wytt.**

wyse *adj.* informed 176, 304, 1364. [OE. *wīs.*]

wyse *n.* manner 1859. [OE *wise.*]

wyt *n.* wisdom 555. [OE. *wit.*]

wyt *v.* See **wytt.**

wyte *n.* punishment 1635. [OE. *wīte.*]

wytnes *v.* bear witness 1372. [f. ME. *wytnes* n.]

wyth *prep.* with 56, 125, 131, etc.; together with 45, 133. [OE. *wiþ* blended with *mid* (*miþ*).]

wythhelde *pt. sg.* engaged in (his) service 522. [*wyth* + *holde.*]

wythynne *adv.* inside 121, 329, 348, etc. [OE. *wiþ-innan.*]

wythowt(e) *prep.* without 205, 859, 940, etc. [Late OE. *wiþūtan.*]

wythowten, -yn *adv.* lacking 12, 86, 215, etc.; exclusive of 137.

wytt *v.* know 2154; *pr. subj. God sone wytt me . . .*, God's son help me 1779; **wote** *v.* 1086 (*var. of wytt*); *1 pr. sg.* 389; *3 pr. sg.* 1367; **wate** *1 pr. sg.* 170, 777; **wys** *1 pr. sg.; I wys* I know (*erroneous present form of wytt*); **wyste** *pt. sg.* 1054, 1578, 1630, etc.; *pt. pl.* 984; **wetyn** *pp.*

1190, 1271; **wyt** *imper.* mark, note 29. [OE. *witan.*]

wytten *v.* blame 1923. [f. ME. *wytte* + *en.*]

wode *n.* woods 1435, 1524, 1697, etc.; **wodes** *n. pl.* 1503. [OE. *wudu.*]

wode *adj.* mad 44, 130, 658, etc. [OE. *wōd.*]

woghe *n.* woe 2013. [OE. *wā.*]

wolde *adj.* old 308. [OE. *ald.*]

woman. See **wemon.**

wondur *adv.* wondrously 186, 684, 1424, etc. [Partly OE. *wundor;* partly OE. *wundrum.*]

wondurs *n. pl.* extraordinary natural occurrences 41. [OE. *wundor.*]

wone *n.* conduct 1344; action of staying, *in phr.: wythowten wone,* without delay 215, 1156. [Aphet. f. ME. *i-wune, i-wone,* OE. *ȝewuna.*]

wones *n., sg.* and *pl.* palace 191. [a. ON. *ván.*]

wonte *pp.* accustomed 843. [OE. *ȝewunod,* pp. of *ȝewunian.*]

woo *n.* affliction 707, 1197, 2076; *adv.* distressed 824. [OE. *wā.*]

worche *v.* cause 1704. [OE. *wyrcan* (*worhte, geworht*).]

worde *n.* word 1021; news 1930; **wordys** *n. pl.* 250, 692, 1081, etc. [OE. *word.*]

worlde *n.* chiefly *this world* 5, 39, 54, etc. [OE. *woruld.*]

worschyp *n.* respect, honour 299. [OE. *weorðscipe.*]

worthe *adj.* equivalent to (something) in value 1268. [OE. *weorþ(e), wyrþe.*]

worthely, -yly *adv.* with elegance 107, 1091, 1572, etc. [f. ME. *worthy* + *ly.*]

worthy, -þy *adj. of persons:* estimable 30; *of things:* good 191, 800, 1344, etc. [OE. *wyrþig,*

merited, infl. by *wyrþe*,
worth(y).]

worthyly. See **worthely, -yly.**

wote. See **wytt.**

woundys *n. pl.* wounds 913, 1848,
1992. [OE. *wund.*]

wowe *v.* woo 1216. [Late OE.
wōȝian.]

woxyn *pp.* become 1975. [OE.
weaxan (Nth. *wōx, weaxen*).]

wrake *n.* occasion of suffering 582,
1975. [OE. *wræc.*]

wrangdome *n.* injustice 153. [ME.
wrang + dome.]

wrange, wronge *pt. pl.* twisted
836, 838. [OE. *wringan (wrang,
wrungon, wrungen).*]

wrate *pt. sg.* wrote 2173. [OE.
wrītan.]

wrathe, wrethe *n.* anger 1611,
2060. [OE. *wræððu.*]

wryttes, -ys *n. pl.* documents
121; formal orders 361. [OE.
writ.]

wroght, wroȝt *pt. sg.* performed
872; caused 2085; *pp.* formed
336, 1091, 1338, etc.; taken (to
wife) 2099. [OE. *wyrcan.*]

wronge. See **wrange.**

wronge *n.* that which is morally
unjust. [f. ME. *wrange* adj.]

X

x the Roman numeral symbol for
ten 154, 190, 202, etc.

Y

ye *pron. pl.* ye 40, 76, 106, etc.;
yow *acc. and dat.* 40, 154, 164,
etc.; **yowre** *poss. pron. and adj.*
your 515, 1239, 1343, etc. [OE.
gē, ēow, ēower.]

yede *pt. sg.* went 388, 658, 919,
etc.; *pt. pl.* 636. See **ȝede.**

yere *n.* year 316, 332; *pl. with
num. expressing a person's* age
61; *with numeral expressing
duration* 674; **yerys** *n. pl.* 83.
[OE. *ȝēr.*]

yoye *n.* joy 853, 1307, 2171. [OFr.
joie.]

yondur *adj.* over there, away
there 484. [ME. *ȝonder, ȝender,*
corresp. to OS. *gendra* adj., on
this side.]

yonge *adj.* young 527, 648, 981,
etc. [OE. *ȝeoung, ȝung, innȝ,*
Nth. *ȝing.*]

yow. See **ye.**

yowre. See **ye.**

yurne *n.* day 315. [a. OFr. *jornee,
journee.*]

INDEX OF PROPER NAMES

Jerusalem 66, 212, 249, 350, 433, 1739, etc.
Jhesu 243, 2186.
Justamownde second husband of the mother of Miles and Emere 413 937, 1255.

Lucyus Jbarnyus founder of Beuerfayre 1888.

Machary Tyrry's steward, one of Florence's persecutors 1592, 1972, 2023, 2071.
Maynelay Menelaus, brother of Agamemnon and husband of Helen of Troy 854.
Mary the Blessed Virgin 1440, 1500, 1852, 1915
Myghell, Seynt St Michael 904.
Mylys, Mylon Miles, son of the King of Hungary and brother of Emere 408, 442, 460, 502, 523, 529, etc.
Mownt Devyse home of Barnard 986.

Narumpy Narnia, described as meadow near the Tiber. See note to line 382.
Naverne Navarre 415.

Otes Emperor of Rome, Florence's father 26, 55, 127, 298, 452, 556, etc.

Petur, Seynt St Peter 434, 514, 694.

Phelyp King of Hungary, father of Miles and Emere 934.
Pyse Pisa 985.
Poyle, Pole Apulia 148, 1937, 1964. See note to line 140.
Rome Rome 16, 25, 50, 71, 89, 150, etc.; **Romes** *gen. sg.* 965.
Rownsevall town in Navarre (scene of battle in *Song of Roland*) 53.

Sampson Roman warrior 491, 982, 1058, 1075, 1082, 1119, etc.
Symond(e) Simon, the Pope 775, 1149, 1372.
Synagot(e) Commander of Garcy's forces 780, 922, 943, 1204.
Spayne Spain 160.
Surry Syria 413, 937.

Tyber Tiber river in Rome 344, 383.
Tyrry(e), Turry one of Florence's rescuers, Beatrice's father 1519, 1591, 1978, 1984, 2061, 2080, etc.
Troy(e) Troy 2, 15, 53, 854.
Turkay, Turky Turkey 553, 947.

Vtalye Italy 119.